PUT YOUR
BEST FOOT FORWARD

ASIA

PUT YOUR BEST FOOT FORWARD

ASIA

A Fearless
Guide to
International
Communication
and Behavior

MARY
MURRAY
BOSROCK

IES
International Education Systems

This publication is designed to provide accurate and
authoritative information in regard to the subject matter
covered. It is sold with the understanding that the publisher is
not engaged in rendering legal, accounting or other
professional services. If legal advice or other expert assistance
is required, the services of a competent professional person
should be sought.

Information contained in this book does not necessarily reflect
the official views of any government. References to
organizations and publications are not endorsements. The
author alone is responsible for errors of omission or commission
in the contents of this book.

Publisher's Cataloging-in-Publication

Bosrock, Mary Murray.
        Put your best foot forward—Asia: a fearless guide to
    international communication and behavior / Mary
    Murray Bosrock. — 2nd ed.
        p. cm.—(Put your best foot forward; bk. 2)
        Includes index.
        ISBN 0-9637530-7-X
        Preassigned LCCN: 93-079394.
        1. Asia—Guidebooks. 2. Asia—Social life and
    customs. I. Title. II. Series: Bosrock, Mary Murray. Put
    your best foot forward; bk. 2.

        DS10.B67 1997   915.04'429
                                                QBI97-40489

Printed in the United States of America
10 9 8 7 6 5 4 3 2

To a woman who at 85 years of age

is still the most

beautiful, charming, intelligent

and loving woman I've ever known—

my Mom

Look for other international education products from IES, including
Put Your Best Foot Forward—Europe
Put Your Best Foot Forward—Asia
Put Your Best Foot Forward—Russia
Put Your Best Foot Forward—Mexico/Canada
Put Your Best Foot Forward—South America

Editor: Terry Wolkerstorfer
Design: Brett Olson
Illustrations: Craig MacIntosh
Research: Kristen Volk

TABLE OF CONTENTS

PART III: COUNTRY INFORMATION

i.
ACKNOWLEDGMENTS

My thanks to the scores of people—
businesspeople, diplomats, scholars and
professionals—who have drawn on their own
experience and knowledge to contribute ideas
and observations to this book, and especially to
those who helped review the manuscript.

Listed by their particular areas of expertise,
they include:

China
P. Richard Bohr, Ph.D.
Derek Chow, Arthur Andersen, Shanghai
Brad and Doris Davis
Dong Ya
Mary King, The Hongkong & Shanghai Bank, Shanghai
Lin Yan
Li King Feng, Minnesota Trade Office
Zhufang Li
Zhanjiang Liu
Dr. Gerlinde Paschinger, First Secretary,
    Austrian Embassy, Beijing
Joseph Schuberg, Shanghai Hilton
Victor Sun, The Hongkong & Shanghai Bank, Shanghai
Norman N. C. Sze, Arthur Andersen, Shanghai

Hong Kong
P. Richard Bohr, Ph.D.
Brad and Doris Davis
Len and Irene Dunning
Gary and Sandy Hawk
Kate Hotchkiss, Asia Trade Representative,
    Minnesota Trade Office

India
Noor Doja, Minnesota Trade Office
Darin Narayana, Norwest Bank
Bhai Analjit Singh
K.R. Sinha, Consul General of India, Chicago

Indonesia
T.S. Ariwanto, P.T. Mitra Andasantika
Jovita Bjoraker, Council on Asia-Pacific Minnesotans
Paul Haroen, Bangun Jaya
Suhaswoto Hidyoningrat, Consul for Information,
    Social and Cultural Affairs,
        Consulate General of Indonesia, Chicago
Martha Schneringer
Peter A. Tanison, P.T. Mika Lestari Kurnia Kencana

Japan
Jeff Arnold
W. Soren Egekvist, Honorary Consul General (retired)
Neal L. Gault, Jr., M.D., Honorary Consul (retired)
Junko Idei
Yo Miyoshi
Inkie Rutgers, International Trade Advisor,
    Minnesota Trade Office
Dr. Erich Schmid, Austrian Ambassador to Japan
Dr. Johannes Skriwan, Charge d'Affaires,
    Austrian Embassy, Tokyo
Evan Williams, Honorary Consul, Minneapolis

Malaysia
Sharisal L. Daniel, Director, Malaysian Tourist Board
Noor Ahmad Hamid, Assistant Director,
    Malaysian Tourist Board

Philippines
Dr. Albert de Leon, Director,
    Council on Asia-Pacific Minnesotans
Pat Escobar, Council on Asia-Pacific Minesotans
Maria Rita Herrara, Cultural Officer,
    Consulate General of the Philippines, Chicago
Ruy Moreno, Arthur Andersen
Diosdado Orocio, Acting Principal Officer,
    Consulate General of the Philippines, Chicago

Singapore
Kate Hotchkiss, Asia Trade Representative,
    Minnesota Trade Office
Jimmy Ong
Jeff Pirie, Arthur Andersen
Steven Plan, Arthur Andersen
Stephen Young, Honorary Consul, Minneapolis

South Korea
Allison R. Mercer, Honorary Consul, Minneapolis
Matthew Oh
Sung Won Sohn, Ph.D.
Yong Jip Kwan

Taiwan
Kate Hotchkiss, Asia Trade Representative,
    Minnesota Trade Office
Michael and Helen Liu
Brad and Doris Davis

Thailand
William D. Black, Regent Hotel
Nanthiya Komindr
Brian Moody, Regent Hotel

Tsanis Nasongksla, Cultural Officer,
    Consulate General of Thailand, Chicago
Jeanne Scherk
Dr. Nikolaus Scherk, Austrian Ambassador to Thailand
Jiraparn Tilapat, Visa and Economic Consul,
    Consulate General of Thailand, Chicago

Vietnam
Bill Cameron, The Hongkong & Shanghai Bank
Le Quy Ming, The Hongkong & Shanghai Bank
Ruy Moreno, Arthur Andersen

Asia/General
Yuval Almog, Coral Group
George Crolick, Executive Director,
    Minnesota Trade Office
Carrie Farrow
Alastair and Sheila Fyfe
Loring Knoblauch, Honeywell
Alfredo Maselli, Honeywell
Sarah E. Seeley
Kris Z. Volk

And to all the others who helped and
encouraged me in ways large and small,
my sincere thanks.

—*Mary Murray Bosrock*
St. Paul, Minnesota
Spring 1994

ii.
WHY ASIA?

In the closing years of the 20th century, businesspeople everywhere understand that their companies will survive and prosper only if they're prepared to compete in a global economy.

Many also understand Asia's major role in that economy—a role that will continue to expand in the early years of the coming century.

Consider, for example, that Asia has more than half of the world's people—some 3 billion, 10 times as many as North America and six times as many as Europe—and some of the world's fastest-growing economies.

Consider that China and India alone have 2 billion people and the potential for sustained economic growth approaching 10 percent annually.

Consider that during the recent worldwide recession, most Asian economies continued to grow—thanks to high rates of saving and investment, relatively low wages, and people who are clever and industrious.

George Yeo, Singapore's minister of information, recently predicted in *The Wall Street Journal* that "In 25 years, the combined GNP of East Asia will be larger than all of Europe's and twice that of the U.S."

No company anywhere in the world can afford to ignore Asia's potential as both producer and consumer.

If Mr. Yeo is right—or even close—no company anywhere in the world can afford to ignore Asia's potential as both producer and consumer. And yet, many Western companies, especially small and medium-sized ones, are reluctant to take the plunge in the Asia market.

For most of them, the reason is simple: Asia seems so... *foreign*, so intimidating, with cultures and customs that differ dramatically from those of the West (and almost as dramatically from country to country within the region).

Admittedly, doing business in Asia and with Asians is a culturally complex undertaking— but one that can be richly rewarding for businesspeople and companies willing to acquire even the most basic grasp of Asian history, culture and customs.

This book is intended to give Western businesspeople the cultural background and communication skills they need to interact effectively with Asians—and to establish the relationships that are the basis for doing business in that part of the world.

Asians do not expect Westerners to be as knowledgeable about their culture as they are about ours. However, the more you know about the history, culture and customs of the country you're visiting—even a few words of the language—the more favorable the impression you'll make and the better your chances of establishing a working relationship.

Knowing something about the culture of your Asian colleagues will allow you to be more sensitive, have more fun and be more effective in pursuing your business objectives. The information in this book will allow you to understand and be understood more easily. You will make mistakes, but they will be sensitive mistakes—mistakes made as a result of trying, not out of arrogance. Remember, it's better to make mistakes by trying than not to try at all.

It's better to make mistakes by trying than not to try at all.

FORMAT

Everyone who reads this book is busy. I have attempted to respect your time by organizing the book into easily accessible sections.

The behaviors discussed in Part I are the first, simplest and most basic rules for communicating with someone in Asia. This information should allow you to move beyond superficial concerns and get more quickly and easily to the business at hand.

In Part II, we'll talk about some important customs that apply generally in Asia.

And in Part III, you'll find country-by-country specifics on communication and behavior in a dozen Asian countries. These quick-reference chapters give you a snapshot of each country that allows you to find the information you need in a matter of moments.

THE WORLD ACCORDING TO ME

This book reflects my personal observations and experiences during nearly two decades of working and traveling in Asia as an international businessperson. I'm just "telling it as I see it."

However, each country chapter has been thoroughly researched through meetings with diplomats, doctors, lawyers, businesspeople, teachers and students from that country.

The book is my attempt to convey to you not only what I have learned, but also what other people with a great deal of experience in Asia have passed on to me.

WHO SHOULD USE THIS BOOK?

Although it was designed primarily as a resource for businesspeople, this book should be equally helpful for leisure travelers, students, teachers, people in the travel and hospitality industry, and hosts who regularly entertain Asian visitors.

Keep this book on your desk or tuck it in your suitcase. Before you meet or talk with someone from one of the countries included, you can quickly learn or review important facts that will assist you in communicating clearly.

THE BOTTOM LINE

The information in this book isn't just "nice to know." It's vital to your success and that of your company if you want to do business in Asia or with Asians. The information in this book can be translated directly into increased revenues and earnings for your company. What you learn in this book literally will go to the bottom line.

Put Your Best Foot Forward

iii.
LETTER FROM ASIA

During the past several years, as I've collected material for this book, I've asked my Asian friends how they view Americans and what points they'd like to make to Americans who'll be visiting Asia. The following letter is a compilation of some of their more trenchant comments.

We like America and Americans. We admire and envy many things about you.

Dear American Friends,

You asked what we Asians think about you Americans. Honestly, we like America and Americans. We admire and envy many things about you. You are free in so many ways. You are free to move around, change directions, express yourselves as individuals and be whoever and whatever you want.

You are also fun to be with. We enjoy sharing our cultures with you because your reactions are enthusiastic, spontaneous and natural. We feel less inhibited just being with you.

Your country's leadership in higher education is widely recognized on our side of the Pacific. In fact, many of the young leaders who are shaping Asia's future have been educated in your colleges and universities.

From blue jeans and makeup to music and movies, American products have a reputation in Asia for quality and value—and moreover, they are a major influence on our changing lifestyles.

However much we like and admire you, we sometimes can't help but feel that you take us for granted. We work hard to understand your history, language and culture, and it often seems as if you make little or no effort to understand ours.

We work hard to understand your history, language and culture, and it often seems as if you make little or no effort to understand ours.

While we have enthusiastically embraced modern, Western culture, remember that there exists in our countries a cultural dichotomy unknown in yours: Beneath the surface culture of computers and credit cards, music videos and McDonald's, we have our roots in a matrix of morals and mores, art and architecture, language and literature that stretches back more than 2,000 years. We are determined to be leaders in the modern world while holding fast to our own traditional cultures.

We don't expect you to know Ramadan the way we know Christmas. We don't expect you to understand the writings of Lao Tzu or Confucius the way we understand Aristotle or Aquinas. We don't expect you to be as familiar with *pad tai* or *kushi-yaki* as we are with pizza and Kentucky Fried Chicken.

When we introduce you to our traditions and foods, we expect you to be respectful, interested and appreciative.

But we do expect that when we introduce you to our traditions and foods, you will be respectful, interested and appreciative.

When we invite you to a restaurant or to our home for dinner, please realize that we are humbly offering you the very essence of our ancient cultures. Grilled fish heads or uncooked sea urchins may seem bizarre to you—even disgusting— but they are prized delicacies to us. We are honored to serve you and introduce you to our culture. If you refuse our hospitality, we are shamed.

When you dine with us, attend business meetings or visit our sacred places, please be aware of the appropriate dress and etiquette. Because we emphasize the importance of the group, rather than the individual, you should try to blend in—not to call attention to yourself or make a statement. Always dress neatly and conservatively. Men, consider shaving off your

beards; women, cut or restrain your hair and
avoid loud colors and excessive makeup.

You need to be aware that we conduct business,
make decisions and socialize as a group. We
also do business on the basis of relationships.
Don't expect to walk in, slap us on the back
and sign a contract—all in one visit. If you
want to establish a business relationship with
us, visit often, enjoy our countries and get to
know us and our cultures. Be patient.

Most of your business discussions will be in
English. If our English sometimes seems less
than perfect, remember that we're making a
great effort to communicate in *your* language.
If you ever feel impatient, just imagine yourself
speaking Chinese or Japanese.

In business meetings, use simple,
straightforward English; avoid jargon
and idiomatic language. On the other
hand, don't talk to us like
kindergartners. We are well-educated,
sophisticated internationalists who
have built thriving economies
through our understanding of export
markets. Many of the items that
make your everyday lives more
productive and enjoyable were made
in our countries.

Please don't denigrate our values or cultures. Don't preach to us about human rights, women's rights or Christianity. Our customs and beliefs are based on centuries of tradition. Unless you have studied our individual cultures in great depth, you're in no position to be judgmental. Our ways aren't better or worse than yours—they're just different. When you're in Asia, accept them.

Try our food, visit our ancient temples and mosques, and participate in our festivals. We're proud of our homes, our countries and our traditions, and we hope you'll enjoy and appreciate them.

Please visit us, but please come informed and with an open mind.

Respectfully,

Your Asian Friends

> "I hope the time has come when the West will be willing to learn from the East."
>
> —Tommy Koh, Singapore columnist

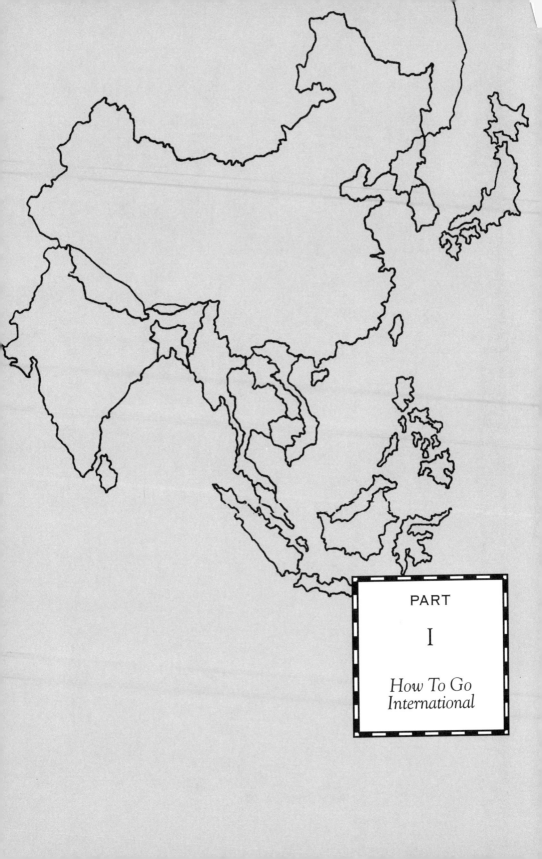

PART

I

*How To Go
International*

1.

THE MYTH OF
THE MONOLITH

From our side of the Pacific, Asia may look
monolithic.

Many Westerners can't tell Hong
Kong from Singapore, Indonesia
from Malaysia or Taiwan from
Thailand. A 1989 survey by the
National Geographic Society
found that only 33 percent of
Americans could identify Japan
on a world map.

Small wonder, then, that we lack even a
basic understanding of Asian history,
culture and social customs—knowledge
that's crucial in developing a business
relationship.

Understanding must begin with the awareness
that Asia is a continent, not a country, and
Asians are not "all the same." Each Asian
country is unique, with its own history, culture,

*Just as the cultures
of Asian countries
are distinct, so too
customs and
behaviors vary
widely from
country to country.*

language, religious tradition and cuisine. To think that Chinese, Japanese, Koreans, Indians and Indonesians are all alike is both ignorant and insulting.

And just as the cultures of Asian countries are distinct, so too customs and behaviors vary widely from country to country.

Trying to describe human behavior is tricky at best. No two people behave in exactly the same way; perhaps even more important, no two people interpret others' behavior in the same way.

Does this make intercultural communication impossible for the ordinary business traveler? Certainly not! My own experience in Asia suggests that the only real prerequisite is a willingness to learn.

This book has some fundamental, country-by-country guidelines that will make your interaction with Asians easier, more comfortable and more fun. They'll get you over some of the first cultural hurdles so you can establish productive business relationships—and eventually, I hope, friendships as well.

Can you survive without this knowledge? Of course you can. As a matter of fact, Asians don't even expect you to have this knowledge. Can this information help you understand potential partners and customers in Asia? Can it help you avoid misunderstandings? Can it help you communicate clearly and effectively what you really want to say? You bet it can!

If you are on your way to Asia for the first time, you are in for a real treat. If you travel often to Asia, you are very lucky. There isn't a country in Asia that I haven't enjoyed. And regardless of how dynamic the business environment or how spectacular the temples, it is always the people—tens and hundreds and thousands of unique individuals—who hold my interest and eventually win my heart.

The people of the world are bigoted and unenlightened: Invariably they regard what is like them as right, and what is different from them as wrong, resulting in mutual recrimination....They do not realize that the types of humanity are not uniform and that their customs are also not one, that it is not only impossible to force people to become different but also impossible to force them to become alike.

Yung-Cheng, emperor of China, in 1727

WORDS OF WISDOM

2.

THE UGLY AMERICAN

I have rarely met an "Ugly American"!

The term became widely known as the title of a 1963 movie starring Marlon Brando, based on a 1958 book by William Lederer and Eugene Burdick about the ignorant and incompetent U.S. ambassador to a fictional Southeast Asian country. It quickly became an epithet for rude, self-centered people who roamed the world with utter disregard—even disdain—for other cultures.

The Americans I know want to understand other cultures.

The Americans I know, work with and meet on my travels are quite the opposite. They want very much to understand and appreciate other customs and cultures. They're just uninformed—not ugly.

It isn't easy to understand other languages and cultures. We share this planet with nearly 6 billion people who speak 6,000 different languages.

In the United States, most of us can travel thousands of miles in several directions without encountering significant cultural or linguistic differences. It is any wonder we find it a little difficult to adjust our thinking to the Asian environment, where a typical journey can take you through several countries, cultures and languages?

Obviously, most of us don't have the time or ability to learn dozens of languages or to become intimately familiar with scores of cultures. So how do we get started in this business of intercultural communication? By being willing to make mistakes.

How do we get started in this business of intercultural communication? By being willing to make mistakes.

An ambassador I know says his wife always learns the language of a new country faster than he does. Why? Because she's not worried about making mistakes as she shops, tours, visits and dines. He, on the other hand—with an official position to uphold—never speaks the language unless he's certain that he'll be correct.

There's a lesson in that story for all of us. We've got to be willing to take a chance—to make a mistake. It's important to understand that there are good mistakes and bad mistakes. Good mistakes are those that say clearly in any language, "I care, I'm trying, I'm sorry if I got it wrong." Sensitive imperfection can be endearing.

It's equally important to remember when interacting with people from other cultures that they too may be struggling to communicate with and understand us.

The West has exported its lifestyle to many areas of the world, but not all. The Chinese, for example—all 1.2 billion of them—were essentially isolated from the Western world from 1949 to 1978. Can you imagine, taking into account the dramatic changes in other parts of the world over those three decades, the difficulty a Chinese person could encounter in dealing with foreigners?

The Beijing government recognized this problem and recently released a list of tips for Chinese to follow while traveling abroad. It read: "Don't squat when waiting for a bus or a person. Don't spit in public. Don't point at people with your fingers. Don't make noise. Don't laugh loudly. Don't yell or call to people from a distance. Don't pick your teeth, pick your nose, blow your nose, pick at your ears, rub your eyes or rub dirt off your skin. Don't scratch, take off your shoes, burp, stretch or hum."

The moral of the story is we all have a lot to learn.

So have fun and make mistakes, but make sensitive mistakes.

It's important to remember that people from other cultures are struggling to communicate with and understand us.

3.
RULES OF THUMB
THE TEN COMMANDMENTS
OF DOING BUSINESS IN ASIA

1. Do your homework! A basic knowledge of your hosts' culture will be richly rewarded.

2. Never embarrass anyone publicly or cause anyone to lose face: It will end a relationship.

3. Take your time and be patient. Relationships develop slowly.

4. When speaking, lower the normal volume of your voice. Never raise your voice in an attempt to overcome language difficulties.

5. Always be sincere. It shows. Sincerity is required to build trust. Trust is required to build a relationship.

6. Show respect for other cultures even if they seem strange. Asian cultures were highly developed while European civilization was still in its infancy.

Take your time and be patient. Relationships develop slowly.

7. Ask, look and listen! Asians are very proud of their culture and enjoy teaching others about their ways. A respectful interest will be appreciated.

8. Asian language and body language are very different. When a problem develops, assume miscommunication was the cause.

9. Likability is the "magic wand." If people like you, they will forgive just about anything you might do wrong.

10. Assume the best about people and their actions. Most people do what seems appropriate to them based on their values, habits and traditions.

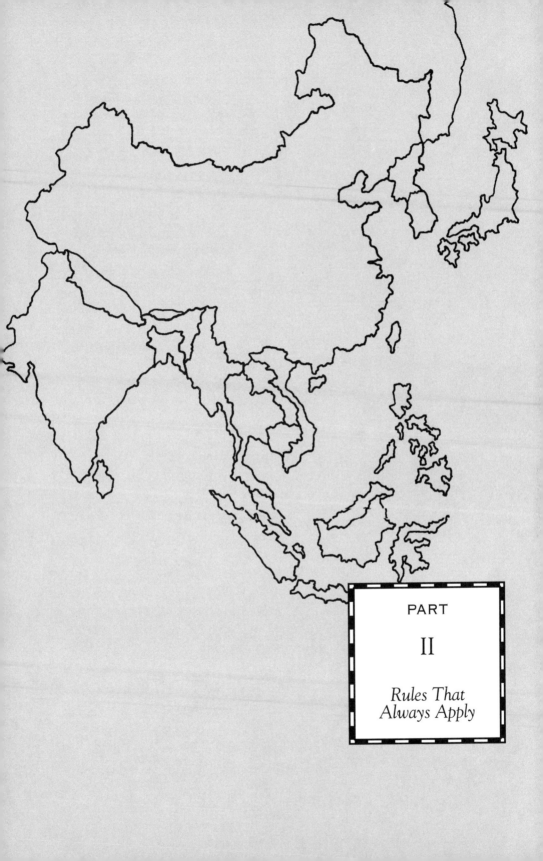

PART

II

*Rules That
Always Apply*

4.

VITAL STATISTICS

The most common negative comment made in other countries about Americans is that we're ethnocentric. Americans often appear to know nothing about anyone, anywhere else in the world; even worse, they don't demonstrate much interest in learning.

Asia is the largest continent in the world in both size and population. The countries in Asia are so diverse and the contrasts among them so great that someone once said, "The only generalization you can make about this part of the world is that almost everyone has black hair!"

Asia includes the world's largest and smallest nations in size and population. In no other area of the world are there such dramatic differences not only in land area, population and population density, but also in geography, climate, ethnicity, religion, standard of living and form of government. To cite a few examples:

Americans often appear to know nothing about anyone else; even worse, they don't demonstrate much interest in learning.

- Singapore, approximately the size of Chicago, has a population of 2.8 million people.

- Japan, slightly smaller than California, has a population of 124.3 million.

- China is larger than the United States and has a population of 1.2 billion.

- India, a little more than one-third the size of the United States, has a population of 883.5 million people—almost four times that of the U.S.

- Japan is one of the most homogeneous societies in the world, with one culture and one language, while Singapore has substantial numbers of Chinese, Indians and Malays with their respective languages, cultures and religions.

- Japan's gross domestic product (GDP) is $29,519 per person; China's is $372.

- The climates vary from snow and freezing temperatures in the winter in Seoul and Beijing to steamy tropical weather year-round in Indonesia, Singapore and Malaysia.

- India is the world's largest democracy, while the Communist Party still has a firm grip on power in China and Vietnam.

- Social life, business life and religion are closely interwoven in Asian cultures. The Islamic, Buddhist, Hindu, Shinto and Christian faiths all have large numbers of adherents, and the influence of Taoist and Confucian philosophies is pervasive.

You can see why it's important when visiting an Asian country to spend at least a brief time reviewing the country's vital statistics.

A well-traveled senior executive of a Fortune 500 company—call him Mr. Smith, though it's not his real name—told me, with some embarrassment, about his visit to Indonesia to negotiate a multimillion-dollar contract with the government. Feeling very confident that his product was superior in quality and value to that of his competitors, he arrived for his meeting with the Minister of Defense.

Greetings were warm and the conversation friendly until the participants got down to business. The minister opened the meeting by saying, "Mr. Smith, we welcome you to Indonesia. Now please tell us what you know about our country."

"Welcome to Indonesia, Mr. Smith. Now please tell us what you know about our country."

The visiting executive knew everything about his company and his product. Unfortunately, this was the last stop on an extensive Asian trip and he knew nothing about Indonesia. He was forced to admit this with an apology.

The minister replied, "Mr. Smith, you've come halfway around the world to ask my government to allow you to set up a system that will cost millions of dollars and will be used for many years by virtually every person in our country.

"Yet you know nothing about us or our country. How could you possibly meet our needs? I suggest you go home, learn something about us, and then come back to us with your product."

Shouldn't a seasoned international executive have known better?

Shouldn't you?

5.

RELIGION AND RITUAL

From the Shinto priest presiding over the opening of a Kentucky Fried Chicken restaurant in Tokyo to the *feng shui* master advising on construction of the Hong Kong & Shanghai Bank's new headquarters, religion and ritual are the cement that binds Asian societies. They are virtually inseparable from business and everyday life.

Knowing, understanding and showing basic respect for a person's beliefs is the key to establishing any business or personal relationship in Asia. You can't begin to understand Asian societies without learning at least the basic tenets of their religions and philosophies.

Most Asians enjoy talking about their beliefs. Once you establish a person's religion, feel free to ask informed, nonjudgmental questions about it.

Rule of Thumb

Understanding and showing basic respect for a person's beliefs is the key to establishing any business or personal relationship in Asia.

To help you ask informed questions, here are some basic facts on Asia's major religions and philosophies:

CONFUCIANISM

Three great religions—Confucianism, Taoism and Buddhism—helped shape China and other countries of East and Southeast Asia. As we'll see, there is significant overlap among the three, in practice even more than in theory; it is not unusual for a person to practice elements of all three, and to see no inherent conflict in doing so.

This reflects the tendency of Chinese religions to be eclectic rather than dogmatic, humanistic rather than theological, and communal rather than personal.

Of these three great religions, Confucianism addresses itself most directly to solving the practical problems of everyday life—to the art of living.

Strictly speaking, Confucianism is not a religion at all; it has no clergy, does not worship a god or gods, and does not teach the existence of an afterlife.

Rather, it is a way of life based on the ideas of Confucius, the Chinese philosopher who lived from about 550 to 480 B.C. It is a guide to personal morality, interpersonal relations, social responsibility and good government.

Three great religions—Confucianism, Taoism and Buddhism—helped shape China and other countries of East and Southeast Asia.

Strictly speaking, Confucianism is not a religion at all, but a way of life.

When you're doing business in Asia, Arthur Andersen can help you take great strides toward global success.

Whether it's helping you solve the corporate complexities of doing business in Asia or helping your employees and their families deal with everyday life in a foreign country, Arthur Andersen is ready.

We've helped companies establish or expand operations in Asia for more than 30 years. We can help you with myriad tax issues such as international tax planning, licensing, individual and corporate compliance, acquisitions and joint ventures. In addition, we can serve your human resource needs, including developing and administering international compensation and benefits policies and outsourcing human resource and expatriate services.

Our experienced professionals are part of our worldwide network of nearly 400 offices in 79 countries, sharing centralized training and a common methodology to assure you high standards and continuity of service throughout the world.

All of which will help you take giant steps toward reaching your goals. Visit us on the Internet at http://www.arthurandersen.com.

John Mott, Partner in charge
International Tax and Business Advisory Services
212-708-6012

Mac Gajek, Partner in charge
International Executive Services
312-507-6810

ARTHUR ANDERSEN

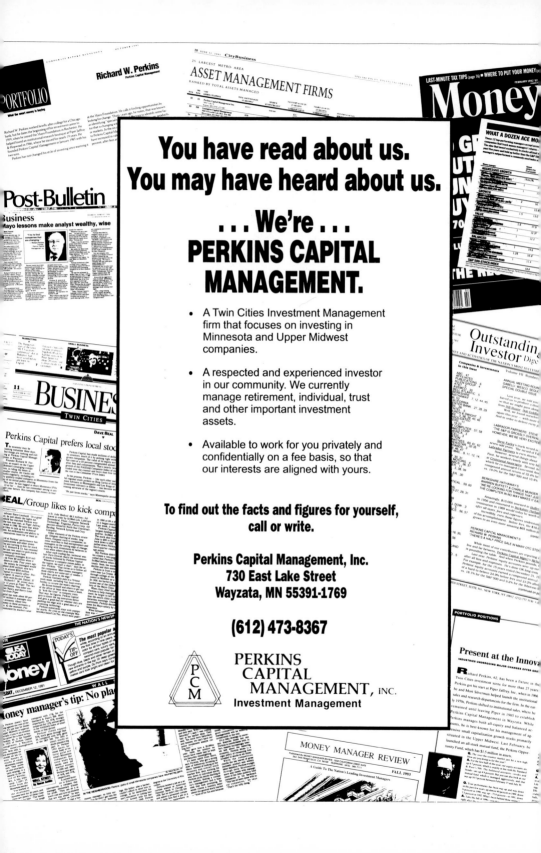

For nearly 2,000 years—from shortly before the birth of Christ to the early 20th century A.D.—Confucianism was the single most important force in Chinese life. Hundreds of millions of Chinese, Japanese, Koreans and Vietnamese have honored Confucius and followed his teachings.

If a single principle underlies his teachings, Confucius said, "It is reciprocity: Whatever you yourself don't want, do not do to the other man." In the West, this same idea appeared some 600 years later in the Gospel of Matthew ("Treat others the way you would have them treat you; this sums up the law and the prophets.") and eventually in the Golden Rule of conventional wisdom.

From this principle evolved the Confucian idea of propriety, or appropriate behavior toward others. Specifically, Confucianism defines correct conduct in "The Five Relations":

- Between parents and children.

- Between elder and younger brothers.

- Between husband and wife.

- Between friend and friend.

- Between prince and minister.

For nearly 2,000 years, Confucianism was the single most important force in Chinese life.

Confucius' ideas about personal conduct further evolved into guidelines for orderly society and effective government. For example, he and his disciples taught that a sound society was built on "The Four Foundations":

- Natural human feeling for others.

- Commitment to the common good.

- Respect for social and religious forms.

- Proper education.

Also central to Confucius' teaching was his concept of the ideal citizen, variously translated as "noble man," "princely man," "superior man," "cultivated man" and—most often— "the gentleman."

Confucius defined a gentleman as a person of good moral character, reverent toward his ancestors and respectful to his father and his ruler; he was expected to study constantly and practice rigorous self-examination.

The Confucian gentleman acted with composure, grace and dignity and always pursued harmony—both internally and in relation to society. Acquisitiveness, passion and attachment to beauty were believed to be among the obstacles to attaining a state of harmony.

When gentlemen are rulers, Confucius believed, their moral example will inspire their followers to lead good lives—bringing about an orderly society more effectively than laws or codes of punishment.

Over the centuries, Confucianism absorbed ideas from Taoism and other philosophies and religions, and Confucians began to practice certain rites or rituals. It's worth noting, however, that the Confucian performs these rites for the sake of his fate in this world—long life, children, wealth—and without any thought for his fate in the hereafter.

Confucianism has been cited as a major factor in the success of modern Asia, where allegiance to the group—family, work unit, company and nation—takes precedence over individual fulfillment.

Confucian ethics have never provided a code for dealing with outsiders; foreigners by tradition have been nonpersons—that is, socially indefinable. Once foreigners become business associates, colleagues or friends, they are treated in a manner appropriate to their position.

TAOISM

Taoism (pronounced *DOW-ism*) has its origins in the teachings of Lao Tzu, the Chinese teacher and philosopher who was a contemporary of Confucius, but it did not develop as an organized religion until about the second century A.D. It differs from Confucianism mainly by virtue of its mysticism and its emphasis on harmony with nature (rather than social harmony).

As a religion, Taoism has some 20 million adherents, but as a philosophy it has had far broader importance in East and Southeast Asia. Taoism was a major influence on classical Chinese art and literature.

Lao Tzu's philosophy is contained in a short book whose title can be translated as "The Way and Its Power." The *tao*, or "way," means understanding the characteristics or behavior that make each thing in the universe what it is.

The word also is used to mean reality as a whole, the absolute value, the one unchangeable element from which all being springs; the divine All-One of which one can partake by rendering oneself absolutely void of worldly interests and passionate desires.

"The truth is infinite; the mind is finite."

—Lao Tzu

If the Taoist concept of divinity seems beyond comprehension, Lao Tzu had an explanation: "The truth is infinite; the mind is finite." In other words, humans can't fully understand the nature of the divinity, which is the first cause or creative force in nature.

Taoists, however, hold that participation in the divinity can be achieved by intuitive or mystical methods, including magic, meditation, special diets, breath control and the recitation of scriptures.

Taoism's objective is to achieve balance and harmony, internally as well as with nature and spiritual forces. The Taoist ideal is a person who avoids conventional social obligations and leads a simple, spontaneous and meditative life close to nature.

Among the tenets of the Taoist life:

- To know nature.

- To be natural (to live a natural life).

- To avoid interfering with nature.

Among the qualities found in the practicing Taoist:

- Care of the body (physical culture).

- Social service.

- A cheerful outlook on life.

The ultimate goal of Taoism is immortality—in this life. Or, as one writer describes the Taoist view: "Life is good and worth living. Let us improve it and prolong it indefinitely."

BUDDHISM

Buddhism was founded in India about 500 B.C. by a teacher and philosopher named Gautama Siddhartha, known as Gautama Buddha ("Buddha" is a form of the Sanskrit word meaning "awakened" or "enlightened").

At various times, Buddhism also has been a major influence in China, Japan, Korea, Thailand, Vietnam and Tibet; it is the most metaphysical of the three great religions that shaped Chinese history. In each area, Buddhism has combined with elements of other religions such as Hinduism and Shinto.

Today, Buddhism's 250 million adherents are primarily in Southeast Asia and Japan.

Buddhism deals with human suffering and final achievement of a state of perfect peace and happiness.

Unlike Confucianism and Taoism, Buddhism deals with the issues of human suffering, the path of escape from that suffering, the existence of an afterlife and final achievement of a state of perfect peace and happiness.

All Buddhists have faith in Buddha; his teachings, called the *dharma*; and the religious community he founded, called the *sangha*.

THE DHARMA

Central to Buddha's teaching are the Four Noble Truths:

- Life is suffering.

- Desire is the cause of that suffering.

- By bringing about the cessation of desire, we can put an end to the cause of suffering.

- The elimination of desire can be accomplished by following the Middle Way and the Eightfold Noble Path.

The Middle Way is a way of life that avoids both the uncontrolled satisfaction of human desires and the extreme forms of self-denial and self-torture.

The Eightfold Noble Path consists of:

- Right views (knowledge of the truth).

- Right resolve (to resist evil).

- Right speech (saying nothing to hurt others).

- Right action (respecting life, morality and property).

- Right living (working at a job that does not injure others).

- Right effort (trying to rid one's mind of evil).

- Right attention (controlling thoughts and feelings).

- Right meditation (practicing proper forms of concentration).

Also central to Buddhist teaching are the related ideas of *karma* and the Wheel of Life.

The Wheel of Life is a way of expressing the idea that existence is a continuing cycle of death and rebirth. Karma, a concept shared with Hinduism, is about cause and effect: A person's position and fate in this life are the consequence of his or her actions in previous lives, and actions in this life will determine a person's fate in the next.

Good deeds, a Buddhist believes, can lead to rebirth as a holy, wise or wealthy person; evil deeds can lead to rebirth as a person of lowly station—ignorant, ill, impoverished.

As long as people remain locked in this cycle of death and rebirth, Buddha taught, they can never be free of pain and suffering. But by ridding themselves of all attachment to worldly things and sensual pleasures—by following the

The related ideas of karma and the Wheel of Life are central to Buddhist belief.

Middle Way and the Eightfold Noble Path—
they can attain a state of perfect peace and
happiness, which Buddha called *nirvana*.

Buddha taught that every person has the
potential for attaining nirvana.

THE SANGHA

Sangha sometimes refers to the ideal Buddhist
community, which consists of those who have
reached the higher stages of spiritual
development, or to the order of Buddhist monks
and nuns. However, the term also means the
total Buddhist community of monks, nuns
and laity.

Monks are expected to live a life of poverty,
meditation and study, and to avoid sexual
activity. Some Buddhists become monks for life,
but others serve in the sangha only for short
periods of time. The monks wear special robes
and are a common sight in all Buddhist
countries.

*Some Buddhists
become monks for
life, but others
serve only for short
periods of time.*

Lay Buddhists are expected to honor Buddha, to
follow basic moral rules and to support the
monks. They also are expected to pay special
honor to images of Buddha and to objects
associated with him.

Buddha urged his followers, including lay
persons, to practice certain virtues:

- Kindness and compassion.

- Meekness and nonviolence.

- Charity and almsgiving.

- Reflection and contemplation.

Major branches or schools of Buddhism include the *Theravada*, the *Mahayana*, the *Mantrayana* and *Zen*.

THE THERAVADA

Theravada means "Way of the Elders." Theravada Buddhism is the dominant religion of Thailand and other countries of Southeast Asia. Theravadans emphasize the importance of Buddha as a historical figure, the virtues of the monastic life and the authority of the *Tripitaka* (teachings of Buddha). For them, the ideal Buddhist is a kind of saint called an *arhat*.

Theravada Buddhism is the dominant religion of Thailand and other countries of Southeast Asia.

THE MAHAYANA

The word Mahayana means "Great Vehicle." Most followers of the Mahayana school live in Japan and East Asia.

The Mahayanists emphasize the existence of many Buddhas—both Buddhas in heaven and people who will become Buddhas in the future. They believe these present and future Buddhas are able to save people through grace and compassion.

The Mahayanist ideal is the *bodhisattva*—a person who vows to become a Buddha by leading a life of virtue.

THE MANTRAYANA

Mantrayana (known as *Shingon* in Japan) means "Sacred Recitation Vehicle." This form of Buddhism is practiced mostly in the Himalayas, Mongolia and Japan.

Mantrayana Buddhism accepts most Mahayanan doctrines, but also emphasizes a close relationship between a spiritual leader called a *guru* and a small group of disciples—who spend much of their time reciting prayers or hymns called *mantras*, performing sacred dances and gestures, and meditating.

ZEN

Zen originated in China but is practiced chiefly in Japan. It is probably the form of Buddhism best known in the West.

Zen accepts Mahayanan doctrines but also emphasizes a close relationship between a master and his disciples. Zen has developed distinctive practices—including methods of meditation— that are designed to lead to a state of spiritual

Zen is probably the form of Buddhism best known in the West.

enlightenment called *satori*. Many followers of Zen believe that satori comes in a sudden flash of insight; others believe it must be achieved gradually through self-discipline, meditation and instruction.

SHINTO

Shinto means "Way of the Gods" and is the oldest surviving religion of Japan. No one knows exactly when or how Shinto began, but it probably originated with Japan's aboriginal people before the massive immigration from mainland Asia. An estimated 80 million Japanese practice Shinto in some form.

Shintoists venerate ancestors and worship many gods, called *kami*. Kami are the spiritual force in mountains, rivers, rocks, trees and other aspects of nature. Shinto also considers the kami a fundamental force in such processes as creativity, disease, growth and healing.

Shinto emphasizes rituals and moral standards, but its main concern is to obtain the blessing of the gods for the events of daily life. Ceremonies are held to bless babies, children (*Shichigosan* festival), weddings and the start of new enterprises. Other ceremonies deal with such basic goals as long life, peace, abundant harvests and good health.

Even large corporations take no chances and enlist the aid of a Shinto priest for ceremonies

Shinto's main concern is to obtain the blessing of the gods for the events of daily life.

involving openings, anniversaries and other special occasions.

Shintoists worship both at public shrines and at small shrines in their homes. Public shrines, called *jinja, taisha* or *jingu* (depending on rank) are generally identifiable by a *torii* gate—two uprights connected by a double crossbar. There usually are carved stone *koma-inu* (guardian lions or dogs) at the entrance. If portrayed correctly, the mouth of one lion is open and the other closed; this symbolizes "ah" and "um," the sounds of birth and death, the beginning and the end, from Hindu mythology. The distance between them is the Path of Life, a reminder to those walking between them of the shortness of their temporal existence.

Influenced by both Buddhism and Confucianism, Shinto developed such moral standards as honesty, kindness and respect for one's elders and superiors.

Some of the New Religions, later movements of Shinto, have encouraged group worship, charity work and the organization of society on a cooperative basis.

Even large corporations take no chances and enlist the aid of a Shinto priest for ceremonies involving openings, anniversaries and other special occasions.

It is common for Japanese to follow both Shinto and Buddhist beliefs without apparent conflict, since each covers certain aspects of life not touched by the other: Shinto is perceived to deal with the here-and-now, while Buddhism is thought to deal with death and the hereafter. It is common for Japanese to be married in Shinto ceremonies but buried in Buddhist ones.

HINDUISM

Hinduism, the major religion of India and the single most important influence on its culture, is one of the world's oldest religions. Its adherents in India number well over 300 million.

Unlike other major religions of Asia, Hinduism was not inspired by one individual, but rather evolved organically, drawing on diverse religious, philosophical and cultural influences.

The multiplicity of Hinduism's sources, along with its great number of sacred texts and the variety of forms in which it is practiced, have tended to make it relatively inaccessible to the uninitiated.

Hinduism has basic beliefs about divinities, life after death, and how its followers should conduct their lives.

The concepts of transmigration and *karman* are central to Hindu doctrine. The basic principle of transmigration is that the soul passes from body to body according to its works. Gods, humans, animals and demons all are linked in this cycle of birth and death and rebirth.

The nature of the new life to which the soul passes is determined by karman (literally "action," "work" or "deed.") As a person acts in one life, so he or she enjoys happiness or sorrow in the next. Similarly, a withered arm in this life must be atonement for an act of violence done by that arm in a previous life.

Hindus believe that this cycle of reincarnation continues until a person achieves spiritual perfection. The soul then enters a new level of existence, called *moksha*, from which it never returns.

Hindus also believe there are terrible purgatories below the earth, where the souls of great sinners suffer until they atone for the worst of their sins and are given another chance on earth.

In karman and transmigration, Hindus share two major beliefs with their Buddhist brethren.

Hindus, however, are polytheistic—they worship many gods. Hindus came to believe that, though divinities appear in separate forms, these forms are part of one universal spirit called *Brahman* (from the Sanskrit word meaning "absolute" or "universal soul"). The three most important divinities are *Brahma*, the creator of the universe; *Vishnu*, its preserver; and *Shiva*, its destroyer.

Gods, humans, animals and demons all are linked in the cycle of birth and death and rebirth.

In karman and transmigration, Hindus share two major beliefs with their Buddhist brethren.

Another important Hindu divinity is Shiva's wife, who has several names: *Durga, Kali, Parvati* and *Uma*. She is the goddess of motherhood—and also the feared goddess of destruction. For many Hindus these contrasting natures of the goddess represent the way in which time and matter constantly move from birth to death and from creation to destruction.

According to Hindu doctrine, animals as well as human beings have souls. Hindus worship many animals as gods. Cows are the most sacred, but Hindus also worship monkeys, snakes and other animals.

Hindus worship as individuals, not as congregations. Most Hindu temples have a principal shrine devoted to an important god or goddess and an array of other shrines devoted to lesser divinities.

Hindus worship many animals as gods. Cows are the most sacred.

The shrines portray the divinities in sculptured images, which Hindus treat as living human beings. Every day, for example, priests wash and dress the images and bring them food. Hindus do not consider this worshiping idols; they believe the divinities are actually present in the images.

Many Hindu observances take place in the home. Most homes have a shrine devoted to a divinity chosen by the family, and daily worship is conducted by the husband or wife. A number of important religious ceremonies are performed at home, including one in which boys officially become members of the Hindu community, marriages, and rituals connected with pregnancy and childbirth.

Hinduism is the basis for India's caste system, which dictates the way of life for many Hindus. There are four castes, called *varnas*. In order of rank, these hereditary groups are:

- *Brahmans*, or priests.

- *Kshatriyas*, princes and warriors.

- *Vaisyas*, merchants and landowners.

- *Sudras*, farmers, laborers and servants.

The caste system includes thousands of subcastes, each of which has its own rules of behavior.

For centuries, one large group, the *untouchables*, existed outside the caste system and ranked below the lowest caste. Through the years, the caste system has weakened in India. Some social distinctions have been abandoned, especially in the cities. Many educated Hindus of different castes mix freely with one another. However, the caste system remains a strong influence in Indian life.

The caste system has weakened in India, and some social distinctions have been abandoned, especially in the cities.

ISLAM

Islam is the religion preached by the Prophet Muhammad in the sixth century. Muhammad, who was born in Mecca about 570 A.D., believed he was sent to warn and guide his people and to call them to worship *Allah* (God).

Its central creed is contained in two sentences called The *Shahada*: "There is no god but God. Muhammad is the messenger of God."

Those who accept and believe in this doctrine are called Muslims. *Muslim* is an Arabic word that means "one who submits (to God)," and *Islam* is Arabic for "submission." Always use the pronunciation *Muslim*, never *Moslem*.

Muslims do not worship Muhammad and are offended when Westerners call Islam "Muhammadanism" and its followers "Muhammadans."

Islam's central creed is contained in two sentences: "There is no god but God. Muhammad is the messenger of God."

As one of the world's largest religions, Islam has more than 550 million followers who are united by the common bond of faith and culture.

The loyal followers of Muhammad preserved his revelations by memorizing them or writing them down during his lifetime. Muslim scholars believe Muhammad approved these teachings. Later, the materials were combined to form the holy book called the *Koran*, from the Arabic word meaning "recitation."

The Koran contains many stories about the Old Testament prophets and also stories from the New Testament about Jesus Christ, whom it calls the Word of God.

The Koran sets forth four principal doctrines of Islamic faith:

- Faith in the absolute unity of God.

- Belief in angels as messengers and helpers of God.

- Belief in revealed scripture and prophetic messengers. Muslims believe Muhammad was the last of these prophets; Jesus and the Old Testament prophets were his predecessors.

- Belief in a final judgment, in which faithful followers of God and his true religion are included in the divine plan of triumph and reward.

The Koran teaches that God is just and merciful and wishes people to repent and purify themselves so that they can attain paradise after death. Like the Bible, it forbids lying, stealing, adultery and murder. It also denounces usury, games of chance, and the consumption of pork and alcohol.

The Koran contains stories from both the Old and New Testaments. It calls Jesus Christ "The Word of God."

Punishment is based on the Old Testament law of retaliation, "an eye for an eye and a tooth for a tooth." Unjust killing is punished by death, unless it is accidental. If it is accidental, "blood money" is paid to the dead person's relatives.

Islam teaches that life on earth is a period of testing and preparation for the life to come. Salvation can be attained through the Five Acts of Worship—also known as the Pillars of Islam:

- Physical and spiritual purification.

- Prayer or worship (*salat*).

- Almsgiving.

- Fasting during the holy month of *Ramadan*.

- Pilgrimage to Mecca (the *Hajj*).

Muslims pray five times daily: at dawn, at noon, in the afternoon, in the evening and at nightfall. A crier, or *muezzin*, announces prayer time from the minaret (mosque tower).

On Friday, which for Muslims resembles the Jewish Sabbath and Christian Sunday, Muslims are expected to attend noon prayers at a mosque. At worship Muslims ceremonially wash their faces, hands and feet immediately before prayer.

Islam teaches that salvation can be attained through the Five Acts of Worship—also known as the Pillars of Islam.

The prayer leader faces Mecca. The men stand in rows behind him, and the women stand behind the men.

The prayers consist of reciting passages from the Koran and other phrases of praise to God. They include such movements as bowing from the hips and kneeling with the face to the ground. Friday prayers are preceded by a sermon.

Ramadan, the ninth month of the Muslim year, is the holy month of fasting during which the faithful may not eat or drink from dawn to sunset. Muslims joyfully celebrate the end of the long fast in a three-day festival.

Ramadan is the holy month of fasting during which the faithful may not eat or drink from dawn to sunset.

All able Muslims are required by the Koran to make the pilgrimage to Mecca at least once. The most important ceremonies required during the pilgrimage include walking seven times around the *Kaaba*, Islam's most sacred shrine, and kissing the sacred Black Stone in its wall (said to have been given to Abraham by the archangel Gabriel). Most Muslims include a visit to the Mosque of Muhammad in Medina.

Islam does not have an organized priesthood. Any virtuous Muslim can lead prayers in most mosques. However, it is usually the imam, a person chosen for piety or scholarship, who leads prayer services and gives sermons.

ANCESTOR WORSHIP

Although the veneration of ancestors is an integral part of such Asian beliefs as Confucianism and Shintoism, ancestor worship as practiced in China, Vietnam and elsewhere goes a step further.

This practice—which assumes that the living can communicate with the dead—is rooted in the belief that if a family worships the spirits of its ancestors it will be rewarded with prosperity and good fortune. There is an inherent belief in an afterlife and a spirit world.

Most ancestor worship takes place at shrines in the home and at the graves of ancestors. Ancestor worship is commonly combined with another religion, such as Buddhism.

ANIMISM AND FENG SHUI

Animism is any belief that attributes to inanimate objects and natural phenomena the qualities of conscious life and an innate soul or spirit; it often embraces the belief that these spirits can exert a good or evil influence.

Animism in some form or other is practiced in many parts of Asia, often in combination with another religion. Among its best-known adherents are the Chinese of Hong Kong, where the understanding of these spirits is known as geomancy or *feng shui*.

Literally, feng shui means the study of wind and water. As practiced, it governs the positioning of buildings, doors and windows as well as furnishings like desks, beds and chairs…and ultimately people.

"The Chinese believe that the earth is a living organism," Yue-Sai Kan writes in *Compass Readings*, the Northwest Airlines magazine. "Like all living matter, it has *ch'i*—'breath' or 'life.' If you situate a building where the earth has good chi, then this will vitalize the people who live or work in it. Essentially, a feng shui master detects a chi area in the earth, pinpointing the best spot to place a building."

Even the august Hong Kong & Shanghai Bank, the British institution that issues the Hong Kong currency, sought a feng shui master to advise on the location of its new multimillion-dollar office building. According to one source, his fee was $50,000 and he worked closely with both architects and engineers.

And the Regent of Hong Kong hotel, often cited as one of the world's best, sheathed its lobby and mezzanine in 40-foot lengths of glass on a feng shui master's advice. According to one report, the hotel rises at a site where "a dragon enters the harbor for his bath." By designing a see-through lobby, the hotel avoided any chance of disrupting the dragon's ritual—an event that could have brought bad fortune to employees and guests alike.

The Hong Kong & Shanghai Bank sought a feng shui master to advise on the location of its new multimillion-dollar office building. According to one source, his fee was $50,000.

Although you don't necessarily have to believe in feng shui, if you're doing business in Hong Kong (or some parts of China), you'd be well advised to respect and observe this tradition. Many Westerners have ignored this custom and paid the price—a business failure.

Here are some feng shui tips:

- Ask a Hong Kong businessperson for the name and number of a reliable feng shui man.

- Do not attempt to open a factory, office or other facility without consulting a feng shui man, who will advise on the location of the facility and the entrance, the moving date and the opening date. He will position furniture and equipment to be in harmony with cosmic forces and will bring *joss* (blessing and good luck) to the business.

- Do not ignore this custom. Many Chinese will not do business without feng shui approval for fear of offending the spirits.

THE FENG SHUI MAN	*An executive with years of international experience was sent to Hong Kong to open the Asia branch of his U.S. bank. After he rented and furnished an elegant office suite, his Chinese employees expressed concern about the position of his furniture. His desk, they warned, was facing the door—a direction that invited evil spirits to cause trouble.*

*After much discussion, he agreed to place a plant
between his desk and the door to satisfy his
employees—not to divert the evil spirits.*

*All went well until he returned from vacation to find
the office in turmoil and the plant dead. The
employees apparently were correct; evil spirits had
killed the plant.*

*He rearranged his furniture immediately and advises
others to consult a feng shui man before decorating
their offices.*

Know and observe the rules for visiting a temple
or mosque in order to show respect for your
host's religious beliefs. Here are some guidelines:

VISITING SACRED PLACES

BUDDHIST TEMPLE

- Remove hats and sunglasses and extinguish
  cigarettes before entering a temple.

- Incense sticks are placed upright in the urn
  at the entrance to the temple.

- Kneel before the altar on one of the red
  pillows and bow your head with
  each beat of the monk's drum.

- Ask sincere questions about
  the different postures of the
  Buddha images—each
  signifying a different stage in his
  life and teaching.

- Your host may invite you to have an astrologer read your fortune. Accept this gift graciously. Your host will probably pay the fee.

WAT (THAI BUDDHIST TEMPLE)

- The *bot* is the most sacred part of the temple, where the main Buddha image resides. Remove your shoes before entering.

- Be careful to step over high thresholds when walking through the *wat*.

- Never climb on statues of the Buddha.

- Don't sit cross-legged or remain standing in the bot. Visitors are expected to be lower than the monks.

- *Wai* (bow and bring your hands together in front of your face) before the Buddha and present your wishes. You may get them!

- If making an offering you will be given flowers, a candle, a piece of gold leaf and three incense sticks. Light the candle and place it with others. Put the flower in the water vessel. Light the incense with the candle. Place the incense sticks in the urn and press the leaf onto the Buddha image.

MUSLIM MOSQUE

- Rules are strictly enforced and few mosques are open to foreigners.

- Take off your shoes at the entrance.

- Wash your hands and face in an adjacent tiled washing area.

- Women should not shake anyone's hand inside a mosque.

- Greet the man at the door with a *salaam* (a low bow while touching right hand to forehead).

- If asked, put on one of the robes at the door before entering.

- Kneel on prayer rugs facing east (toward the holy city of Mecca).

- The interior of mosques is devoid of icons or statues because Muslims believe it is blasphemous to imitate the work of Allah. The mosque is for undistracted and uninterrupted prayer.

Regardless of which Asian country you're in to visit, study or do business, the more you understand and respect local religious traditions, the more successful you'll be.

RESPECTING LOCAL BELIEFS

C. William Carey, Town & Country's chairman and CEO, talked to *World Trade* magazine about opening his company's highly successful plant in Thailand:

"Our challenge was to become acceptable at the grass-roots level. Buddhists from the beginning, Thais are motivated by security and respect from the employer. That's why it was important to sit cross-legged for a 3 1/2-hour ceremony where nine Buddhist monks blessed the seven-story, 27,000-square-foot factory when it opened. A Buddhist spirit house was built at the factory so workers can recite daily prayers and make offerings—on their own time."

6.

MEETING AND GREETING

The first impression is powerful! A good first impression creates the expectation of a positive relationship. A bad first impression, on the other hand, can be overcome only with a lot of work over a long period of time—and sometimes we don't get that chance.

First impressions are completely different in Asia than in the West. When two Asians meet, there is an immediate and mutual assessment taking place. A person's language, deference, formality, posture, manners, degree of bow or wai, eye contact, education, age, company and position all are being appraised. Only after each person's status is clear can two acquaintances communicate comfortably. First impressions have been formed; each knows where the other fits into the group. The relationship can proceed.

You can see why making a positive first impression in Asia may be difficult for

Westerners who are unaware of or insensitive to this process. Flagrant displays of individuality, loudness, arrogance or aggressiveness, back-slapping (or any touching) and sloppiness in posture, dress or speech will offend or embarrass your Asian host.

You may be uncomfortable with people who are formal and impersonal. You may regard these greeting rituals as a waste of time and unrelated to accomplishing your business objectives. If this is the case, you'd be better off staying at home.

Your chances of creating a good first impression improve enormously if you've done your homework. Your host may appear in a three-piece pinstripe suit, shake hands, smile and say "How do you do?" But, on the other hand, you should be prepared to observe the local meeting customs—to bow or wai or salaam, to exchange business cards in the appropriate way, to make or not make eye contact, to speak a phrase or two in the local language.

Being prepared—and flexible—will allow you to react comfortably regardless of the greeting offered.

You'll also be well served by restraint, common sense and good taste. The "Well, here I am, folks" or "How y'all doing?" greeting combined with a knuckle-breaking, arm-pumping handshake is not common in other parts of the world and not likely to get a relationship off to a good start. It is much more acceptable to show a polite reserve combined with an open and friendly attitude.

GENERAL RULES
FOR MEETING AND GREETING

Rule of Thumb

- Be yourself but be prepared to observe local greeting customs. Bow, wai, salaam or *namaste* (in India, a slight bow while bringing palms together at chest level) as appropriate. (See country chapters in Part III.) These greetings are not expected, but are very much appreciated.

Be yourself but be prepared to observe local greeting customs.

- Be prepared to give and receive a lighter, less firm handshake in Asia.

- Don't stand too close.

- Never shake hands with a glove on or one hand in your pocket.

- Eye contact may be brief.

- Maintain correct posture.

- Always establish and use a person's correct name.

- Introduce yourself properly. Say your full name, your title and job description and your company name:

  > Dr. John Moore
  > Vice President and head of the Asia-Pacific division
  > H.B. Stevens Company.

- Be reserved in speech, posture and dress.

- Do not touch, back-slap or give a knuckle-breaking, arm-pumping handshake.

- Save your friendly, exuberant personality for later meetings.

- If possible, allow a respected and well-connected third party to introduce you.

- Always give and receive a business card properly.

BOW OR HANDSHAKE?

Bowing is a typical form of greeting in Korea and Japan.

Bowing is a typical greeting in Korea and Japan and to a lesser extent in China and Taiwan. The bow imbues an encounter with formality and can express gratitude, devotion, sympathy, loyalty, apology, congratulations or a simple "hello" or "goodbye."

The bow is a highly regarded way to show respect. The depth of the bow depends upon the relationship between the people involved, the situation in which bows are exchanged, and the country in which you are bowing.

Most Asians will greet Westerners with a handshake, and Japanese and Korean businesspeople also will usually offer a slight bow. Do not attempt a full-fledged bow with all its nuances unless you have taken the time to learn the proper bow for each country. Failing this knowledge, shake hands and bow slightly.

7.

NAMES AND TITLES

Don't use first names until explicitly invited to do so by your host. Asians know that the United States is a "first name" country. We shift from last names to first names almost on first meeting.

We consider it warm, comfortable and friendly to do so. We think everyone else would like to do the same. That's not the case in Asia. Most Asians address each other by their formal names indefinitely. Asians, in general, do not want to call you by your first name, and— except in Thailand and Indonesia, where last names are long and difficult to pronounce— they don't want you to call them by theirs.

Titles in Asia are indicative of status and rank. They are important and should be used whenever they apply. President, secretary, mayor, doctor and director should be used. Some countries use the title without the name, e.g., Mr. President or Mr. Secretary. Some countries place the name before the title and others place the title before the name. Do your homework!

For Americans who have been reared with a "Just call me Bill" attitude, the concern much of the world has about names and titles seems superficial. In Asia proper use or misuse of someone's name and/or title can make the difference between a successful negotiation and an international incident. That's just the way it is. Correct use of a person's name and title shows respect; incorrect use is an insult.

Correct use of names and titles is one of the most complicated and difficult things for an international traveler—even an experienced one—to learn. Many specifics vary from country to country. Surnames, middle names and given names appear in different orders and different rules apply to their proper usage.

Each country chapter in Part III illustrates the correct way to use names in that place. Because these rules are so different from country to country, you will probably want to review this section every time you visit a country, talk on the phone, correspond with or host an Asian colleague.

Correct use of a person's name and title shows respect; incorrect use is an insult.

Correct name usage is challenging. However, it's worth making the effort. It shows consideration for your hosts and will win friends if done correctly. I'm sure President Clinton wishes he'd refreshed his memory on correct name usage during his last visit to Korea.

As the Associated Press reported:

"President Clinton, in a series of protocol missteps, embarrassed South Korean officials, confused his translator, baffled guests and briefly delayed his first state dinner abroad.

"As if that wasn't enough, he repeatedly referred incorrectly to the wife of President Kim Young Sam as Mrs. Kim. In Korea, a woman keeps her maiden name and the president's wife is Sohn Myong Suk, or Mrs. Sohn.

"When Clinton stepped to the microphone to deliver his dinner speech, he unexpectedly invited a translator to stand between himself and Kim, who was seated. In South Korea, it is an insult for anyone to stand between two heads of state. Korean officials were stunned by Clinton's move.

"Meanwhile, Clinton apparently realized that the translation was delaying dinner so he skipped some of his remarks, further confounding those trying to follow along.

"Protocol is taken seriously in Korea, where there are strict rules of behavior even among family members. A slight, however unintentional, can mar a friendship and ruin a business relationship...."

"The two presidents spoke...before Clinton stepped into his limousine and bade farewell. 'Good night, Mrs. Kim,' he said."

GENERAL RULES FOR USING NAMES AND TITLES IN ASIA

Rule of Thumb

Do not use first names unless and until specifically invited to do so.

- Do not use first names unless and until specifically invited to do so.

- Do your homework. Know the correct rules of name usage in each country. Each Asian country has very different and very distinct name usage rules.

- Remember, many Asian women keep their maiden names when married.

- Ask for a business card so you can *see* the correct spelling and correct title.

- Listen carefully to the pronunciation of the name when you're introduced to someone. Try to avoid having them repeat their names—but do so if it's absolutely necessary. It's better than getting it wrong.

- Ask each person by what name he or she prefers to be addressed.

- As soon as possible, jot down the phonetic pronunciation of a name.

- Err on the side of formality.

- When in doubt, use a title.

- If uncertain about the correct title, use a higher title but never a lesser title.

- Help the introducer or host with your name.

- Say your name slowly and pronounce it clearly.

Family history, rank and status are very important to Asians. Their names and titles are a source of pride, tradition and continuity. Understanding and respecting this tradition is essential to doing business or making friends in Asia.

Just think of it as "The Comfort Zone." If your aim is to make your hosts comfortable—and amenable to doing business—respect their cultural comfort zone when it comes to using names and titles.

THEM'S FIGHTIN' WORDS

Mispronouncing a person's name is an affront. In some countries, it is considered a grave insult. Speculation is that during the Gulf War, President George Bush intentionally mispronounced "Saddam" as "SAY-DEM" in order to anger Saddam Hussein. If that was his intention, he apparently was very successful. It was reported that Saddam was continuously infuriated by the mispronunciation of his name!

8.
LANGUAGE AND BODY LANGUAGE

If every businessperson's primary job is to serve his or her customers, then it follows that the language of international business is the language spoken by the customer.

Language is a great gift! It is given not only with your mouth but with your eyes, your hands and your body. It is your initial act of sharing yourself. It is the best way to win friends for yourself, your company and your country. This is where you shout, "I care about you, your country and your culture."

Nothing bespeaks your interest and concern more than taking the time to learn someone's language. The warmth, appreciation and welcome you will receive in return is incomparable.

Learning at least one of the local languages spoken in the dozen countries covered by this book would mean learning 10 languages. Let's

The language of international business is the language spoken by the customer.

face it: None of us has the time, let alone the ability, to learn 10 languages fluently.

So, what's the best approach? Learn a few simple, polite phrases in the language of whatever country you're going to visit—enough to show that you respect your hosts enough to try. Remember, trying counts and mistakes made while trying are good mistakes.

Learn how to greet and thank your hosts in their language. Learn a short toast. It doesn't have to be perfect; the effort will be greatly appreciated.

Most Western businesspeople expect Asians to overlook their lack of competence in the local language. Most will. In fact, many Asians speak English, which they have learned through years of studying and with great effort.

Remember, it is as difficult for a Japanese or Chinese to achieve fluency in English as it is for a Westerner to learn Chinese or Japanese fluently. Most of us wouldn't even attempt it. So when your hosts speak English as a courtesy to you, show appreciation, respect and patience. Remember, English is usually their second or third language.

CULTURAL MISPERCEPTION

A look at two "typical American sentences" from a recent textbook used to teach Japanese how to speak American-style English illustrates how erroneous perceptions of foreign cultures might lead to some comic misunderstandings.

Typical sentence #12, reportedly something an American might say to a bartender: "I'm sorry I clogged the sink. I didn't want to vomit on the floor."

Typical sentence #44, as used by an American man in conversation with his wife: "This is not a hickey, it's from scratching my neck."

Alas, similar cultural misperceptions often color our attempts to communicate with Asians.

To avoid misunderstandings with your Asian colleagues:

- Speak slowly and clearly.

- Use simple, straightforward words—no idioms, jargon or slang. And no sports analogies!

- Never assume the listener understands your meaning; if there's any doubt, repeat what you said in a slightly different way.

Faux Pas

Avoid idioms, jargon or slang and sports analogies.

- Nod when you understand. Remember, a nod means "I understand," not "Yes."

- Use audio-visual aids in the local language.

- Translate business documents into the local language.

- Remember, never correct an Asian's English pronunciation in front of anyone. This would cause embarrassment and loss of face, and could seriously jeopardize a promising relationship.

- Leave room for error; assume the best.

- Always be patient.

- Never jump to conclusions.

You probably remember the tragic story of Yoshihiro Hattori, the Japanese teenager who was an exchange student in Baton Rouge, Louisiana, and went to the wrong home for a Halloween party. He was shot and killed by the homeowner apparently because he didn't stop when the man ordered him to do so by shouting "freeze."

To the average Japanese who has grown up in a nonviolent society and studied English for six years in school, the homeowner offered no threat and "freeze" meant "ice cold." So be aware! When you're communicating across a language barrier, the words may sound familiar, but the speaker's meaning may be quite different from what the listener understands.

Most Asian languages are tonal, and the way a word is pronounced can change its meaning entirely. Also, the transliteration of Chinese or Japanese ideograms and Arabic or Sanskrit words into English is a purely phonetic rendering, and there often are multiple spellings. Some examples: *hadj, hajj, haj,* a Muslim's pilgrimage to Mecca; *Lao Tzu, Lao-tsu, Lao-tse,* Chinese philosopher; *Mao Zedong, Mao Tse-tung,* Chinese political leader.

Asian languages are different in other ways too: Most of them contain honorific pronouns that express a level of intimacy, social rank, age or gender and higher or lower status. Strangers do not strike up conversations; a person wouldn't know how to speak to a stranger without knowing his or her rank and status.

Language is indirect and vague with sentences left unfinished. Speech is filled with delicate nuances and delivered with courtesy and respect in a soft voice. "Yes" often means "I'm listening" or "I understand," not "I agree." "Let's wait and see" or "I'll try, but it could be difficult" may mean "No."

A task-oriented, time-conscious, frank and aggressive Westerner may find this way of communicating frustrating and difficult to understand. The face-conscious Asian, on the other hand, will not be favorably inclined to do business with someone he or she regards as blunt, crude, aggressive and confrontational.

CONFLICT AND COMPROMISE

Harmony may seem like a strange value in the United States, which graduates some 40,000 lawyers yearly and is by far the most litigious society in the world. We thrive on conflict— some companies regard it as energy to be managed constructively. Problems are solved through an adversarial process.

Business associates, friends—even strangers— openly discuss, debate and disagree on any issue that might arise. Many people consider the debate—win or lose—the fun of conversation.

This is not true in Asia. In a society that's oriented to the group rather than the individual, conflict is to be avoided. Problem-solving is nonconfrontational—that is, by consensus.

When you openly attack an Asian's idea, it will be viewed as an attack on him or her personally—which would cause a loss of face and could doom any relationship.

Silence may be Asians' response to conflict. They may smile and change the subject. They may pull back from the discussion and ultimately withdraw from the relationship.

The Westerner who travels to Asia generally is adventuresome and outgoing, anxious to forge friendships and business deals quickly. Asians remain formal and impersonal until trust is established.

However, once trust is established and friendship offered, Asians will share confidences about personal lives, children, family, business, even intimate thoughts and feelings. When an Asian offers this kind of confidence, it must be handled sensitively and taken seriously. To take this relationship lightly could be devastating to the confiding Asian.

USING INTERPRETERS

You've hired an interpreter. Your communication problems are solved, right? Watch out! Your problems may just be starting.

Clear communication of ideas in a business negotiation is difficult, even when the parties share a common tongue. When business is conducted in more than one language, misunderstandings cannot be avoided. Effective use of your interpreter is crucial to clear communication.

Here are some tips for using an interpreter:

- Apologize to your counterparts for being unable to converse in the local tongue.

- Ask your interpreter to advise you on the expected meeting style—punctuality, preliminary small talk, getting down to the major issues, identity of key counterparts.

- Discuss with your interpreter in advance the subject of the meetings and the main points you plan to make.

- Remember, it is very rude in Asia to place an interpreter between yourself and the party to whom you are speaking.

- Look at and address your remarks to your counterpart, not the interpreter.

- Take your time; speak slowly and clearly.

- Keep your language simple and direct.

- Pause frequently to allow for interpretation—after every verbal

Pick up the phone.

Pick up the miles.

1-800-FLY-FREE

Now when you sign up with MCI® you can earn up to 8,000 bonus miles on any one of the airlines below.* Then earn another 5 miles for every dollar** (or 1 flight credit for every $150) you spend on MCI long distance, cellular, paging, or calls with your MCI Card® from anywhere in the world. You're going to use these services anyway. Why not rack up the miles while you're doing it?

Is this a great time, or what? :-) **MCI**

Pick Up The Phone
Pick Up The Miles

MCI Calling Card
123 456 7890 1234
J. D. SMITH

You earn frequent flyer miles when you travel internationally – why not when you call internationally?

- Callers can earn frequent flyer miles with one of MCI's airline partners.

- Access to the U.S. from more than 125 countries and places around the world

- Operators who speak your language

- 24-hour customer service

MCI

Please call MCI for complete program details at 1-800-444-1616

MCI

Reference Guide for MCI Card Calling in the U.S. and Worldwide

Calling Card
123 456 7890 1234
J. D. SMITH

MCI

COUNTRY		WORLDPHONE TOLL-FREE ACCESS #
American Samoa		633-2MCI (633-2624)
# Antigua	(Available from public card phones only)	#2
# Argentina		0800-555-1002
# Aruba ÷		800-888-8
# Australia (CC) ■	To call using OPTUS ■	1-800-551-111
	To call using TELSTRA ■	1-800-881-100
# Austria (CC) ÷		0800-200-235
# Bahamas (CC)		1-800-888-8000
Bahrain		800-002
# Barbados		1-800-888-8000
Belarus	From Brest, Vitebsk, Grodno, Minsk	8-800-103
	From Gomel and Mogilev regions	8-10-800-103
Belgium (CC) ◆		0800-10012
# Belize	From Hotels	557
	From Payphones	815
# Bermuda ÷		1-800-888-8000
# Bolivia ◆		0-800-2222
# Brazil (CC)		000-8012
# British Virgin Islands ÷		1-800-888-8000
Brunei		800-011
# Bulgaria (CC)		00800-0001
# Cayman Islands		1-800-888-8000
# Chile (CC)	To call using CTC ■	800-207-300
	To call using ENTEL ■	800-360-180
# China ◆	(Available from most major cities)	108-12
# Colombia (CC) ◆		980-16-0001
# Costa Rica ÷		0800-012-2222
# Cote D'Ivoire		1001
# Croatia (CC) ★		99-385-0112
# Cyprus ◆		080-90000
# Czech Republic (CC) ◆		00-42-000112
# Denmark (CC) ◆		8001-0022
# Dominican Republic (CC)		1-800-888-8000
# Ecuador (CC) ÷		999-170
# Egypt (CC) ÷	(Outside of Cairo, dial 02 first)	355-5770
El Salvador ◆		800-1767
Federated States of Micronesia		624
# Finland (CC) ◆		004-890-10012
# France (CC) ÷		0800-102-80
French Antilles (CC)	(Martinique, Guadeloupe)	0800-99-0019
French Guiana (CC)		0800-99-0019
# Gambia ◆		00-1-99
# Germany (CC)		0130-0012
# Greece (CC) ◆		00-800-1211
# Grenada ÷		1-800-888-8000

COUNTRY		WORLDPHONE TOLL-FREE ACCESS #
# Guam (CC) ÷		950-1022
Guatemala (CC) ◆		99-99-189
# Guyana		177
# Haiti (CC) ÷		193
Honduras (CC) ÷		122
# Hong Kong (CC)		800-1121
# Hungary (CC) ◆		00▼800-01411
# Iceland (CC) ◆		800-9002
# India (CC)	(Available from most major cities)	000-127
# Indonesia (CC)		001-801-11
Iran ÷		(SPECIAL PHONES ONLY)
# Ireland (CC)		1-800-55-1001
# Israel (CC)		1-800-920-2727
# Italy (CC) ◆		172-172-1022
Jamaica		1-800-888-8000
# Japan (CC) ◆	To call using KDD ■	0039-12
	To call using IDC ■	0066-55-121
	To call using ITJ ■	0044-11-121
# Jordan		18-800-001
# Kazakhstan (CC)		8-800-131-4321
# Kenya	(Available from most major cities)	080011
# Korea (CC)	To call using KT ■	009-14
	To call using DACOM ■	0039-12
	Phone Booth◆÷	Press red button, 03, then ★
	Military Bases	550-2255
# Kuwait		800-MCI (800-624)
# Lebanon ◆		600-MCI (600-624)
# Liechtenstein (CC) ◆		0800-89-0222
# Luxembourg		0800-0112
# Macao		0800-131
# Malaysia (CC) ◆		1-800-80-0012
Malta		0800-89-0120
# Marshall Islands		1-800-888-8000
# Mexico		95-800-888-8000
# Monaco (CC) ◆		800-99-0019
Morocco		00-211-0012
# Netherlands (CC) ◆		0800-022-9122
# Netherlands Antilles (CC) ÷		001-800-950-1022
# New Zealand (CC)		000-912
# Nicaragua (CC)	(Outside of Managua, dial 02 first)	166
# Norway (CC) ◆		800-19912
# Panama	Military Bases	108
		2810-108
# Papua New Guinea (CC)		05-07-19140
# Paraguay ÷		008-11-800
# Peru		0800-500-10
# Philippines (CC) ◆	To call using PLDT ■	105-14
	To call using PHILCOM ■	1026-14

COUNTRY		WORLDPHONE TOLL-FREE ACCESS #
# Poland (CC) ÷		00-800-111-21-22
# Portugal (CC) ÷		05-017-1234
# Puerto Rico (CC)		1-800-888-8000
# Qatar ★		0800-012-77
Romania (CC) ÷	To call using ROSTELCOM ■	01-800-1800
Russia (CC) ◆ ★	To call using SOVINTEL ■	747-3322
		960-2222
		950-1022
San Marino (CC) ◆		172-1022
# Saudi Arabia (CC)		1-800-11
# Singapore		8000-112-112
# Slovak Republic (CC)		0021-00112
# Slovenia		080-8808
# South Africa (CC)		0800-99-0011
# Spain (CC)		900-99-0014
Sri Lanka	(Outside of Colombo, dial 01 first)	440100
# St. Lucia ÷		1-800-888-8000
St. Vincent (CC) ◆		1-800-888-8000
# Sweden (CC) ◆		020-795-922
# Switzerland (CC) ◆		0800-89-0222
# Syria		0080
# Taiwan (CC) ◆		0080-13-4567
# Thailand ★		001-999-1-2001
# Trinidad & Tobago ÷		1-800-888-8000
# Turkey (CC) ◆		00-8001-1177
# Turks and Caicos ÷		1-800-888-8000
# Ukraine (CC)		8▼10-013
# United Arab Emirates ◆		800-111
# United Kingdom (CC)	To call using BT ■	0800-89-0222
	To call using MERCURY ■	0500-89-0222
# United States (CC)		1-800-888-8000
# Uruguay		000-412
# U.S. Virgin Islands (CC)		1-800-888-8000
# Vatican City (CC)		172-1022
# Venezuela (CC) ÷ ★		800-1114-0
# Vietnam ■		1201-1022

Automation available from most locations.
(CC) Country-to-country calling available to/from most international locations.
÷ Limited availability.
▼ Wait for second dial tone.
■ When calling from public phones, use phones marked LADATEL.
★ International communications carrier.
◆ Not available from public pay phones.
● Public phones may require deposit of coin or phone card for dial tone.
◆ Regulation does not permit Intra-Japan calls.
▲ Local service fee in U.S. currency required to complete call.

The MCI Card® with WorldPhone® Service… The easy way to call when traveling worldwide.

123 456 7890 1234
J. D. SMITH

If you already have a MCI Card, take the attached WorldPhone access guide on your next trip.

To get your MCI Card, call 1-800-444-1616.

MCI Card StepSavers

Your MCI Card has FREE built-in time-saving features and services for calls in the U.S. Just dial the orange 1-800 number on the back of your MCI Card, enter your MCI Card # and PIN. Then choose one of the ✱ features⁺ below:

✱91 Speed Dial Home
We've programmed your home phone number into your speed dialing system.

✱90 Speed Dial
You can store up to 8 other frequently called numbers and make changes as often as you like.

✱ Misdial
If you make a mistake dialing, press ✱ and re-enter the correct number.

Other MCI Card Features^

Request an MCI Operator to connect you to:

✚ Travelers Assist
Get local medical, legal, translation, restaurant and entertainment referrals.

? Directory Assistance
Obtain telephone numbers in the U.S. and worldwide.

🌐 Free Customer Assistance
Speak with a WorldPhone Operator in one of 19 languages, or request to be connected to an MCI Customer Service Professional.

Next Call
Don't hang up! To place consecutive calls, simply press # for 2 seconds. At the double tone, dial the area code and the next number.⁺

⁺ Available from touch tone phones only. Star (✱) features also available overseas except ✱91 and ✱7.
^ Rates and surcharges apply to all MCI Card calls.

Calling From the U.S. and Canada

To place a call from anywhere in the U.S., Canada, Puerto Rico, or the U.S. Virgin Islands:

❶ Dial **1 800 888-8000** and listen for the chime.

❷ Enter your MCI Card number + PIN and listen for the double tone.

❸ Dial the Area Code + Phone Number you are calling.

To call internationally:
Follow steps ❶ & ❷ then dial 011+ Country Code + City Code + Phone Number.

Calling From Overseas

To call back to the U.S. or from one country to another:

❶ Dial the WorldPhone toll-free access number of the country you are calling from.

❷ Follow the voice instructions in your language of choice or hold for a WorldPhone Operator.

❸ Give the WorldPhone Operator the telephone number you wish to call.

WorldPhone

Call the WorldPhone Hotline at **1 800 444-4141** within the U.S., or outside the U.S. call collect **916-567-5151** for a new country access availability, travel updates, and customer service assistance.

http://www.mci.com

MCI

"paragraph" and, when the subject matter is especially important or complicated, after every sentence.

- Ask questions and get feedback to make sure your ideas are being interpreted correctly and understood.

- Repeat your main points.

- Assume your counterparts can understand English, even if they're using an interpreter; never say anything you don't want others to hear.

- Follow up with a written summary of what was said and agreed.

VOLUME

A loud-mouthed Westerner is offensive to almost all Asians. Americans, in particular, seem to raise their voices when they are not being understood or do not get their way. This could cause an Asian to pull back from the discussion in an effort to avoid confrontation.

Americans seem to raise their voices when they are not being understood.

In Asia, the higher a person's status, the less volume he or she uses in speaking. To emphasize a point, Asians lower their volume. Try to avoid being loud or raising your voice; this is viewed as crass and could ruin the mood of a meeting.

BODY LANGUAGE

Eye contact, posture, where we put our hands, our feet, our arms, our legs, all send messages—positive or negative—to other people. We misread these signals constantly within our own culture. Can you imagine the mixed signals we can send and receive when dealing with another culture?

Behavioral scientists say there are 700,000 nonverbal signals given through body language. What one person views as proper behavior, another may consider an affront.

Surely, you say, there must be some common ground. How about the smile? It's the universally understood gesture. Not quite. By all means, smile. Smiling warms up any environment. However, be aware that your smile may not be returned; in some cultures, people don't smile at strangers. Also, the smile has different meanings in different cultures. Asians often smile to cover up embarrassment, confusion or anger. So even a smile can be misunderstood.

Body language figures prominently in a relationship with Asians. However, nonverbal signals are often misunderstood. Asians tend to control, or even deliberately manipulate, their facial expressions for effect. Americans' faces normally become stern when they're trying to make a serious point. An Asian, on the other

hand, may smile or laugh while making a
serious point in order to reduce the tension.

A smile or a laugh may be used to soften bad
news. Would you be shocked if an Asian told
you with a smile that his father died of lung
cancer? Remember, a smile or a laugh can mean
fear, humiliation, anger or apology. Be sensitive
to the context, and respond appropriately.

GENERAL BODY LANGUAGE RULES

- Never mimic anyone's behavior.

- Never mimic what you think is a national
  gesture.

- Never slap people on the back.

- Don't display affection in public.

- Don't put your hands in your pockets.

- Never stare at anyone.

- Cover your mouth when you yawn.

- Don't beckon someone with your index
  finger.

- Asians revere the head as the seat of the
  soul and consider feet the lowliest part of
  the body. (See "Taboos" section below.)

- Never touch an Asian person (and especially not a child's head).

EYE CONTACT

Westerners generally look into one another's eyes when meeting, greeting and conversing. How often have we said to our children, "Look at me when I'm speaking to you"? A person who doesn't look you in the eye is not to be trusted.

Not so in parts of Asia. Japanese children are scolded by their parents with a long, hard stare. Many Asians learn from an early age that continued, direct eye contact is rude and threatening.

When Asians do not look you in the eye it does not mean they aren't listening and paying attention. On the contrary, silence and lack of eye contact usually mean things are going well.

A lack of eye contact certainly should not be interpreted as a sign of dishonesty.

| A TEST OF CHARACTER? | *My father had a simple test for every young man who attempted to date his daughter. The boy's first handshake had to be a knuckle-buster and he needed to look directly into my father's eye's while introducing himself. Failure to do either of the above, my father felt, meant the young man had a severe character flaw. Luckily, I didn't fall in love with an exchange student from Asia.* |

TOUCHING

- Asians for the most part are non-touchers. Japanese spouses won't show any affection in public. Even children returning after long absences will stand three feet away from their parents and bow.

- If you attempt to back-slap or hug, most Asians will be very uncomfortable.

- Asian men do not touch foreign women. Confucius taught that men should not even pass an object to a woman.

- Do not touch an Asian of the opposite sex unless a close friendship has been established.

- During drinking sessions persons of the same sex may touch each other.

TABOOS

- Don't be loud! A persistent criticism of Americans all around the world is that we're too loud and boisterous. Cultivate a moderate tone and volume in speaking with Asians.

Feet

- Never point your feet or foot at anyone. Keep both feet on the floor. It is easy to accidentally point the sole of your shoe at someone if your legs are crossed.

- Don't swing a crossed leg or tap your foot on the floor.

- Don't prop your feet up on furniture.

- Don't talk about feet. That includes fallen arches, a corn, a bunion, etc.

Arms and Hands

- Talking with your arms and hands is considered unrefined. Do not put your hands in your pockets. Do not put your hands on your hips. Do not fold your arms over your chest. Rest your hands in your lap.

- Use both hands to give and receive objects—even a paper or pencil, and especially a business card. Passing objects with one hand shows a lack of respect. In some countries, it's customary to pass an object with the right hand and the palm of the left hand placed under the right forearm.

- Muslims in Asia, however, give and receive objects with right hand only. The left hand is considered very unclean.

9.

TRADITION AND SUPERSTITION

Tradition and superstition are threads running throughout the fabric of Asian society. Your Asian counterparts take these matters seriously—and so will you if you want to succeed in Asia.

The Asian concept of "face" combines the Western notions of honor, integrity, respect and reputation; the major difference is that face is far more important to an Asian than any of those other attributes is to a Westerner. The better your reputation in Asia—the more face you have—the more power and prestige you have and the more respect and deference you are shown.

FACE

A person maintains face by avoiding embarrassment, failure and defeat; by being consistent and avoiding inherently contradictory ideas, statements and behavior; and by achieving harmony with the group.

To "lose face" is to lose honor and reputation. To do so brings shame upon an individual, his family, his company—even his country. Worst of all, in a society focused on the group rather than the individual, loss of face can bring ostracism by colleagues and other peer groups. This makes Asians extremely sensitive to criticism, especially public criticism. Asians will go to great lengths to save face for themselves or others.

Asians will go to great lengths to save face for themselves or others.

One consequence of this desire to save face is that mistakes are often minimized, covered up or ignored. A superior, for example, would never think of criticizing a subordinate in the presence of his or her fellow workers; to do so would cause the subordinate to lose face and essentially would make him an ineffective member of the group or team. The subordinate, on the other hand, would take very seriously his or her responsibility to avoid mistakes that could embarrass his superior.

Faux Pas

In Asia, never cause anyone to lose face.

Similarly, in the interest of avoiding conflict and causing disharmony, disagreement may be covered up by a vague, ambiguous or overly polite response. When your Asian counterparts mean "no" but say "maybe" or suggest that further study is needed, they're just trying to save face—*yours*.

In Asia, never cause anyone to lose face. To do so will almost certainly end a relationship.

SAVING FACE FOR ASIAN COLLEAGUES

- Respect a person's rank or status;
  use titles properly.

- Resolve problems and conflicts privately.

- Never reprimand anyone publicly;
  never make statements that could
  embarrass or offend someone.

- Never ask a question in a manner that
  would cause loss of face if it were
  answered honestly.

- Follow the local protocol for bowing,
  apologizing, deferring, toasting, gift-giving, etc.

RESPECT FOR ELDERS

Age is honored in Asia. Elders are treated deferentially, even reverently. This tradition should be strictly observed by visitors under all circumstances. If you treat an older person without proper respect, it will seriously damage your Asian colleagues' opinion of you and could end a relationship on the spot.

When in the company of an older person:

- Greet older people before others in the group. Follow the appropriate greeting ritual.

- Pay attention to and converse with the older person.

- Give your seat to an older person.

- Stand when an older person enters the room.

- Never raise your voice in an older person's presence.

- Always remove sunglasses when speaking to older people.

- Maintain good posture—feet on the floor and knees together when seated.

- Ask permission before smoking or drinking.

ASTROLOGY

The Chinese Zodiac consists of a 12-year cycle, each year of which is named after a different animal that imparts distinct characteristics to its year. Three examples are the Year of the Tiger, the Year of the Monkey and the Year of the Rat.

Many Chinese believe that the year of a person's birth is the primary factor in determining that person's personality traits, physical and mental attributes and degree of success and happiness thoughout his or her lifetime.

Believers in Chinese astrology would, for example, never enter into a marriage without knowing whether the proposed partner had a compatible sign.

Many numbers and colors have special meaning in Asia—and those meanings vary from country to country. Check Chapter 13 and the "Gifts" section of each country chapter to find out what colors and numbers bring good or bad luck. These superstitions are very important to many people—and not observing them could bring *you* bad luck by offending your Asian colleagues. Here are a few examples of numbers and colors with special meaning:

NUMBERS AND COLORS

NUMBERS

Three is a lucky number in Thailand and Hong Kong. Give gifts in threes.

Four is bad luck in Japan and Korea. The word "four" sounds like the word "death." Many hotels and hospitals don't have fourth floors or rooms numbered four. Give odd numbers of items for gifts, if possible.

Eight is a lucky number in Hong Kong and parts of southern China. The word "eight" sounds like the Cantonese word for "prosperity."

Nine is a lucky number in Hong Kong. "Nine" sounds like "eternity" in Cantonese.

IT'S ALL IN THE NUMBERS

A recent episode in Hong Kong attests to the great symbolic power numbers have for many Asians.

The Hong Kong stock market was where the action was in early 1992, with a bull market driving stock prices to record heights. Then, rumors began circulating that Chinese leader Deng Xiaoping had died. Trading abated as investors closely monitored the Hang Seng Index for clues about the validity of the rumor and the direction of the market.

At midday, the Hang Seng Index stood at 4,444.14, and they had their answer. For the Chinese, "four" is associated with death and "one" with eternity. Thus the index had rendered its verdict: "dead, dead, dead, dead, certainly dead." Needless to say, a large selloff ensued and the market dropped sharply.

COLORS

White symbolizes sorrow in Japan, purity in Indonesia.

Purple is not to be worn to a wedding in Japan. Purple fades and might cause the couple's happiness to fade.

Green is associated with disease in Malaysia.

Red symbolizes anger in Indonesia, *black* violence and *yellow* happiness.

10.

DINING, DRINKING
AND ENTERTAINING

Food—how you eat it and how you react to it—long has been considered an important ingredient in the art of diplomacy. Your behavior at the table is one of the quickest ways to make or lose foreign friends.

When dining in Asia, be prepared for surprises. You could be offered dog meat, snake meat, sea slugs, chicken blood, raw fish, monkey brains or a thousand-day-old egg.

When your hosts offer you a food that's a local delicacy or a national specialty, they are offering you their friendship as well as a sample of their culture.

They are giving you the best they have, and if you reject it, you are rejecting their culture, their friendship—and them personally. This is not an auspicious way to begin a mutually beneficial relationship. So....

When you refuse an offered food, you're rejecting your hosts' culture and their friendship.

What's on your plate may swim, crawl, fly or look at you. Never mind! Taste it—you may even like it. If you don't, eat a reasonable portion anyway. I have eaten dozens of exotic dishes all around the world—a number of which, I freely admit, I wouldn't choose to have in my own home—and I'm still here to write about it. What's more, I still enjoy eating.

Eat what you're served. You'll survive.

Eat what you're served. You'll survive, too, and eating sea slugs, *sushi* or shark fin soup with your hosts likely will be the first step toward a fruitful friendship. Put your best foot forward!

THE ART OF NOT EATING—POLITELY

If you have a weak stomach or really dislike the food served in a particular country, here are some helpful hints:

- Take a big gulp of the pink stuff (Pepto-Bismol) before you go to dinner.

- Mentally prepare yourself for the unexpected.

- Never ask what a dish is until you've finished eating it.

- Don't chew particularly unpleasant food, just swallow fast. Sometimes the consistency is worse than the taste.

- Taste everything, and try to eat at least a little of it. If you truly can't eat something, a taste is polite.

- Never, never joke or make a negative comment about what is served; try not to grimace.

- Engage in conversation with your dinner partners; it will get your mind off the food and take up time until the next course is served.

- When offered seconds of something you don't like, say "Thank you, but let me finish this portion first." Eat slower and talk more.

- If you're really afraid a particular dish might make you ill, decline politely. It is certainly preferable to gagging at the table. (We all remember what happened to President George Bush in Japan.)

The above caveats notwithstanding, my own experience is that, by and large, Asian cuisine is a delight and the major challenge is to limit my intake.

And while we're on the subject of limiting intake, you need to be aware of the number of courses served in Asia. An ordinary business dinner can have several courses or a variety of dishes. A formal banquet can have more than a dozen courses, and the higher-ranking the guest of honor, the more courses are likely to be served. Pace yourself. If you enjoy the first four or five courses too much, the last half dozen will be an ordeal.

TRIAL BY BANQUET

Jim Walsh, CEO of Ampex Corp., says he has eaten such delicacies as snake and cockroach in order to establish relationships in Asia. "In some ways this is a test of Westerners," he says. "You mustn't show your disgust even if you're served roast rat. Keep in mind that with Asians you're aiming to develop long-lasting, trusting personal relationships. A contract is nice but it's not the final word, so the basic integrity of both parties has to be there. These banquets are not Asians practicing one-upmanship but rather a check on your pretensions. Eyeballs of all sorts, fish heads and duck feet are all common fare in response to 4,000 years of not having enough to eat. Our Western arrogance wears off quickly once you travel the banquet circuit."

—World Trade *magazine*

DINING, ASIAN STYLE

GENERAL TABLE MANNERS

- If you have special dietary restrictions, mention them to your host ahead of time.

- Don't appear overly concerned about the cleanliness of dishes, utensils or the kitchen—even if you are.

- Taste every dish offered. You needn't eat a lot, but a taste is polite.

- Never complain about or make fun of the food served.

- Eat slowly. You'll embarrass your host if you finish a course first and have an empty plate in front of you.

- You may smack and slurp soup and noodles. It is taken as a compliment to the hosts.

- Leave the table if you must blow your nose.

- Cover your mouth with your hand while using a toothpick.

- Don't smoke at the table unless your hosts smoke. They probably will. You will be offered a cigarette whenever your hosts light up. Make a similar offer to everyone present each time you light up.

- There is no "Dutch treat" in Asia. The person who invites pays the bill.

- In Asia, forget your mom's admonition to "Clean your plate." Always leave at least a small amount of food on your plate when you have finished each dish or course. If you clean your plate, it will be refilled until you leave some food.

THE SIXTH CHINESE BROTHER?

Do you remember the story of "The Five Chinese Brothers" by Claire Bishop? One of the Chinese brothers could hold the entire sea in his mouth. During his first visit to China, I thought my husband would become the sixth Chinese brother, who could hold all the rice in China in his mouth. He does, or did, like fried rice and told our Chinese hosts that it was his favorite dish. Coming from a post-Depression "clean-your-plate" family, he cleaned his plate of fried rice—the eighth of 12 courses—once, twice, three times. The polite Chinese continued to refill his plate. The polite American continued to clean his plate until all the rice was gone. I don't remember who quit first, but now I know why my husband always gained five pounds on his trips to China.

BANQUET ETIQUETTE

- When you are hosting a banquet, make the initial invitation by phone. Send a formal written invitation once the date has been established.

- Choose a restaurant that will be acceptable to and convenient for your guests. Check with your interpreter or the hotel concierge for restaurant recommendations.

- If you are reciprocating for a banquet at which you were the guest, the number and lavishness of the courses should be similar to those at the previous banquet. Don't try to outdo your counterpart, but don't skimp, either.

- A banquet usually lasts 2 to $2\frac{1}{2}$ hours— from 6:30 or 7 p.m. to 8:30 or 9 p.m.

- Always be on time or a little early for a banquet.

- If you're the guest, you will always be met by your host upon arrival; if you're the host, be on hand to meet your guests.

- The guest of honor enters the dining room first. If you're the host, insist that your Asian guests enter first.

Banquets normally include from 12 to 15 courses.

- Banquets normally include from 12 to 15 courses—possibly more for a very high-ranking guest of honor.

- Wait to be told where to sit.

- The guest of honor sits at the center of the table, facing the entrance to the dining room and to the right of the host.

- Generally, if you are the guest of honor, the ranking Asian person is seated on your left and the second-ranking person is seated on your right.

- If your Asian host's wife is present, she will sit opposite her husband. Foreign wives generally will be seated next to their husbands.

- Tables are generally large and round with a turntable in the center for serving.

- The host places food on the guests' plates to start the meal.

- Do not refuse any food. Slowly eat small amounts of each course served. Always leave some food on your plate as you finish each course.

- The host invariably makes the first toast shortly after the banquet begins. Do not drink until the toast has been offered.

- The guest of honor is expected to reply with a short toast immediately, or after one or two more courses have been served. (See the "Toasting" section below.)

- Toasts may be offered to the entire table or just to those sitting near you.

- Guests may toast with water, juice or soft drinks if they do not drink alcohol.

- You may be applauded after an introduction or toast. If this happens, join in the applause to express your thanks.

- Beer and tea are served with the meal, and tea is served again after the meal. *Maotai* or other local liquor may be served at some point during the meal.

- Drink as much as you want, but do not become loud or obnoxious. Intoxication is frowned upon at formal dinners.

- If you are the guest of honor, you will be expected to leave with the members of your party before your hosts.

*Try not to ask for a
knife and fork.
Attempt to use
chopsticks.*

CHOPSTICK ETIQUETTE

- Try not to ask for a knife and fork. Attempt to use chopsticks.

- Pick up chopsticks with your right hand and transfer them to your left hand. Then take the proper grip with the fingers of your right hand.

- Hold the chopsticks between your fingers, never in your fist.

- Always return your chopsticks to the chopstick rest with the tips pointing to your left when not in use. Never place them on top of the rice bowl.

- Do not plant your chopsticks vertically in the rice. (This is how rice is offered to deceased ancestors by Buddhists.)

- Do not point or gesture with chopsticks.

- Never cross your chopsticks.

- Don't tap or drum on the table with your chopsticks.

- Never use one chopstick to spear pieces of food.

- Do not lick the ends of your chopsticks.

- Do not push dishes around with chopsticks.

- Do not sort through food with your chopsticks, picking out the tastiest morsels.

- Do not pick up a dish with the hand that's holding your chopsticks.

- Don't put food from the serving bowl directly into your mouth. Place food from the serving bowl on your plate, then eat off the plate.

- Do not take food from a common serving plate with the same end of the chopsticks you put in your mouth; use the "handle" end.

- The rice bowl is on the left. Rice is eaten with chopsticks after the rice bowl is brought to your mouth. Never mix morsels of food in with your rice.

- The soup bowl is on the right; liquid is drunk directly from your bowl after solid morsels are eaten with chopsticks. Noodles are eaten by bringing the bowl to your mouth and slurping them from the chopsticks. Replace the lid of the soup bowl when you have finished.

- Sauces are for dipping food lightly, not for dunking or soaking or for pouring over rice.

- When finished eating, place your chopsticks neatly on the table or the chopstick rest.

DRINKING

Asians drink a lot of alcohol when entertaining guests. Appreciate the local drinks. Try *sake* in Japan, *soju* in Korea, *maotai* in China.

There are exceptions. Devout Muslims don't drink alcohol (or smoke tobacco). If your Asian counterpart is a Muslim and is abstaining, it's a courtesy for you to do likewise. Some Thais, if they are devout Buddhists, also abstain from alcohol.

Western women should not drink alcohol or smoke tobacco in bars or other public places unless Asian women are present and doing so. It's chauvinistic, but that's the tradition.

Drinking is a social event and is viewed as an opportunity to open up and converse on a more personal level.

In Japan and Korea, do not be surprised if an evening of social drinking ends in intoxication; drunkenness is accepted as normal behavior on such occasions. Remember not to call attention, be critical, or show pity or disapproval even if someone falls over in front of you.

Malaysia, Indonesia and the Philippines, however, do not tolerate or accept public drunkenness. Filipinos view drunkenness as greedy and self-indulgent, and it is thought to be very crude behavior.

NO THANK YOU

Remember, to refuse a drink from a host could cause embarrassment and loss of face. Never flatly decline a drink with "no." If you cannot drink alcohol, explain to your host that you have a stomach ailment or other medical problem. Ask for a soft drink or fruit juice rather than alcohol. Alternatively, accept the glass and don't drink.

Drinking is a social event, an opportunity to converse on a personal level.

TOASTING AT HOME AND ABROAD

Drinking is a national sport in much of Asia and visitors are expected to play.

Toasting is a very important part of entertaining in Asia. Be prepared to make a short toast to friendship, to your hosts, to their country, etc. If possible, make a toast in your host's or guest's language— even a word or two. If it's not perfect, don't worry—it will be enjoyed and appreciated by your Asian colleagues.

- An accompanying anecdote (in English) is generally appreciated.

- Don't tell jokes—they seldom cross cultural lines.

- Use toasts to establish a closer, friendlier relationship.

- Enjoy toasting and being toasted; it's a way of building bridges between people and cultures.

- In much of the Orient "bottoms up" is the standard toast. In Japan, that's *kampai* (kahm-PIE); in Korea, *gon bae* (GAHN-bay); in China, *ganbei* (GAHN-bay).

ENTERTAINING FOREIGN GUESTS

There is no place like home. Your city's best restaurants can't compare with an invitation to your home. Visitors always enjoy seeing how you live, how you decorate your home, what music and art you enjoy and, especially, meeting your family. An invitation to your home is a special event not soon forgotten by your guests.

Some points to remember:

- Check for dietary restrictions.

- Serve American-style food; it's hard to compete with the Asian food they'd get at home.

- Avoid (huge) American-sized servings of beef. Most Asians eat much smaller portions of meat than we do.

- Do not offer guests a tour of private areas of your home; they'll be more comfortable in "public" rooms like the living room, dining room and den.

- Always ask your guests if there is a particular event they would like to attend or participate in while visiting your city. Some possibilities: picnic or barbecue; baseball or American football game (if they like sports); concert or theater; museums; shopping; hiking; local sightseeing; boating or sailing; golf (especially appreciated by Japanese visitors).

11.

TIPPING

Tipping is less common in Asia than in the
U.S. or Europe, and tips are smaller.
Americans, especially, are used to tipping—but
it's just not done in some Asian countries.

When Americans visit another country and
throw money at service people, they're trying to
be kind and appreciative, not abrasive or
arrogant. But they often create the impression
that they're boorishly flaunting their wealth—
or worse, trying to take over the country!

Even people without material wealth have a
sense of personal worth, and that sense can be
violated by a tip that's inappropriately large or
small.

Tip too little, and a service person is likely to
feel cheated out of fair compensation for his or
her work. Tip too much, and a service person
can feel like you're making him or her a charity

*Americans often
create the
impression that
they're boorishly
flaunting their
wealth—or worse,
trying to take over
the country!*

case. But if you tip fairly and appropriately, it will be appreciated without being demeaning.

In some Asian countries, good service is given without any expectation of a tip. To give poor service would cause a loss of face for the person rendering the service. This is not an economic issue but a cultural phenomenon.

The key to tipping is to know both local customs and the value of what you're giving.

Most hotels and restaurants in Asia add a 10 or 15 percent service charge to your bill. Nothing extra is expected, and an offered gratuity may even be rejected.

The key is to know both local customs and the value of what you're giving. Not only do rules for tipping vary from country to country, but inflation, fluctuating currency exchange rates and rapidly changing local attitudes all affect appropriate tipping.

Although the country information chapters in Part III of this book give guidelines for tipping, it is crucial to ask a local colleague or the concierge in your hotel for the current tipping practice. This simple step can save you considerable embarrassment.

That said, it's worth noting that service personnel in hotels and restaurants that

cater primarily to a Western clientele are more likely to expect tips.

If someone has performed an exceptional service for you, you can put an appropriate amount of local currency in an envelope, write the service person's name on the envelope, and unobtrusively give it to the person or leave it in your room (for the maid) or at the desk.

A MATTER OF COMMON CENTS

President Ronald Reagan, during his 1984 visit to China, embarrassed a shopkeeper and his hosts— and made headlines—while shopping in China. In what he thought was a gracious gesture, he told a Beijing shopkeeper to "keep the change" from a small purchase. The change amounted to a few cents, which was insulting in itself. However, even worse, tipping was still officially illegal in China. Needless to say, far from appearing munificent, our president appeared (at least to Chinese) vulgar and ill-informed.

12.

DRESS

Dress is another form of nonverbal communication. Dressing appropriately and attractively says to our hosts that we respect their culture and gives us the opportunity to make a good first impression. There is no worse feeling than "sticking out like a sore thumb" because of inappropriate dress, especially in Asia where you'll hear sayings like, "The nail that sticks up get hammered down."

Dress conservatively in Asia and you'll never be wrong. The traditional business suit for men and a simple dress for women will serve you well everywhere in Asia.

Men should take a dark suit, a blazer or conservative sport coat, slacks and sport shirts, dress shoes and casual shoes.

The dark suit should be worn for all first business meetings, banquets in China and all formal dinners.

Rule of Thumb

Dress conservatively in Asia and you'll never be wrong.

Do not make the mistake of going native—or what you *think* is native. A vice president of a large American company visited Indonesia recently and, on arrival, purchased a batik shirt. Because the weather was extremely hot, he was certain a batik shirt and slacks would be appropriate for his meeting. As he entered the office of his prospective customers, he was embarrassed to find himself facing three gentlemen wearing dark suits, white shirts with French cuffs, and silk ties!

Women should wear suits, dresses, skirts and blouses in subdued colors. The women in many of Asia's major cities dress elegantly—and they're setting the standard you'll be expected to meet. Cotton and other natural fibers will be more comfortable in hot, humid areas than polyester and other synthetics.

Be aware: Especially in Japan, you may be seated on the tatami mats covering the floor of a restaurant or home. Women wearing tight and/or short skirts will find this a difficult maneuver.

In Japan, you may be seated on the tatami mats covering the floor of a restaurant or home. Women wearing tight and/or short skirts will find this a difficult maneuver.

GENERAL RULES FOR DRESS IN ASIA

- Avoid loud clothing, such as plaid pants or brightly colored sport coats.

- Women should never wear suggestive, tight or low-cut dresses.

- Beards may not be appreciated. Body hair on men is considered ugly in most of Asia. If you can't part with your beard, at least trim it a bit.

- Always dress modestly.

- Don't dress like an American cowboy.

- Cover up what is inappropriate to expose.

- Don't go native.

- Do not wear a kimono, sarong or other traditional Asian garment unless you are certain of the proper way to wear them, as well as the appropriate time and place. There is nothing sillier than a foreigner trying to look like a local and not succeeding.

- Shorts and jeans should be worn only at the beach or pool, or for rugged outdoor activity; regardless of the heat, do not wear tank tops or shorts in the cities.

Rule of Thumb

Cover up what is inappropriate to expose.

- Be aware: Shoes are removed in many Asian restaurants, homes and temples. Slip-on (rather than lace-up) shoes will make this easier.

- Because shoes are often removed, always wear clean socks without holes.

13.

GIFTS

Although Webster defines a gift as "something bestowed voluntarily without compensation," this is not true in most countries of Asia. Gift-giving is obligatory at all levels of Asian society.

Gift-giving is obligatory at all levels of Asian society.

Giving and receiving gifts in Asia can be a very complicated and, for some, a very intimidating experience. In many countries a "proper" gift is expected and better be given if you hope to begin or continue a relationship. In other countries an "improper" gift—or a gift given at the wrong time—may be an insult.

Giving a gift before a meeting begins or after a meeting ends has different meanings in different places and can be viewed as a bribe, not a gift.

Knowing what gift to give and to whom, when to give it and under what circumstances, and how to present it is a vital part of developing a friendship or doing business in Asia. It would be a shame if ignorance of gift-giving customs led you inadvertently to insult someone with whom you were trying to develop a relationship. It can and does happen in Asia.

Asians do not expect Westerners to understand or participate in gift-giving to the same degree that Asians do. Nonetheless, business relations are built through the giving of gifts, and you need to be aware that there's a "tracking system" in which everyone is conscious of gifts and favors given and owed.

A gift or favor received is evaluated and remembered; a gift received carries with it the obligation to return a gift of equal value, and a favor received must be balanced by returning a similar favor in the future.

In Asia, any gift or favor carries with it an obligation to reciprocate.

Remember that, in Asia, any gift or favor carries with it an obligation to reciprocate. Failure to reciprocate will be seen as a breach of the social contract and will jeopardize any further relationship.

All of these rules may seem overwhelming to a Westerner, but don't despair. Courtesy and common sense—coupled with the information below and the "Gifts" section of each country chapter in Part III of this book—will give you a good foundation. Build on it by consulting a knowledgeable person, such as a local colleague or your hotel's concierge, in each country you visit.

The perfect gift is in the eyes of the beholder. It is a gift that says you took the time to listen to someone and learn about his or her interests, tastes and personality—and the trouble to find a gift suited to those characteristics.

In the mid-1980s while working in Australia, I visited the remarkably beautiful beaches of Sydney. In an attempt to observe local customs without— quite—going topless, I bought a bikini. The combination of the intense February Australian sun and fair, Irish-American skin that had rarely seen the light of day proved to be the perfect formula for a nasty sunburn around my middle.

Some time later, when I had finished my work in Australia, my friends presented me with a farewell gift—a beautiful one-piece swimsuit made by one of the women in the office.

I was pleased and flattered. This was a personalized gift and it said to me that my associates had thought enough of me to remember my personal experience. That's a perfect gift.

IN GENERAL, GIFTS SHOULD

- Never be cheap or tacky.

- Never be intimate items.

- Never be practical items.

- Never violate a tradition.

- Never be vulgar or insulting.

- Be appropriate to the relationship and culture.

- Be of good quality.

- Be brand names with international prestige.

SOME GIFTS TO GIVE IN ASIA

- Arts and crafts from your state or region.

- Native American arts and crafts.

- Photo books about your city, state or region.

- Cellular telephones.

- U.S.-made chocolates.

- Smoked salmon from the Pacific Northwest or Alaska.

- Lenox china.

- Amish handmade products.

- T-shirts/sweatshirts from universities in your state (for young people).

- Fine U.S. or European whiskeys or liqueurs (except in Muslim countries).

- Ginseng. It's a root that is the basis of traditional Chinese herbal medicine and is believed to possess a wide variety of therapeutic properties. North American ginseng is considered excellent and would be a prized gift in many Asian countries.

- American or European wines and gourmet food items are appropriate *only after you've established that your counterpart has a taste for such things.* Many Asians do not.

North American ginseng is considered excellent and would be a prized gift in many Asian countries.

GIFT-GIVING RITUALS

- Never give a gift unexpectedly. Alert your host that you will be bringing a gift.

- Allow your host to present a gift first.

- Give individual gifts in private.

- Give group gifts during a scheduled meeting.

- Present a group gift to the leader of the group.

- Write a thank-you note for any gift or entertainment offered to you.

- Refer to the gift you were given during a later visit.

GIFT TABOOS

I don't know of any area of the world where you can get in more trouble by giving the wrong gift than you can in Asia. There are many taboos based on the perceived meaning of certain colors, numbers and items. Please read and observe the taboos noted in each country chapter in Part III. A few examples:

There's no area of the world where you can get in more trouble by giving the wrong gift.

- Giving 13 of anything is taboo in most Asian cultures.

- Even numbers of gift items, especially pairs, are considered unlucky in some places.

- Clocks are associated with death in many countries.

- Knives, scissors and other sharp items can symbolize the severing of a relationship.

- Flowers are usually a lovely gift, but don't give them without checking into local customs. Certain numbers, colors or types of flowers have special meaning—sorrow, death, anger, courtship—that vary from country to country.

- Never give the same gift to the same person a second time. Keeping a written record of gifts given will help avoid this problem.

- Never give a gift that is inexpensive and easy to purchase in the country you're visiting. A gift that says, "Made in China" isn't special in Hong Kong.

- Always check the religious customs before giving a gift. For example, never give Muslims alcoholic beverages, pork, cigarettes or ashtrays.

APPROPRIATE VALUE

Always attempt to give a gift comparable in value to the one you've received. Giving a gift that is noticeably more or less valuable than the one you've received can cause a loss of face for your counterpart—and possibly a loss of your relationship.

Faux Pas

Never give a gift that is inexpensive and easy to purchase in the country you're visiting.

Never get into a battle-of-the-gifts with an Asian counterpart, in which each of you tries to outdo the other (leading to a steady escalation in the lavishness of gifts). You will always lose. Always.

If you are interacting with people at different levels of an Asian company, you'll need gifts of different value. For example, you might give the chief negotiator in your joint venture discussions a high-quality pen set and the factory manager a less-expensive appointments calendar or notebook. Giving the factory manager the same pen set as the executive would be demeaning to the executive—and would at the same time embarrass the factory manager.

WRAPPING

Always wrap a gift before presenting it. In some Asian countries, the way a gift is wrapped and presented is more important than the gift itself. Enclose a signed card.

- Never use red ink. A relationship is severed by sending someone a letter or card written in red ink.

UNWRAPPING

Do not unwrap a gift or expect your Asian recipient to unwrap your gift upon receipt. In many countries, a gift is received graciously, but not opened in the presence of the giver. Just receive your gift with both hands, thank the giver and place it next to you. If you would like to open your gift, you may ask politely, "May I open my gift?" You may be invited to do so. If you are, do it graciously. Don't rip off the paper and toss the card aside carelessly. Instead, read the card with interest and nod acceptance, then carefully open the paper. After discreetly examining the present, quietly thank the giver with an appropriate comment on the gift.

WHEN TO GIVE

Each country has occasions when gifts are
given and expected. Chinese New Year,
Christmas, national days and other such
occasions are listed in each country chapter.

HOSTESS GIFTS

Most entertaining in Asia is done in
restaurants. However, if you are invited to
someone's home, always take a gift for the
hostess—a wrapped gift, presented correctly. A
small gift of candy, crayons, coloring books or
toys for the children also is a nice touch.

BUSINESS GIFTS

Business relationships at all levels of society—
high and low—are maintained through gift-
giving. Be prepared to give a business gift at all
levels.

Do not initiate gift-giving or embarrass anyone
by giving a gift if the person has nothing to give
in return—but always be ready to reciprocate.
Tuck several appropriately priced and wrapped
gifts in your luggage and carry one in your
briefcase so you'll always be prepared in case
you are given a gift in a factory, home or office.

In Asia, business gifts are often given at
meetings—sometimes at the first meeting,
sometimes at the successful conclusion of

Rule of Thumb

*Be prepared to give
a business gift at all
levels. Do not
initiate gift-giving,
but always be
ready to
reciprocate.*

negotiations, sometimes just to continue a relationship. In some countries, gifts are exchanged before business meetings begin, in others after meetings are adjourned.

If there are several people present, give everyone a gift, give a group gift or wait until the intended recipient is alone to give your gift.

Faux Pas

Do not stop giving gifts because previous gifts haven't been acknowledged.

THANK-YOU NOTES

Although you should write a formal thank-you note whenever you receive a gift, be aware that people in many Asian cultures usually do not do so. This doesn't mean the gift isn't appreciated, and it doesn't in any way negate either your obligation or your counterpart's to give gifts at appropriate times in the future. Do not stop giving gifts because previous gifts haven't been acknowledged—it could end a relationship.

14.

PUNCTUALITY AND PACE

Learning the local sense of punctuality and pace is one of the most difficult things about adjusting to an unfamiliar culture. Asians generally expect foreigners to be on time for appointments. Be on time—or better yet, be early—for an appointment or social function in Hong Kong, Japan or Singapore. However, be prepared for Malays, Thais, Filipinos and Koreans to be late, especially for social occasions. If you're uncertain about your hosts' attitude toward punctuality, the best rule is to be on time for all meetings, but be patient if your hosts are a bit late.

In countries where punctuality is a habit, being late says to people that you are:

- Lacking in respect (for them).

- Sloppy or undisciplined in your personal habits.

- Potentially unreliable as a partner or supplier.

If you are an "Oh, well, what's a few minutes late?" person, I suggest you become an on-time person when traveling abroad.

Former Vice President Dan Quayle learned this lesson the hard way during his visit to Indonesia a few years ago. The vice president arrived two hours late because his tennis match with an Australian dignitary ran overtime.

The front-page headline in the *Jakarta Post* read, "Quayle Arrives Behind Schedule." This apparent disregard of the schedule was interpreted by Indonesians, correctly or incorrectly, as indicating a lack of respect for their country. It damaged Quayle's reputation and reflected badly on other Americans.

The generally accepted attitude toward punctuality is covered in each country chapter in Part III. Follow this guide. If uncertain, ask! Ask your host, a colleague or the hotel concierge. It is always better to err on the side of punctuality.

Be sure to allow plenty of time to get from one appointment to another. Traffic congestion is horrendous in most major cities of Asia, and addresses are sometimes difficult to find, even for a taxi driver. I recently waited more than

Rule of Thumb

It is always better to err on the side of punctuality.

Smarte Carte keeps you moving.

When your baggage becomes a burden, Smarte Carte can help. Our convenient and reliable baggage carts will keep you moving so you can reach your final destination quickly and easily. Smarte Carte has been providing international travelers with dependable, easy-to-use baggage carts for more than 25 years, making us the baggage cart system of choice in more than 100 airports worldwide. So, the next time you travel, look for Smarte Carte. We'll keep you moving.

smartecarte®

two hours for a friend to make his way from Bangkok's famed Oriental hotel to a restaurant only a couple of miles away. Fortunately, he was able to report his progress—or lack of it—by cellular phone.

Asia is modernizing and its economies growing as fast as skyscrapers sprout in Hong Kong, Bangkok and Singapore. And there is no more frenetic economic activity anywhere than on the stock and commodities exchanges of Asia's financial centers.

Nonetheless, Asians do business at a distinctly different pace than Westerners. Pace deals with a sense of urgency (or the lack of it), with making or postponing decisions, getting the job done, keeping promises and meeting deadlines.

These differences in pace are not a matter of either malice or incompetence. They have their roots in deeply ingrained habits and attitudes—in culture itself. The local pace seems natural and right to the person performing the task.

PACE

Rule of Thumb

Asians do business at a distinctly different pace than Westerners.

To understand the Asian sense of pace, it's essential to see Asians as they see themselves: as part of a nation, a people, a culture that has endured for thousands of years and will continue for thousands more.

This is a vastly different historical perspective than we have in a country that's little more than 200 years old. For Westerners generally, and Americans in particular, if we can't get something done now, today, this week, this month, this year—certainly in our lifetime—then it just doesn't exist. It's not worth bothering with.

But from the Asian perspective, this year, this decade, this generation, this century are mere pinpricks on a historical continuum that stretches millennia into the past and millennia into the future.

If their goal isn't achieved in their own generation, it will be in their children's or their grandchildren's. If there is famine or disease or war, this too eventually will pass—as it has countless times before. Their race, their family, will endure.

This sense of historical continuity is one of the things that enabled Vietnam to outlast both France and the United States. The Vietnamese were prepared to fight and suffer and die for generations if necessary to achieve their objectives. The French and Americans weren't—and worse, they grossly underestimated the commitment and staying power of their opponents.

There is also in Asia a related sense of fatalism: the notion that life brings an endless succession of changes, that those changes bring with them an endless series of opportunities, and that opportunities are better taken advantage of if they're awaited patiently rather than forced. This tends to make Asians both flexible and resilient—ready to turn a seeming disaster into an unforeseen business opportunity.

Westerners need to cultivate patience and flexibility.

The obvious implications of these differences are that a Westerner who wants to do business in Asia needs to cultivate both patience and flexibility; to pursue relationships rather than transactions; and to focus on long-term gains rather than quick profits.

As one veteran China trader put it: "If you're the kind of person who has trouble waiting for a red light to change, then China is not for you."

A well-known Chinese fable illustrates the Asian understanding of continuity and fate:

A SENSE OF CONTINUITY

There once was a farmer, Sei Weng, who owned a beautiful horse that was admired by the whole village. One day the horse ran away. When the villagers came to express sympathy for the loss, Sei Weng said simply, "Such things happen."

Not many days later, the horse returned leading a group of beautiful stallions. So the villagers came again to visit Sei Weng, this time expressing congratulations on his good fortune. Once again, Sei Weng replied, "Such things happen."

Not long afterward, the son of Sei Weng fell off the beautiful horse, breaking his leg. The villagers came to Sei Weng to express their sympathy. The farmer responded simply, "Such things happen."

Soon after, war broke out, and all the young men of the village were drafted into the army. Because of the injuries sustained in his fall from the horse, Sei Weng's son was not taken with the others. The young men of the village all died in a fierce battle, so Sei Weng's son was the only young man left. The villagers again congratulated Sei Weng on his good fortune. And again, in reply he said only, "Such things happen."

This story illustrates the Asian concept of life as an endless stream and the belief that, although the direction of the stream changes over time, one must remain flexible when evaluating its course at any given moment.

15.

STRICTLY BUSINESS

The long-anticipated and much-predicted emergence of Asia as an economic power is happening—not next year, next month, next week or even tomorrow. It is happening now. By the end of the decade, the economies of the Pacific Rim together will be bigger than those of the European Community, and at least equal to those of North America.

How can any company afford to ignore a market with more than 40 percent of the world's people—many of them educated, industrious and clever, people who have learned to live by their wits and get the most out of sometimes limited resources?

It's also hard to ignore the kind of return Western companies are getting on their investments in Asia. A recent survey by the U.S. Department of Commerce showed that American companies were getting an average annual return of 31.2 percent on their

How can any company afford to ignore a market with more than 40 percent of the world's people?

investments in Singapore, 28.8 percent in Malaysia, 23.6 percent in Hong Kong, 22 percent in Taiwan, 17.9 percent in South Korea and 14.1 percent in Japan. The average return on U.S. investments in all foreign countries was 15.2 percent. These are pretty compelling numbers.

The business opportunities in Asia are enormous—and those opportunities are attracting a rapidly increasing number of Western companies. The challenge will be to ensure that your company will be one of those that succeeds and prospers.

Over and over again, businesspeople with decades of experience in Asia have told me that the key to success is learning as much as possible about the history, culture and customs of the region.

The key to success is learning as much as possible about the history, culture and customs of the region.

Cultural differences affect every facet of doing business in Asia. Recognize and respect those differences, and you'll have a leg up on the competition.

Business customs and culture vary widely from one part of Asia to another, so you'll want to consult the appropriate chapter in Part III before visiting a particular country. Following in this chapter are some general guidelines for conducting business that apply throughout Asia.

SOME GENERAL RULES

- Try to understand and adapt to the Asian style of doing business without compromising your principles. Remember, the followers of Confucius emphasize the welfare of the group, while Western humanism stresses the achievements of the individual; Asians tend toward ambiguity while Americans prize directness; ritual, etiquette and ceremony are part and parcel of Asian life, while they're increasingly disdained in the West. Just keep telling yourself that some adjustment is going to be necessary if you want to succeed in Asia.

Rule of Thumb

Just keep telling yourself that some adjustment is going to be necessary if you want to succeed in Asia.

- Appearance and status count! How you dress, where you stay, where you dine, and how you travel (first class, business class or coach; taxi or chauferred car) will be carefully noted by your Asian colleagues, and from this information they will draw some conclusions about how seriously you should be taken and whether you're a person of substance. So if you're attempting to sign a big contract in Hong Kong, stay at the Regent, the Mandarin or one of the other prestigious major hotels.

- Networking is essential. Who you know is more important than what you know. Get introduced by a respected third party who will speak for you in advance. Introductions are taken seriously: The introducer takes responsibility for the person being introduced, and with the introduction comes a guarantee of credibility; to violate this trust would cause the introducer to lose face.

- Have a high-quality product or service that is available in a timely manner.

- Establish and maintain some form of local presence.

Saving face and achieving harmony are highly valued.

- Allow the details of money issues to be discussed by a go-between or lower-ranking staff.

- Being too blunt and too aggressive can offend reserved and face-conscious Asians. Saving face and achieving harmony are highly valued.

- Do not engage in argumentative and adversarial exchanges.

- Be prepared to commit time, energy and money to any project in Asia. Patience is essential. Decisions are by consensus and therefore are made slowly. However, implementation of a decision may be rapid, even by Western standards.

- Be prepared to move quickly as opportunities arise; move before the competition does rather than waiting for the formal announcement of a project.

- Research may be difficult in Asia. Asians prefer not to answer pointed questions or to say what they really think. They may tell the interviewer what they think he wants to hear.

- Focus groups should include people of the same business or social level. Mixing people from different strata of a company or society will result in those of lower status deferring to those with higher status.

- Listen to the requirements of buyers. Don't tell them what they need.

- Make certain that products are appropriate for the market and meet local standards.

- Make a technically compliant bid.

PERSISTENCE PAYS

To some American companies, the prospect of selling their products in Japan seems as daunting as climbing Mount Fuji.

However, some American businesspeople have made the trek. In their efforts to crack the Japanese market, for example, salespeople for TRW have literally hiked with their customers 12,338 feet to the summit of Japan's sacred mountain.

Fortune magazine reports that TRW's dedication and commitment have paid off: The company has seen its auto parts sales in Japan skyrocket over 700 percent since the mid-1980s and projects that its sales in Japan will triple to $1.5 billion by 1997—a figure equal to TRW's current auto parts sales to the Big Three in Detroit.

And TRW is not alone. Total American exports to Japan have increased from $44.49 billion in 1989 to over $47.76 billion in 1992.

The moral of the story? To succeed in Japan, American companies must be prepared, if necessary, to scale Mount Fuji. And for those American companies prepared to understand and persist in the Japanese market, the rewards are great.

When establishing, renewing or continuing a business relationship in Asia, be prepared to socialize. This is no time for a "No, thank you." Asians insist on getting to know potential partners and suppliers before doing business with them. They establish these necessary relationships through business entertaining. This is one crucial step in the development of a business relationship you'd be well advised not to skip or take lightly. The time, money and energy spent should forge a lifelong relationship. So whether you're invited to a 23-course Chinese banquet, for drinks at a sing-along bar, or for a quiet meal in a restaurant or home, make a point of accepting the invitation.

Reading each country chapter should make you aware of what to expect and what's likely to be expected of you. Then, wherever you are invited to go or whatever you are invited to do, join in! It'll be a new experience and it'll be fun.

SOCIALIZING

Socializing is crucial in developing business relationships.

BEING ENTERTAINED

- Climb a mountain, visit a temple, sing a song, dance a dance, participate in whatever you're invited to do.

- Appreciate and join in the drinking ritual—but with caution. Pace yourself.

- Be prepared to perform if you are asked to do so. Yes, you may have to sing, even if it is just your college fight song. You might expand your repertoire with "Jingle Bells," "New York, New York," "My Way" or anything else by Ol' Blue Eyes.

- Be prepared to make a toast for every occasion.

    - If invited to a banquet, reciprocate by hosting a banquet of comparable quality before you leave.

        - Enjoy the local food.

- Be prepared for long evenings and late hours. These can make or break a business deal.

CORRESPONDENCE

Addressing an envelope to Asia:

Recipient's name
Building and block address
District and postal service
City
Country

Example:

Yo Mijoshi
3-8 Kanda Wishikicho
Minato-ku 106
Tokyo
JAPAN

- Never use red ink! Chinese use red ink to sever a relationship forever. Japanese funeral notices are written in red.

- When corresponding with Asians in writing, do it in English unless you hire a translator who can translate a document perfectly. It is much better to use English than to send business correspondence translated poorly.

BUSINESS CARDS

The exchange of business cards in much of Asia is done with great formality and ceremony. Remember, this is your first opportunity to make an impression and the business card remains long after you have left. It is a very important communication tool. Using it correctly in Asia is a must.

The ritual involved in exchanging business cards varies somewhat from country to country, but the following rules will serve you well in most places.

The business card is a very important communication tool.

- Take time to have your business card translated into the local language to show respect for the culture and commitment to doing business in the country.

- Print your cards in English on one side and in the appropriate Asian language on the other. Be aware that you may encounter (at least) two forms of written Chinese: classical (or complex) characters are used in Taiwan and Hong Kong, while simplified characters are used in the People's Republic of China.

- Present your card with the Asian-language side up and your name facing the receiver.

- Present your card with both hands. At the same time, bow slightly and say your name.

- When a person hands you his or her card, bow and receive it with both hands.

- Look at the name, title, company and address.

- Nod in recognition.

- Ask a polite question related to the information on the card.

- Place cards in front of you in the order in which people are seated.

- Place cards carefully in your briefcase at the end of the meeting.

- Travel with plenty of cards—everyone gives and takes business cards.

- Never write on your card or anyone else's. This is a sign of disrespect.

- Enclose your business card in all correspondence, making certain that it's clean and in good condition.

PERSONALIZING RELATIONSHIPS

The "Hi, how are you? Let's sign the contract" approach doesn't work in Asia. If you want to get an Asian's business, you must be prepared to invest the time and effort needed to personalize your relationship. Here are some ways of doing that:

- Make high-level visits as often as possible to countries and companies with which you hope to do business (Americans have a reputation for disappearing).

- Phone, write and fax often; stay in touch.

- Contribute to local charities.

- Join appropriate associations in the local community.

- Learn about local issues; get involved if appropriate.

- Adjust your pace. Don't come on too fast or too strong. Take a low-key approach.

- Allow time to build your counterpart's confidence in the relationship.

- Make it clear you are there for the long haul rather than a quick sale or profit.

- Be yourself—warm and friendly but initially more formal than you would be at home.

- Discreetly demonstrate your knowledge of and interest in the local culture; your knowledge will help build a closer and stronger business relationship.

HOLIDAYS AND FESTIVALS

Each country in Asia (and many of the regions within larger countries) has special holidays and holy days on which businesses close. There are typical vacation periods—Chinese New Year, Ramadan, Christmas, New Year's and the week preceding Easter—during which it is virtually impossible to do business in various countries. Check the holiday schedule for the countries you're going to visit when planning an Asian trip.

Travelers also should check normal workdays and business hours in each country.

A business aquaintance told me this story about a recent Asian trip on which he visited six countries:

He had scheduled his arrival in Malaysia for a Thursday afternoon, with departure on Sunday. Upon arrival, he phoned several companies, asking if he could make a courtesy call the following day. To his dismay, he wasn't able to get a single appointment. The companies he wished to visit were run by Muslims and were closed from noon Friday until noon Saturday. He left on Sunday morning without having made a single contact. It was a wasted trip.

16.

ESPECIALLY FOR WOMEN

Women in Asia and their roles in family, home and business are as diverse as anywhere in the world. The only word that describes all of them is "changing."

The family is at the very heart of Asian society. Asians believe that governments come and go, but the family endures. The family both nurtures such traditional values as hard work, thrift, filial piety, loyalty and scholarship and promotes such newer ones as economic growth. As a result, some Asian women are still reluctant to relinquish their traditional role in the family.

Despite all we hear about male-dominated Asian cultures, attitudes are changing rapidly in most countries. Many Asian employers are quite pragmatic—more concerned about performance than gender.

Male-dominated cultures are changing in many Asian countries.

Some indications of these changing attitudes:

- When *Asian Business* asked its female readers in 1993 to rate the business climate for women in 17 different countries, the results surprised many in the West. Hong Kong was rated the most friendly business environment for women, closely followed by Singapore. Malaysia earned fourth place behind the United States. The Philippines, Taiwan, Thailand, China, Japan and Indonesia all finished ahead of France and Germany.

- The government of Vietnam now grants a six-month paid maternity leave to all new mothers—regardless of marital status.

- Many Philippine women are educated at American universities in law, medicine and business. Corazon Aquino was Philippine president in the 1980s, and Miriam Refensor-Santiago almost won the 1992 presidential election.

- The first woman to serve as United Nations High Commissioner for Refugees, Sadako Ogata, is Japanese. Ms. Ogata is the highest-ranking Japanese official, male or female, to serve in an international organization.

Much of the Asian resistance to women in business is directed at local women, not Westerners.

- While some top jobs remain closed to
  Asian women, in general women have been
  moving steadily up the corporate ladder.
  Consider the following statistics collected
  by *Asian Business*: From 1971 to 1991, the
  percentage of female managers and
  administrators in Hong Kong nearly tripled;
  women now occupy 20 percent of such
  positions. In 1980, Malaysian women
  occupied 5 percent of such positions; eight
  years later, this percentage had doubled.

Much of the Asian resistance to women in
business is directed at local women, not
Westerners. As I have done business in Asia, I
have generally found that being a woman is an
advantage. It is sometimes easier for a woman
to get in the door to tell her story.

Once you are in the door, interpersonal
communications make the difference. A women
is at least as likely as a man to have the following
traits (all considered desirable in Asia):

- Reads nonverbal cues.

- Speaks in a soft, well-modulated voice.

- Listens to all opinions.

- Explores common ground and clients' needs.

- Makes an effort to build bridges.

- Takes time to build consensus.

- Never tries to rush a decision.

- Shows personal interest in people and their lifestyle.

Women are still something of a novelty in Asian business circles, so you'll certainly get your counterparts' attention; what you do with that attention is up to you. If you follow a few simple rules, being a woman can be a definite advantage when doing business in Asia.

GENERAL RULES FOR WOMEN IN ASIA

- Establish your position and professionalism immediately.

- Send biographical materials spelling out your educational background, professional experience, honors and awards, title and current responsibilities in advance of your visit.

- Establish credibility by being introduced by a mutually respected person.

- Define your role clearly.

- Never lose your cool.

- Do nothing that can be misinterpreted as a sexual invitation or a come-on.

- Allow men to open doors, light cigarettes and otherwise be gallant.

- Do not be embarrassed or angry if someone treats you in a sexist manner.

- Aggressive behavior is considered unseemly in most Asian countries; it is even less seemly for a woman.

- Dress conservatively and modestly for all occasions.

- Dress in a feminine style, but without flaunting your sexuality.

- Research local customs toward women, respect them and follow them when appropriate—even if you think they're outrageous.

- Expect cultural misunderstandings to arise from the interaction between genders; try not to be judgmental.

- It may be a new experience for some people to do business with women; be patient.

Rule of Thumb

Research local customs toward women, respect them and follow them when appropriate.

- Roll with the punches. If you are clearly dealing with someone who is incapable of working with a woman, consider asking a male colleague to join you or to handle that particular deal.

Be aware that many Asian men have formed their image of Western women from magazine ads, television commercials, pop art, videos and Madonna. As a result, a blond-haired, blue-eyed woman may suddenly find herself the object of more attention than she might have hoped for. This sort of attention can be discouraged by dressing modestly and conservatively, and by making it clear from the outset that you are interested only in a business relationship.

| CREDENTIALS, PLEASE | *Before I was granted an interview with Singapore's Prime Minister Lee Kuan Yew, I was asked to submit a written request accompanied by a* curriculum vitae *specifying the college I had attended, the undergraduate degree I had received and the graduate work I had completed—as well as professional experience. The Singaporeans didn't care that I was a woman—they just wanted to be certain I was a qualified one!* |

17.

HYGIENE, HEALTH AND SAFETY

There are diseases endemic in Asia that most Westerners don't commonly encounter—malaria, cholera, plague, typhoid fever, hepatitis A and parasitic infections among them. It's imperative that you check with a reliable, informed medical source to determine whether immunizations or other precautions are needed for your trip.

- If possible, visit a travel clinic—like those found at many university hospitals and major metropolitan medical centers—when planning a trip to Asia. Most primary care physicians simply aren't familiar with health problems in and immunization requirements for Asian countries.

- Alternatively, call the Centers for Disease Control Fax Information Service in

Rule of Thumb

If possible, visit a travel clinic when planning a trip to Asia.

Atlanta at (404) 332-4565. You can order the International Travel Directory, which lists more than three dozen documents, and it will arrive on your fax machine in 15 to 30 minutes.

Using the directory, you can order the documents appropriate to your planned trip. Disease risk and prevention information for East Asia, for example, is document 220190; for Southeast Asia, 220200; for the Indian Subcontinent, 220220. These documents also will be delivered via your fax machine in less than an hour—at no charge. They'll give you and your doctor a pretty good handle on what precautions and/or immunizations are needed for your trip.

- Another source of travel health information is the "Tips for Travelers" booklets published by the Department of State. Write to the Superintendent of Documents, U.S. Government Printing Office, Washington, D.C. 20402 and specify the countries you're interested in. There is no charge.

- And, of course, U.S. embassies in the countries you plan to visit will have up-to-date health information.

- Check your medical insurance before you travel. Make certain it covers emergency care in a foreign country. If it does not, take out a supplementary policy that does.

- Keep all medication in the original, labeled containers to make customs processing easier.

- Take with you all prescription and nonprescription medication you may need.

- Pack all medication in your carry-on bag; if your checked luggage goes astray, you've still got your medication.

- Pack a small first aid kit.

- Take your physician's phone number with you.

- Our simple advice about the blood supply in Asia is—*don't trust it!*

- Rh-negative blood is virtually impossible to find in China (no Chinese have this blood type).

- Wash your hands with soap before eating or putting them near your mouth.

- Eating at sidewalk or roadside food stalls is risky at best. *Never* eat at food stalls in the

Rule of Thumb

Check your medical insurance before you travel.

Our simple advice about the blood supply in Asia is— don't trust it.

areas around hospitals, where hepatitis is often endemic.

Be wary of eating fruits or vegetables unless they are cooked or peeled.

- Except in major hotels and first-class restaurants, be wary of eating fruits or vegetables unless they are cooked or peeled, and avoid dairy products.

- Always wear shoes, sandals or shower shoes. Never walk barefoot on grass, pavement, beaches—or even in your hotel room.

- Swimming in freshwater lakes or streams is not recommended in most areas of Asia because of possible exposure to schistosomiasis and other parasitic diseases. Water in or near major harbors is often polluted; otherwise, saltwater swimming is safe.

- Wear insect repellent whenever you are on an outing outside a major city.

- If you're traveling in tropical or subtropical areas, carry sunscreen and use it regularly. A nasty sunburn is a real distraction in those crucial negotiations.

WATER

The quality of drinking water varies drastically in Asia. Water purification systems in some countries are among the best in the world, while in other countries (or regions within countries) all tap water must be regarded as nondrinkable.

- Try to drink bottled or boiled water regardless of the country you're visiting. While the water might meet international standards for drinkability, even the different chemicals used to purify tap water could make you ill.

In countries where water is notoriously poor:

- Drink bottled colas, juices and waters only after watching a waiter open the bottle in your presence.

- Don't even brush your teeth with tap water.

- Do not have ice in your drinks.

HOSPITALS/ CLINICS

The standard of health care available at hospitals in Asia varies from excellent to nonexistent. As a general rule, your hotel can refer you to an English-speaking physician for help with minor medical problems. However, if you even suspect your medical or dental problem is serious, check with your country's nearest embassy or consulate before seeking treatment.

Remember that some hospitals require immediate payment for health services. Also, you may need to be evacuated to another country for emergency care of a serious medical problem. Don't wait until it's too late.

TOILETS

A friend's 10-year-old daughter, Joan, who accompanied him on a recent trip to Southeast Asia, emerged from toilets discreetly explaining that they were either "Eastern style" or "Western style."

Asia has some of the world's finest restaurants and most modern hotels. All of these have excellent toilet and bath facilities—including "Western style," sit-down, flush toilets. However, in rural areas or older buildings, you're likely to encounter "Eastern style" squat toilets; some old Asia hands say if you haven't used a squat toilet, you haven't really been to Asia.

If you haven't used a squat toilet, you haven't really been to Asia.

Squat toilets range from a hole in the ground to a shiny porcelain fixture with "footprints" flanking the aperture; some may have a cover that must be removed before use. In any case, be psychologically prepared to squat, facing the wall and the hooded end of the fixture.

Ladies, beware: You should avoid wearing pantyhose, tight pants, high heels or any clothing that restricts your ability to squat and can't survive a little contact with a not-so-clean floor.

Take wet-wipes and tissues or toilet paper with you at all times in Asia. The time you fail to do so will be the time you need to use a public restroom without toilet paper, sink, running water, soap or towels.

If you find using a squat toilet difficult, console yourself with the knowledge that many Asians find sit-down, flush toilets just as strange and puzzling to use.

Take wet-wipes and tissues or toilet paper with you at all times in Asia.

SECURITY

Be sure to take all the safety precautions when abroad that you would at home. No matter how safe a city or a country is reported to be, there are potential dangers anyplace.

Remember that the time to make important decisions is not after traveling 20 or more hours across a dozen time zones. Robert Burke, director of corporate security for Monsanto, says, "The fatigue and sleep deprivation caused by jet lag, plus strange sights, sounds, smells and customs, can add to disorientation and make it easier to be victimized."

International travelers are advised by Monsanto in its eight-page booklet to:

- Whenever possible, explore foreign cities in the company of a local person.

- Know how to use public phones, and learn key phrases in the local language so you can communicate with the police if necessary.

- Carry with you at all times phone numbers and addresses of your company's local representatives, the nearest U.S. embassy or consulate and your principal business contacts in the city you're visiting.

- Don't carry documents or packages for anyone else, and store your own important papers in a hotel safe.

- Always carry your passport on your person (not in a briefcase or purse) or leave it in the hotel safe. Make photocopies of the identification pages of your passport and keep one copy in a separate place from your passport. Travel with several extra passport photos. The photos and a copy of the identification pages will make it much easier to get a replacement passport if the original is lost or stolen.

- If you're a private citizen, carry no papers that link you with the U.S. government or the military. Even a card that says you're an "honorary Kentucky colonel" could be misinterpreted by a terrorist. (Military personnel and government employees will have their own guidelines for carrying identification.)

SOME OTHER SECURITY TIPS

- Do not carry identification, airline tickets, credit cards or other valuables in your briefcase or purse. Carry them on your person or leave them in the hotel safe.

- Do not wear a money belt or document pouches where they're visible; they could make you a target for theft.

- Do not set your bag down at your feet while checking schedules or using a phone.

HOTEL SAFETY

- Bring a little flashlight.

- Take note of fire exits.

- Upon entering your room, check emergency phone numbers; check to ensure that the phone line to the front desk works.

- Verify who is at your hotel door before opening the door.

- Secure the door whenever you are in your room by using all locking devices provided.

- Never leave cash, jewelry or other valuables lying around; put them in the room safe that you'll find in many Asian hotels, or put

Faux Pas

Never leave cash, jewelry or other valuables lying around.

them in a safe-deposit box at the hotel's front desk.

- Secure any sliding doors or windows and check locks on doors to any connecting room.

- Enter the hotel through the well-lit main entrance.

- Be especially careful in parking lots and ramps; take advantage of an escort service if available.

DRIVING

> Make every attempt not to drive in Asia.

Make every attempt not to drive in Asia. Mass transit, taxis and chauffeur-driven cars are readily available in most countries. The rules of the road are a matter of local custom, and driving can be dangerous if you don't know them; the traffic congestion is maddening; you have an excellent chance of hitting a pedestrian or cyclist; and in several countries you have no legal rights if you are involved in an accident. In other words: Don't drive. If you can afford it, a chauffeur-driven car from your hotel is the best and safest means of transportation.

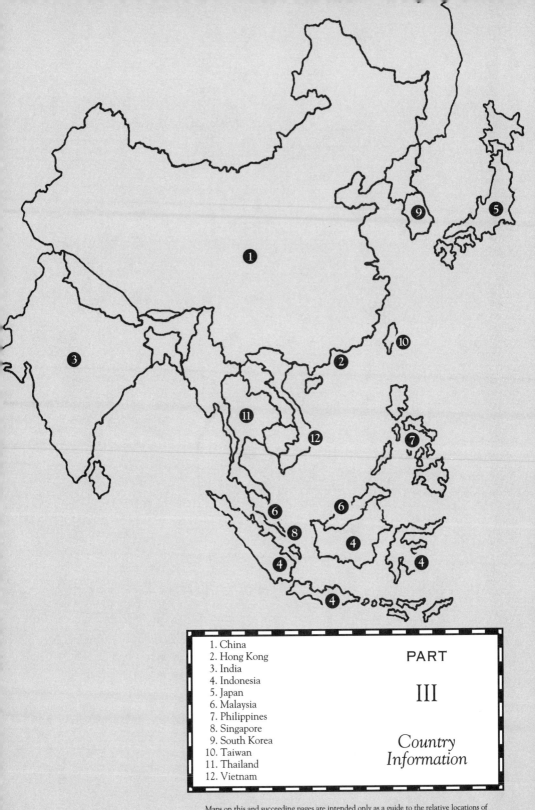

1. China
2. Hong Kong
3. India
4. Indonesia
5. Japan
6. Malaysia
7. Philippines
8. Singapore
9. South Korea
10. Taiwan
11. Thailand
12. Vietnam

PART

III

Country Information

Maps on this and succeeding pages are intended only as a guide to the relative locations of countries and cities. They are not to scale and are not intended to be authoritative representations of national boundaries.

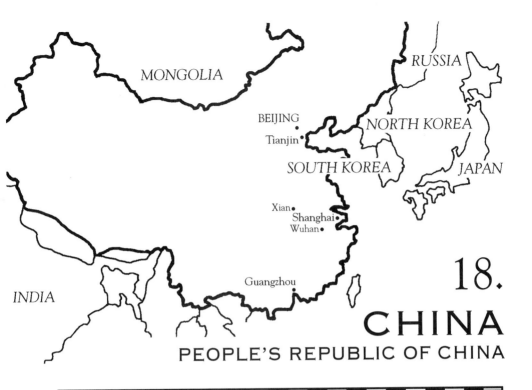

18.
CHINA
PEOPLE'S REPUBLIC OF CHINA

VITAL STATISTICS

POPULATION:
1.24 billion, largest in the world. One-fifth of all the world's people live in China.

CAPITAL:
Beijing, with an estimated population of 7.6 million.

MAJOR CITIES:
Shanghai (13 million), Tianjin (5.5 million), Guangzhou (3.2 million).

LAND SIZE:
3,692,000 square miles, slightly larger than the U.S.; the overall population density is 295 persons per square mile.

GOVERNMENT:
Socialist republic consisting of 22 provinces, five autonomous regions and three municipalities. The president is head of state, and the premier is head of government. The Chinese Communist Party

holds all political power and exercises leadership and control through its central committee and politburo, which are elected every five years. The politburo sets policy; the government executes it.

The National People's Congress has 2,970 deputies elected indirectly by regional bodies and the People's Liberation Army. The NPC in turn elects its standing committee and the state council (including the premier, vice premiers, cabinet ministers and president).

LIVING STANDARD:	GDP = US$720 per person, one of the lowest in the world but improving steadily. Continued double-digit growth will give China the world's largest economy by the year 2020.
NATURAL RESOURCES:	Coal, iron ore, crude oil, mercury, tin, tungsten, antimony, manganese, molybdenum, vanadium, magnetite, aluminum, lead, zinc, uranium, world's largest hydropower potential.
AGRICULTURE:	Accounts for 26 percent of GNP; among the world's largest producers of rice, potatoes, sorghum, peanuts, tea, millet, barley and pork; commercial crops include cotton, other fibers, and oilseeds; produces a variety of livestock products; basically self-sufficient in food.

INDUSTRIES:	Iron, steel, coal, machinery, armaments, textiles, petroleum, cement, chemical fertilizers, consumer durables, food processing.
CLIMATE:	Subtropical in the southeast, but continental in the interior. January is the coldest month, July the warmest. Average rainfall exceeds 33 inches in the humid southeast, 22 inches in China's semihumid northeast and the North China plain. The remainder of China receives less than 13.5 inches a year. About 80 percent of all precipitation falls between May and October; July and August are the wettest months. Monsoons drench the coastal regions every summer, especially in the south and east. Average summer temperatures normally exceed 68°F (20°C) throughout China; average January temperatures range from 46°F (8°C) in the south, to 5°F (-15°C) in the north.
CURRENCY:	Chinese currency is called *renminbi*—literally "the people's money"—and often abbreviated RMB. The unit of currency is the *yuan*; each yuan is composed of 100 *fen*. On January 1, 1994, the Chinese government abolished the Foreign Exchange Certificates (FEC) previously issued to foreigners, ending the system of dual currencies. Renminbi cannot be purchased outside of China.

THE PEOPLE

CORRECT NAME: Chinese.

ETHNIC MAKEUP: 92 percent Han Chinese, 8 percent minority groups (55 types).

VALUE SYSTEM: Centuries-old ideas shape the Chinese way of life. Age and rank are highly respected. The need to belong and conform to a unit—whether family, political party or other organization—is deeply rooted in Chinese society. Collective responsibility makes the group answerable for the individual's behavior.

To the dismay of the older generation, today's young people are wearing blue jeans and sunglasses, drinking Coke and driving motorbikes. Discussions of Chinese politics or foreign affairs hold little interest for most Chinese except in Beijing. After a half-century hiatus, getting rich through private enterprise is again fashionable in China.

FAMILY: The family is the focus of life in China. Most elderly people rely on their children for support. Although the Cultural Revolution weakened families as people were sent to remote areas to work or study, there is a resurgence of family loyalty today. Marriages are still arranged in rural areas, but in major cities—and particularly among university students—marriages are based on mutual attraction. Many people marry late, partly because of the chronic housing shortage and partly because of pressure to have only one child.

RELIGION: While its practice has been officially discouraged by the government, religion remains an important part of traditional Chinese life. The influences of Buddhism, Taoism and Confucianism have evolved into the "three religions in one" that characterizes Chinese belief. Some 2 percent of the population is Muslim. Christianity, although its adherents comprise less than 1 percent of the Chinese population, has had a significant influence.

SPORTS: Table tennis, swimming and soccer are the favorite sports.

IMPORTANT DATES

2205 B.C.	First Chinese state.
221 B.C.	Qin Dynasty founded; Chinese empire unified under one leader. (The Western name "China" is thought to be derived from the name "Qin".)
206 B.C.	Han Dynasty founded, launching period of territorial expansion and trade.
618 A.D.	Tang Dynasty founded with capital at (present-day) Xian; arts and culture flourish; China becomes the world's most powerful state.
1842	British defeat Chinese in Opium War. The Treaty of Nanjing cedes Hong Kong to Great Britain.
1894-95	Sino-Japanese War severely weakens China.
1900	Secret societies attack and kill Westerners and Chinese Christians during the Boxer Rebellion.
1911	Qing Dynasty falls ("The Last Emperor").
1912	The Republic of China declared and Dr. Sun Yat-sen becomes president.
1926-28	Chiang Kai-shek and his Nationalist forces form a government at Nanjing, purge opponents and attempt to reunify China.
1931	Japan seizes Manchuria.
1937	War with Japan begins.
1934-35	Mao Zedong leads the Long March, saving the Communists from defeat by Chiang Kai-shek's forces.

1946	Civil war breaks out between Nationalists and Communists.
1949	The Chinese Communists defeat the Nationalists and proclaim the People's Republic of China with Beijing as its capital.
1950	China invades Korea in support of North Korean forces.
1953	First Five-Year Plan for economic development.
1958	The Great Leap Forward severely weakens China's economy; rural communes formed.
1963	China breaks with the Soviet Union.
1966-69	Red Guards lead the Cultural Revolution, severely disrupting all aspects of daily life.
1972	President Richard Nixon visits China.
1976	Mao Zedong and Premier Zhou Enlai die.
1977	"Gang of Four," led by Mao's widow Jiang Qing, formally denounced. Deng Xiaoping becomes deputy premier, initiates economic reform.
1979	The United States establishes diplomatic relations with China.
1981	Central Committee labels the Cultural Revolution a "grave blunder."
1984	Government reforms loosen control of the economy.
1989	Pro-democracy demonstrations in Tiananmen Square crushed by the military.
1997	Death of Deng Xiaoping in February. China resumes sovereignty of Hong Kong on July 1.

MEETING AND GREETING

- Shake hands upon meeting. Chinese may nod or bow instead of shaking hands, although shaking hands has become increasingly popular.

- The Chinese bow, unlike the Japanese bow, is from the shoulders rather than the waist.

- When you're introduced to a Chinese group, they may greet you with applause. Applaud back.

- Chinese introductions can be very formal, even austere. Chinese may not smile when introduced (they are taught not to show emotions openly).

- A common greeting is *ni hao ma* (nee how ma), which means, "How are you?"

- The senior people present initiate the greetings. Greet the oldest, most senior person before any others. In group introductions, line up according to seniority with the senior people at the head of the line.

Rule of Thumb

Greet the oldest, most senior person before any others.

- Officially, mixing with foreigners is discouraged. Foreigners are still viewed as intruders. In practice, however, Chinese are usually friendly and polite to foreign guests.

NAMES AND TITLES

- Use family names and appropriate titles until specifically invited by your Chinese hosts or colleagues to use their given names.

- Do not use "comrade."

- Traditionally, Chinese family names are placed first, followed by the given name (which may have either one or two syllables).

  Example: Deng Xiaoping ("Deng" is the family name, "Xiaoping" the given name).

- Address Chinese using family name + the appropriate courtesy title:

  - Mr. = *Xiansheng* (Syen-shung).

  - Mrs. = *Taitai* (Tigh-tigh) or *Furen* (Foo-run).

  - Miss = *Xiaojie* (Sheeow-jyeh).

  - Ms. = *Nushi* (Noo-shee).

  The family name comes first, followed by the courtesy title.

Faux Pas

Do not use "comrade."

Example: Mr. Li is addressed as Li Xiansheng.

Mrs. Li is addressed as Li Taitai or Li Furen.

Miss Li is addressed as Li Xiaojie.

Ms. Li is addressed as Li Nushi.

- You cannot tell women's names from men's names. Chinese women continue using their maiden names even after marriage, but may indicate marital status by using Madam, Mrs., Taitai or Furen with their maiden name. Mrs. Wang may be married to Mr. Li.

Mrs. Wang may be married to Mr. Li.

- Xiaojie is also a very polite form of address for a waitress, cashier, or elevator attendant (female).

- Chinese are often addressed by their government or professional titles.

  Example: Address Li Pang using his title—Mayor Li or Director Li.

- When someone's name and title are not known, address him or her simply as Xiansheng (Mr.) or Nushi (Ms.).

- Never address a Chinese by his or her family name alone.

Example: Never address Li Pang as just "Li."

- Chinese may address foreign women by using Miss plus their first name.

Example: Mrs. Mary Jones might be addressed as Miss Mary.

- Attempt to make the translation of your name as short and easy as possible. Omit initials.

- Chinese may call close friends and family members by their given names.

Example: Wang Chien may be addressed by close friends as "Chien."

- Remember, you're very unlikely to be on a first-name basis with your Chinese counterparts—at least not until your relationship is firmly established.

- Some Chinese use their names in Western order (family name last) on business cards. Those who frequently work with foreigners may take a western style given name, e.g., David Li.

- Chinese generally introduce their guests using their full title and company name. You should do the same when introducing yourself.

Example: "Doctor John Smith, CEO of American Data Corporation."

- Among themselves, Chinese may call you *quei lou* or *lao wai* (foreign devil or barbarian), or perhaps *mei guo lao* (Yankee). If you happen to pick up on this, don't take it personally. While these terms are condescending, they are applied to foreigners generally and reflect China's traditional view of its exalted position as the "Middle Kingdom," the center of the world.

LANGUAGE

- The national language is *putonghua* ("common language"), a version of the Beijing dialect. Known to Westerners as Mandarin, it is the language of instruction in school. Other principal dialects include Cantonese, Fukienese, Hakka and Wu; 93 percent of Chinese speak one or more of these five main dialects.

Since 1956, more than 3,000 of the most commonly used Chinese characters have been simplified.

- Written Chinese includes 50,000 characters, or ideograms, but fewer than 6,000 are in common use; between 3,000 and 4,000 are required for reading fluency. Since 1956, more than 3,000 of the most commonly used characters have been simplified.

- The transliteration of Chinese ideograms into English is purely phonetic, and there are three main systems for doing it: Wade-

Giles, developed by two British scholars in the 19th century; Yale, developed by the U.S. university; and *pinyin*, declared the official system of the People's Republic in 1958.

Pinyin is gradually being adopted by Western news media, scholars and language teachers, but the other systems are still in use. As a result, you'll see multiple spellings of Chinese words rendered in English: *Lao Tzu*, *Lao-tsu* and *Lao-tse*; *Peking* and *Beijing*, *Mao Tse-tung* and *Mao Zedong*. In general, try to use the pinyin system.

- English is not widely spoken or understood, except by students. Employees of major hotels and restaurants catering to foreigners speak English, but workers in smaller hotels and restaurants often do not.

- Chinese find "no" difficult to say. They're more likely to say "maybe" or "we'll see" in order to save face.

BODY LANGUAGE

- Chinese dislike being touched by strangers. Do not touch, hug, lock arms, back-slap or make any body contact.

- The concept of lining up (queuing) is foreign to Chinese. People will push in large crowds and do not mind being crowded.

- People of the same sex may walk hand-in-hand as a gesture of friendship..

- Chinese point with an open hand. Never point with your index finger.

- Never put your feet on a desk or a chair, gesture with your feet, point your foot at someone or slide an object over to someone with your foot.

- It is common for Chinese to spit or blow their noses (without a handkerchief) on a street or sidewalk. This is not considered rude. Blowing one's nose in a handkerchief and returning it to one's pocket, on the other hand, is considered vulgar.

- To beckon Chinese, extend your hand palm down and flex your fingers in a scratching motion. Never use your index finger to beckon anyone.

- Sucking air in quickly and loudly through one's lips and teeth expresses distress or surprise at a proposed request. Attempt to change your request, allowing the Chinese to save face.

- Clicking fingers or whistling is considered very rude.

PHRASES

English	Chinese	Pronunciation
Hello	*Ni hao*	Nee how
Hello (phone)	*Wei*	Way
Good morning	*Zao*	Dzow
Good afternoon	*Ni hao*	Nee how
Good evening	*Ni hao or Wanan*	Nee how or Wahn-ahn
Please	*Qing*	Ching
Thank you	*Xie xie*	Syeh syeh
You're welcome	*Bu xie*	Boo syeh
Yes	*Shi*	Sher
No	*Bu shi*	Boo shi
Excuse me	*Duibuqi*	Dwei-boo-chi
Goodbye	*Zaijian*	Dzigh-jyen
How are you?	*Ni hao ma*	Nee how ma

MANNERS

DINING

- In general, manners are more relaxed in China than in Hong Kong or Taiwan.

- The restaurants of major hotels catering to foreigners usually have Western-style food available. Reserve early.

- Given a choice between Western or Chinese food, it's a rare Chinese who would opt for Western-style cuisine. And eating slabs of rare beef is considered barbaric.

- Chopsticks are used for all Chinese-style meals (see "Chopstick Etiquette" in Chapter 10).

- Chinese generally eat dinner earlier than Westerners.

- Chinese are superb hosts. Twelve-course banquets with frequent toasts are a Chinese trademark. (See "Banquet Etiquette" in Chapter 10 for more details.)

- When eating in rural areas or small urban restaurants serving local clientele, carry your own chopsticks or discreetly pour boiling water or tea over those provided. If making a scene over the chopsticks is going

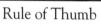

Rule of Thumb

When eating in local restaurants, carry your own chopsticks or discreetly pour boiling water or tea over those provided.

to insult your Chinese hosts and adversely affect your chances of closing the big deal...well, that's what the gamma globulin shots were for.

- Never tap your chopsticks on the table. It's considered very rude.

- It is bad manners for a Chinese host not to keep refilling guests' plates or teacups. Leave a small amount of food on your plate at the end of each course to demonstrate appreciation for your host's generosity— otherwise you'll keep getting more.

- Seating is very important. The guest of honor at a meal is always placed at the head of the room, facing the door.

- Allow the host to begin eating before joining in.

- Do not discuss business at dinner unless Chinese initiate the discussion.

- Slurping soup and belching are acceptable. Cover your mouth with your hand when using a toothpick. Never place bones, seeds or other debris in your rice bowl. If a plate is not provided for this purpose, put them on the table.

- When finished eating, place your chopsticks neatly on the table or on the chopstick rest.

- If you're hosting, you might offer to let your Chinese colleague choose the restaurant. Most Chinese prefer Chinese food, but may be too polite to say so.

- You seat yourself in less formal Chinese restaurants; other people will share a table with you if the restaurant is crowded.

- Most tables are round and have a revolving tray in the center. Several dishes are placed on the tray so guests can sample all of them. Try each dish at a meal or banquet.

- If you're the host, order one dish for every person present and one extra. In addition, order rice, noodles and buns. Soup usually comes at some point during the meal. The host should tell his guests to begin eating a new dish before he digs in himself.

- The host (the person who has made the invitation) pays the bill for everyone.

- Government-owned or -managed restaurants have poor service and food and often close by 8 p.m. Government restaurants often seat foreigners in an area separate from locals. Sit where you are seated without objection.

- If you are invited to dinner, your Chinese host may ask you to make reservations, because some Western-style restaurants only accept reservations from foreigners.

- If you are the guest of honor at a dinner, leave shortly after the meal is finished, since no one will leave before the guest of honor.

DRINKING/TOASTING

- Beer is the alcoholic beverage of choice for most Chinese.

- Try not to refuse a drink when offered by a Chinese colleague; sipping is quite acceptable.

- At banquets, three glasses—a large one for beer, soda or mineral water, a small wine glass, and a stemmed shot glass (usually for *maotai*, a 120 proof sorghum liquor) are at each place. The shot glass is the one used for toasting.

- Be prepared to make a small toast on any occasion.

- *Ganbei* (GAHN-bay), meaning "bottoms up," is a standard toast. It is not necessary to drain your glass, but it's often done. Try to follow your host's example.

Ganbei, meaning "bottoms up," is a standard toast.

- The first toast normally occurs during or after the first course, not before. After the next course, the guest should reciprocate. Toasts may be accompanied by long speeches or merely by the raising of glasses.

  - Do not drink until you toast others at the table. Chinese consider drinking alone to be rude. Simply raising your glass and making eye contact is sufficient. If you are toasted, sip your drink in reply.

- Toasts are often made after the arrival of a new dish on the table, especially when shark's fin soup is served.

- A toast to friendship among companies will help cement a business relationship. If a foreign woman is the leader of the delegation, it is acceptable for her to make a toast.

- A toast may be offered to the whole table and even include surrounding tables. Sometimes a host may move among the tables, offering an individual toast at each one, but this is usually done only at large banquets.

HOME

- Guests are rarely invited to a Chinese home. It is an honor to be a guest. Be on time or a little early, and take a small gift.

- Bedrooms and kitchens are private. Don't enter these rooms unless you are invited.

- All dishes are served at once in a home. The host will place portions of each dish on guests' plates. Sample each dish.

- Chinese hosts walk their guests to the car and wave goodbye until the car is out of sight.

TIPPING

In the past, tipping was considered degrading— tips were only offered by a person of superior rank to someone clearly inferior. While Chinese do not expect tips from other Chinese, tips are expected from foreigners. Tipping in a foreign currency is still officially illegal; despite this, it is often done and appreciated in establishments frequented by foreigners.

- Restaurants: Extra change is sufficient— except at a banquet you host, where you may want to offer a gratuity for exceptional service.

- Taxis: Extra change, unless the driver helps with bags.

- Toilet attendants, coat-check attendants, porters: Small change.

- Drivers and maids: Minimal (token).

- Hairdressers and barbers: No tip or very small change.

- Ushers: No tip necessary.

- Guides: 50 RMB for half a day.

DRESS

- Toilets are often squat style. Dress accordingly.

- Unpretentious, modest clothing is the norm, but trendy clothes and fancy fabrics are making a comeback. Young people wear bright colors and jeans.

- Women should avoid bare backs, shorts, low-cut tops and extravagant jewelry.

- Take wash-and-wear fabrics with you. Laundry facilities are poor.

- Warm clothing, hats, thick-soled shoes and sweaters are essential in winter in northern China.

BUSINESS

- Men: Sport coats and ties. Slacks and open-necked shirts are generally suitable in the summer for business meetings—jackets and ties are not necessary. Follow the local custom.

- Women: Dresses or pant suits. No heavy makeup and no dangling, gaudy jewelry. Wear subtle colors and styles.

RESTAURANT/BANQUET

- Men: Jackets should be worn at a banquet, but may be removed during dinner in the summer. Jackets and ties may be more comfortable in cold weather.

- Women: Simple, floor-length dresses or slacks. Slacks are acceptable even on formal occasions. Plain and simple is the rule.

CASUAL

- Men: Pants, short- or long-sleeved, open-necked shirts.

- Women: Pants, blouses.

GIFTS

- Gift-giving previously was against the law, but now is generally accepted.

- Present a gift with both hands. Gifts generally are not opened upon receipt. Give a gift to everyone present or don't give any. A gift may be presented to a group.

Gifts generally are not opened upon receipt.

- Never give a gift of great value until a clear relationship is established; this would embarrass the recipient. Gifts may be given singly or in sets (e.g., dishes), but never in sets of four—in Chinese, "four" sounds a lot like "death."

- Older Chinese usually refuse a gift at first to be polite. Offer it a second time.

- Chinese customs officials may scrutinize items that look unusual. This is merely curiosity. If asked, "What is this?" or "How does this work?" respond with a friendly explanation. Bringing in relatively inexpensive items like framed photos, ties, pens, books or calendars will seldom cause a problem.

WRAPPING

- Wrap a gift simply. Red is the preferred color.

- However, avoid red *writing* on a card or note; it has negative connotations from the Cultural Revolution.

- Do not wrap gifts before going through customs, which may require a gift to be unwrapped for inspection.

- Avoid white, which is symbolic of death (especially of parents), and black, which also is associated with tragedy or death.

HOSTESS

- When invited to someone's home, always bring a small gift for the hostess.

- Suggested gifts: Brandy, chocolates, cakes.

BUSINESS

- Be prepared to exchange a modest gift with your business colleagues at the first meeting. Not giving a gift could start a potential business relationship off on the wrong foot.

- Avoid giving gifts of great value. Only after all business dealings are completed is it appropriate to exchange a gift of value.

Rule of Thumb

Be prepared to exchange a modest gift with your business colleagues at the first meeting.

- Always give a gift to *each member* of the Chinese delegation that meets you—*in the order in which they were introduced.*

- Suggested gifts: Cognac or other French brandy, whiskey, pens, lighters, desk items, books, framed paintings or other decorative items for the home. Western-grown ginseng is a popular gift in China. Calculators and watches are good gifts for younger people or children. Give a somewhat more prestigious gift like a cellular phone or small CD player to a senior person.

- Give a group gift from your company to the host company. Present this gift to the leader of the group.

AVOID GIVING

- Do not give foreign currency (including commemorative coins).

- Do not give cheese—it is not in the Chinese diet and Chinese generally do not like it.

The English word "clock" is a homonym for the Chinese word "funeral."

- Do not give Western-style table wine, which is not popular in China.

- Do not give clocks, especially to an older person: The English word "clock" is a homonym for the Chinese word "funeral."

- Do not give fruit or basic foods until a friendship is established. This could be insulting—it implies poverty.

- Do not give anything in sets of four, or with the numbers 4 or 40 on the cover.

- Do not give green headwear; it signifies that somebody in the family is committing adultery.

DO

- Always refer to China as "China" or the "People's Republic of China."

- Always refer to Taiwan as "Taiwan" or the "Province of Taiwan."

- Always show respect for older people. Always offer a seat or first passage through a door to a colleague or an older person as a polite gesture.

- Ask permission before photographing anyone.

- Expect people to push and shove as crowds enter trains, buses, etc. Chinese do not queue (form lines).

- Ask a Chinese friend to purchase an item you would like from a Chinese shop. The

Rule of Thumb

Always refer to China as "China" or the "People's Republic of China."

price charged a Westerner will be two or three times greater than the price charged a Chinese.

- Ask questions that can't be answered "yes" or "no."

  Example: Ask "What material is this dress made from?" rather than "Is this a silk dress?"

- Always return applause when you are applauded.

- Expect to be stared at, especially in small villages.

- When telephoning to a hotel in China, it is best to ask for a room number rather than a name. Western names are difficult for operators to understand.

DO NOT

- Never refer to China as "Red China," "Communist China" or "Mainland China."

- Never refer to Taiwan as "China," the "Republic of China" (the name adapted by the Chiang Kai-shek's forces after they fled to Taiwan) or "Free China."

- Never be loud, boisterous or flamboyant. Never interrupt conversations or periods of silence.

Faux Pas

Never embarrass, criticize or contradict a Chinese publicly. Reputation and honor are the highest values in society. To cause loss of face can cause loss of friendship.

- Do not be insulted if Chinese ask personal questions such as, "How much money do you make?" "How many children do you have?" or "Are you married?" This is the Chinese way of making small talk.

- Do not photograph anything related (even remotely) to the military—this includes airports, railroads, bridges, etc.

- Never ask about divorce. This would cause a Chinese to lose face.

- Never force a Chinese to say "no." This will quickly end a relationship.

- Never bargain except for antiques, second-hand goods, or at a bazaar or "free market."

- Do not in any way suggest that Taiwan is not part of China.

- Never say or act like you are starving. Never ask for a doggy bag.

Faux Pas

Do not photograph anything related (even remotely) to the military.

Faux Pas

Do not in any way suggest that Taiwan is not part of China.

PUNCTUALITY

- Punctuality is important for foreign businesspeople; Chinese expect strangers to be on time.

- Always arrive exactly on time for a dinner or banquet. Never arrive early: It shows you are hungry, and you will lose face.

STRICTLY BUSINESS

- The Chinese are practical in business matters and realize they need Western investment, but they dislike being dependent on foreigners. They are suspicious and fearful of being cheated or pushed around by foreigners, whom they perceive as culturally and economically corrupt. Moral: It's vital to establish trust at the very outset of a relationship.

BUSINESS CARDS

- Business cards are exchanged upon meeting. See the "Business Cards" section of Chapter 15.

- Business cards should be printed in English on one side and Chinese on the other. Make sure the Chinese side uses "simplified" characters, and not "classical" characters, which are used in Taiwan and Hong Kong. If you are planning to visit the People's Republic of China and either Hong Kong or Taiwan, you should mark your boxes of business cards in some way to avoid mix-ups.

CORPORATE CULTURE

Structure: *Guanxi* refers to the web of relationships and obligations that ties the business system together. Guanxi is vital to any successful business arrangement.

The Chinese organization is vertical, with strong emphasis on seniority, rank and title. Rank is often demonstrated through such symbols as clothes, car and driver, and servants.

Personal interests are subordinated to those of the group, and independent expression is discouraged. People express themselves through the group and the group is accountable, not the individual.

Meetings: Endless meetings are held to reach consensus. Decisions and their implementation are slow and cumbersome. Be prepared for long meetings and protracted negotiations (10 consecutive days is not unheard of) with many delays. Multiple visits will be required.

Meetings always begin on time. Chinese enter a meeting with the highest-ranking person first, and they will assume the first member of your group to enter the room is the leader of your delegation.

The foreign team enters the room together and shakes hands with the Chinese side. The senior Chinese welcomes everyone. The foreign leader introduces his or her team, and each member distributes his or her card. The leader invites the Chinese to do the same.

Seating is very important. The host sits with the most important guest on his right. Small talk is exchanged before business discussions begin, with the foreign side opening discussions.

Meetings are characterized by monologues from each side—and endless cups of tea.

Meetings are usually characterized by long monologues from each side—and endless cups of tea. There may be periods of silence; do not interrupt these silences. Either the Chinese or the foreign side can end a meeting by politely requesting the scheduling of the next meeting.

Negotiations: Technical competence should be the prerequisite for your negotiating team. It is best to begin negotiations with middle managers and technical experts. The Chinese will match whatever level of management is present in the visiting team. Continuity and relationships are important, so always send the same team to continue negotiations.

Make sure your Chinese counterparts are fully authorized to take whatever action you're working toward (although the real authorities may be acting far behind the scenes). It may be hard to determine who holds the ultimate authority.

Foreigners should establish the agenda and get an agreement on its major points at the outset. Present your proposals in detail, and back them up with technical and factual data. The Chinese will be slow to divulge information; be patient but persistent.

Be prepared to make sizable concessions. Chinese prefer to make concessions at the end of negotiations, rather than as the negotiations progress. Never show that you are under any time constraints. Senior executives should be brought in if pressure is needed to speed approvals or break an impasse.

If negotiations break down, do not formally end them; rather, employ a euphemism ("temporary cessation," for example) to save face. If the deal falls through, do not speak badly of your Chinese counterparts; you may want to do business with them in the future.

To the Chinese, *a contract is not considered binding!!!* It's viewed more like a draft subject to change. Chinese are more interested in a strong commitment of cooperation than in a solid legal document.

Rule of Thumb

Foreigners should establish the agenda and get an agreement on its major points at the outset.

To the Chinese, a contract is not considered binding!!!

Communication: English is not spoken in business meetings, though some Chinese may understand English without making it known.

Arrange to hire an interpreter or ask that one to be provided. If you're planning to have someone from your own company interpret, make sure he or she is fully competent in the subject matter to be covered.

Use simple words and short sentences.

Send as much information as possible before you arrive; Chinese do not like surprises in meetings or negotiations.

Communicate in writing whenever possible. Verbal communication, especially on the telephone, tends to lose something in the translation. Written communications (including faxes) are there in black and white to be examined and referred to.

BE AWARE

- Patience is essential. The time required to successfully enter the Chinese market—or to show a return on your investment—may be measured in years, not months.

- If the Chinese know that you are under pressure to return home with a signed agreement, they will use this to their full advantage in extracting concessions.

- The status of the people who make your intitial contact with the Chinese is very important. Don't insult the Chinese by sending a junior sales rep; on the other hand, don't lose face by sending your CEO to haggle over arcane details.

- Chinese may try to make foreigners feel guilty about any setbacks in the negotiations, and may manipulate this sense of guilt to achieve concessions.

- Other negotiating tricks designed to make you agree to concessions: staged temper tantrums and a feigned sense of urgency (when none exists).

- If the Chinese side no longer wishes to pursue the deal, they may not tell you. To save their own face, they may become increasingly inflexible and hard-nosed, forcing you to break off negotiations. In this way, they may avoid blame for the failure.

If the Chinese side no longer wishes to pursue the deal, they may not tell you.

- Try to arrange your negotiations in a conference room that is larger than necessary. Chinese negotiators like to smoke, and 13 hours in a small, smoke-filled room can test even the toughest negotiators.

- Brand loyalty is very strong.

ENTERTAINMENT

- A formal banquet is the most popular form of business entertainment. Banquets or dinners are a means of forming the informal ties that nurture negotiations.

- As a rule, business is not discussed directly at meals, but dinner conversation may provide a chance to probe the other side's position indirectly and without commitment.

- The sponsoring Chinese organization generally hosts the welcome banquet. Foreign guests should reciprocate toward the end of the visit. Invite everyone with whom you have dealt to the banquet you host.

- Spouses are not usually included in business entertaining. Businesspeople may bring their secretaries.

- Business breakfasts are not customary, but you may request one.

APPOINTMENTS

- Most businesses work a 48-hour week—Monday through Saturday, 8-11:30 a.m. and 1:30-6 p.m.

- The best time to schedule an appointment is 10 a.m. to 3 p.m., Monday through Thursday. Business lunches are OK. Appointments are absolutely necessary.

- Many people leave their offices by 4 p.m., and some are not in their offices on Friday.

- Avoid scheduling appointments the weeks before and after the Chinese New Year.

ESPECIALLY FOR WOMEN

- China is a difficult place for foreigners of either gender to do business. A woman may gain acceptance, but it will take time and will not be easy.

- China is a male-dominated society. However, there are many women in business in China and some occupy high ranking positions and important managerial jobs. One of the principles of the Chinese communist system is to work toward sexual equality.

- Women have the power in the family, but allow men to appear powerful in order to save face. Socially, men dominate.

- Negotiating teams may have women members, and they may be used to deflect criticism or respond negatively to proposals by the other side.

- Businesswomen attend business dinners, but rarely bring their spouses.

- The chivalrous attitude of "ladies first" does not apply in China.

- Chinese women rarely smoke or drink in public. However, it is acceptable for Western women to do so in moderation.

- Asians consider Chinese women to be the most assertive in Asia.

- Women should dress modestly.

- China is relatively safe for women, but Guangzhou requires greater attention to safety.

HEALTH AND SAFETY

- Bring ample supplies of medicine. Western prescription and over-the-counter medications are not widely available. Prescription drugs are sold to foreigners only in hospitals for cash.

- Do not attempt to get a doctor, dentist or emergency treatment in China. Call your embassy if a medical problem arises. Take out medical insurance that will fly you to Hong Kong for emergency medical care.

- Do not drink tap water, consume ice cubes, or eat fruits and vegetables that haven't been cooked or peeled. Although some major hotels have a water purification system, the best rule is to drink only bottled or boiled water. Avoid dairy products or cold foods because refrigeration is poor.

- Emergency numbers: Vary from city to city.

HOLIDAYS AND FESTIVALS

January	New Year's Day (1).
January/February	Chinese New Year (three days—set by lunar calendar).
March	International Working Women's Day (8).
May	Labor Day (1), Youth Day (4).
June	Children's Day (1).
July	Founding of Communist Party of China (1).
August	People's Liberation Army Day (1).
October	National Day (1-2).

Lantern Festival, 15th day of first lunar month, and Dragon Boat Festival, fifth day of fifth lunar month, are widely celebrated but are not official holidays.

Both New Year's are celebrated.

CHINA

NEW TERRITORIES

Sha Tin

Tsuen Wan

Kwun Tong

Kowloon

VICTORIA

LANTAU ISLAND

Aberdeen

HONG KONG ISLAND

Stanley

LAMMA ISLAND

19.

HONG KONG

SPECIAL ADMINISTRATIVE REGION OF THE PEOPLE'S REPUBLIC OF CHINA

VITAL STATISTICS

POPULATION:

6.32 million. The overall population density of 15,000 per square mile is the highest in the world; population density reaches an astounding 480,000 per square mile in one area of Kowloon.

CAPITAL:

Victoria (now usually known as Central District) on Hong Kong Island.

LAND SIZE:

410 square miles.

GOVERNMENT:

Hong Kong was a British territory until July 1, 1997, when it became a Special Administrative Region of the People's Republic of China.

LIVING STANDARD:

GDP = US$27,130 per capita.

NATURAL RESOURCES:	Outstanding deepwater harbor, feldspar.
AGRICULTURE:	Minor role in the economy; rice, vegetables, dairy products; less than 20 percent self-sufficient.
INDUSTRIES:	Textiles, clothing, tourism, electronics, plastics, toys, watches, clocks.
CLIMATE:	Subtropical. Average temperature is 84°F (29°C) in July, 61°F (16°C) in January. Winters (October to April) are dry and sunny, summers (May to September) very humid with occasional typhoons. Annual precipitation is high—over 100 inches (223 cm) a year.
CURRENCY:	Hong Kong dollar (HK$). Notes are in denominations of HK$1,000, 500, 100, 50, 20, 10. Silver coins are for HK$ 5, 2, and 1, and bronze coins for 50, 20 and 10 cents.

THE PEOPLE

CORRECT NAME: Hong Kong resident.

ETHNIC MAKEUP: 98 percent Chinese.

VALUE SYSTEM: Young and old work hard and play hard, with a sense of uncertainty about their future under the Chinese government. Hong Kong Chinese value family, tradition, religion, eating, gambling and making money—especially making money. They flaunt their wealth and social status with cars, clothes and cellular phones.

FAMILY: An individual's actions, prestige, education, wealth and reputation reflect positively or negatively on the entire family. Chinese families traditionally have been strong, with loyalty, obedience and respect for elders highly valued. Today, families are smaller and traditional values are being challenged by young people adopting Western mores.

RELIGION: The three great religions of China—Buddhism, Taoism, and Confucianism—influence the beliefs of most Hong Kong residents. Hong Kong is 18 percent Christian.

SPORTS: Table tennis, soccer, cricket, and making money, not necessarily in that order.

IMPORTANT DATES

1842 AD	British defeat Chinese in Opium War, gain island of Hong Kong under Treaty of Nanjing.
1898	Chinese lease New Territories to Great Britain for 99 years.
1915	Large migration to Hong Kong after overthrow of Manchu dynasty in China.
1937	Large numbers of Chinese flee to Hong Kong after Japan invades China.
1941-45	Japanese troops occupy Hong Kong.
1949	New wave of immigration begins as Communists assume control in China.
1966-69	Cultural Revolution causes another wave of immigration to Hong Kong.
1970s	China begins large-scale investment in Hong Kong.
1984	China and Great Britain work out agreement for return of Hong Kong to Chinese sovereignty in 1997.
1997	July 1: Great Britian returns Hong Kong to China.

- Shake hands with everyone—men, women and children—upon meeting and again on leaving. Handshakes may be less firm than you're accustomed to.

- Higher-ranking persons are introduced before those of lower rank, older persons before younger ones, and women before men. Family members are greeted in order of age, oldest first and youngest last. When greeting people, it's polite to inquire about their health or activities.

- At a social function, feel free to introduce yourself.

- Use family names and appropriate titles until specifically invited by your hosts or colleagues to use their first names.

- Chinese names have two parts: family name and given name. The family name comes first, followed by the given name, which may have one or two syllables.

  Example: Luo Gan Lei ("Luo" is the family name, "Gan Lei" the given name).

- Address Chinese using the appropriate courtesy or professional title + family name.

  -Mr. = *Sinsaang* (Seen-sahng)

  -Mrs. = *Taaitaai* (Tigh-tigh)

  -Miss = *Siuje* (See-oo-jeh-eh)

  The family name comes first, followed by the courtesy title.

  Examples: Mr. Luo is addressed as Luo Sinsaang.

  Mrs. Luo is addressed as Luo Taaitaai.

  Miss Luo is addressed as Luo Siuje.

- Many Hong Kong Chinese have Christian given names.

  Example: Lau Gan Patrick may also be known as Mr. Patrick Lau.

- In correspondence, the correct form of salutation is Dear + Mr., Mrs., Miss or professional title + family name.

  Examples: Dear Mr. Luo, Dear Professor Lau.

Hong Kong Chinese may have Christian given names.

- If you're unsure of a person's title or marital status, you can use the full name.

  Example: Dear Lau Gan Lei.

- Younger executives may write their names in Western style, given name first and family name last. They also may ask to be called by their given or Christian names.

- The Chinese are famous for communicating by "saying it without saying it." It's important to learn how to read between the lines.

- Chinese (Cantonese) and English are the official languages.

- The written form of Chinese used in Hong Kong employs "classical" Chinese characters, not the "simplified" characters used in the People's Republic.

Chinese are famous for "saying it without saying it." Learn how to read between the lines.

- English is taught in all schools. American English is understood, but British English is spoken. Employees of most major hotels and restaurants speak English.

- Few taxi drivers speak English. Ask the concierge in the hotel to write your destination on hotel paper for your taxi driver. Carry a hotel card with its name and address in Chinese for use when taking a taxi home. Police with a red patch on the shoulder speak English.

- Government documents, street signs, etc., are written in both Chinese and English.

- Speak in simple, short sentences. Do not assume the Chinese understand you just because English is widely spoken.

- Chinese is a tonal language and very difficult to speak correctly, but polite phrases are usually understood without correct tones. Try to speak a few words of Cantonese. Hong Kong Chinese greatly appreciate the attempt to speak their language.

- Chinese often use stories and anecdotes to express ideas.

- When Chinese say "OK," it does not mean "I agree"—it means "I understand."

- In China, Hong Kong may be referred to as *Xiang Gang* ("Fragrant Harbor" in *putonghua* or Mandarin). Hong Kong, the name given to the island and the colony by the British, is adapted from the Cantonese *Heung Gong.*

Try to speak a few polite phrases in Cantonese. The effort will be appreciated.

- Hong Kong Chinese may stand close when talking, but they tend to be uncomfortable with body contact. Do not hug, kiss or pat people on the back.

- When sitting, do not swing your legs. Women, however, may cross their legs.

- Never wink at anyone. This is a very rude gesture.

- A woman may hold hands with another woman. This is simply a show of friendship.

- To beckon someone, extend your arm and hand, palm down, and make a scratching motion with your fingers.

- Never point with your index finger. This is done with animals. Point with your hand open.

Hong Kong Chinese stand close when talking, but tend to be uncomfortable with body contact.

PHRASES

English	Chinese	Pronunciation
Hello (telephone)	*Wai*	Why
Good morning	*Jou sahn*	Dyoh sahn
Good afternoon	*Ngh on an sahn*	Ng awn ahn sahn
Good night (not used)	*Jou tau*	Dyoh tow
Goodbye	*Joigin*	Dyoy-geen
Please	*My goi*	Mm goy
Thank you	*Dojeh*	Daw-dyeh
You're welcome	*M'sai m'goi*	Mm-sigh mm-goy
Excuse me	*Deui mh jyuh*	Der-mm-dyoo
Yes	*Haih*	High
No	*Mh-haih*	Mm-high
How are you?	*Neih hou ma?*	Nee how ma?

- Cantonese cuisine is considered one of the best in the world.

- The Oriental or Western style of eating is used according to the food being served.

- Every cuisine in the world can be found in Hong Kong. Western food is available in many restaurants and most hotels.

- When eating Chinese or other Asian food, chopsticks are used. See "Chopstick Etiquette" in Chapter 10.

- Banquets of eight to 14 courses are not unusual in Hong Kong. See "Banquet Etiquette" in Chapter 10.

Be sure to eat and show appreciation for shark fin soup, which is offered only to special guests and is very expensive.

- If you've been the guest of honor at a banquet given by your Chinese hosts, be sure to reciprocate with a banquet of equal quality. Your hotel can assist you with arrangements.

- Be sure to eat and show appreciation for shark fin soup if it is offered. This delicacy is offered only to special guests and is very expensive.

- Rice is served as a filler. Do not eat large amounts—it implies the host has not served enough food.

- The guest of honor is seated facing the entrance. If a couple are the guests of honor, they are seated opposite each other, with the host to the left of the female guest and the hostess to the right of the male guest.

- Food is generally placed in the center of the table and all help themselves. The host may place special delicacies on your plate. Try to eat them.

- At very formal banquets, the waiters will serve all courses to each guest, including the hosts.

- To place food in individual bowls, use the serving spoon provided, your porcelain spoon, or the large end of your chopsticks (the end not put in your mouth). When serving yourself, don't take the last serving of anything.

- A whole fish may be served. The head of the fish will point to the guest of honor. The guest of honor uses his or her chopsticks to divide the fish. Others then help themselves. Do not turn the fish over—this is bad luck, signifying the fisherman's boat capsizing.

- Always leave some food on your dish when you're finished with a course. The host will continue refilling a guest's plate or bowl until the guest politely leaves food on the dish.

- Don't be afraid to dirty the table cloth. Bones, shells, etc., are put on the table unless a special plate is provided for this purpose. Do not put them in your rice bowl. Chinese find belching, slurping, clanging utensils and making loud noises at the dinner table acceptable, sometimes even complimentary.

- Lay your chopsticks on your chopstick rest or neatly on the table when you are finished eating. Never stick them in a bowl of rice!

- Oranges or other fruits are served to signal the end of the meal. Leave soon after the meal ends.

- When dining with Hong Kong British, use your best Western dining manners.

- Wait for the host or hostess to seat you in a restaurant. You may be seated with other people if the restaurant is full.

- You may be given a hot towel for your hands and face before and after your meal, and may not be given a napkin.

- To obtain your bill, make a writing gesture, with your other palm as the imaginary piece of paper. Ask if a service charge is included.

DRINKING AND TOASTING

- Tea is the customary beverage for all occasions. Your teacup will be refilled continually. Leave your cup full if you are finished. Chinese find adding sugar and cream to tea a very strange Western habit. Place the teapot lid upside down, or open if attached, to signal the waiter for more tea.

- Toasting is an important part of a Chinese dinner. Typical toasts include:

  -*Yum boui*, which means "Cheers."

  -*Yum sing*, a challenge to drain your glass.

  -*Gan bei*, which means "Bottoms up." You only need to drain your glass the first time; sips are sufficient after that.

- If you are the guest of honor and are toasted, smile, raise your glass, make eye contact, drink, raise your glass and thank the host and guests.

- The banquet host visits each table and makes a toast. A toast is often made in the

middle of a banquet when the shark fin
soup is served.

- At the end of dinner, the guest of honor
  rises and thanks the host on behalf of
  everyone present. Make a simple, polite,
  short toast to friendship, success and
  cooperation.

HOME

- Never drop in on anyone. Arrange a visit
  in advance. Shoes are generally not
  removed when entering a home. Follow
  your host's example.

- Do not go into your host's kitchen.

- If offered a drink (tea, bottled water or a
  soft drink), always accept.

- Tipping is mandatory in Hong Kong. Tip
  everyone for everything.

TIPPING

- Restaurants: Service charge of 10 percent is
  included in the bill, but leave an additional
  tip—usually extra change. For excellent
  service, leave waiters an additional 5
  percent.

- Taxis: Small change for short rides; 10
  percent for longer rides if the driver helps
  with the luggage.

- Toilet attendants: HK$5.

- Coat check: HK$10.

- Bellmen and porters: HK$10 per bag for good service or HK$20 total.

- Hairdressers and barbers: 10 percent.

- Maids: Minimal.

- Guides: Depends on amount of time and service rendered.

DRESS

- Hong Kong residents dress ostentatiously, with designer labels and lots of jewelry. You'll feel uncomfortable if you're too staid.

- All types of clothing are worn in Hong Kong. However, taste and fashion look more toward Japan than Britain or the U.S. Clothing should be light for summer, with sweaters and jackets for winter.

Hong Kong residents dress ostentatiously, with designer labels and lots of jewelry.

BUSINESS

- Men: Lightweight, Western-style suits and ties. Bankers wear pinstripes.

- Women: Dresses, suits or skirts and blouses. Conservative styles and colors.

- Wear a good watch. It will be noticed.

RESTAURANT

- Men: Suits and ties.

- Women: Cocktail dresses or evening pants.

- People tend to dress up when going out in the evening. Most European-style hotel restaurants require a coat and tie in the evening.

PRIVATE CLUBS

- These are popular places to do business. A coat and tie are required at most clubs.

CASUAL

- Men: Open-neck shirts, cotton trousers. Designer labels preferred.

- Women: Dresses, skirts or slacks, and blouses. Women do not wear shorts in the city.

GIFTS

- Gift-giving is a tradition in Hong Kong that communicates respect and friendship. Never go to a Chinese home without a gift.

- Present and receive a gift with both hands. Do not open a gift upon receiving it.

- The word for the number "3" in Chinese sounds like the word for "life" and the word

Gift-giving communicates respect and friendship. Never go to a Chinese home without a gift.

for the number "8" sounds like the word for "prosperity." The Chinese word for the number "9" is a homonym for the word "eternity." Give gifts in these numbers, if possible. Do not give gifts in a group of four; the Chinese word for "4" sounds like the word for "death."

- Almost every imaginable product can be purchased in Hong Kong. For a special gift, try to bring something from your home city or state.

- Give brand-name, high-quality—even ostentatious—gifts.

WRAPPING

- Red, green and gold are good colors for gift wrap. Make sure the wrapping is elegant.

HOSTESS

- Suggested gifts: Fruit, candy, cookies.

BUSINESS

- Be prepared to present a small gift at the first meeting with Hong Kong business contacts.

- Give: Quality cognac, brandy, candy, pens. Scotch whiskey is widely available in Hong Kong, so it has no special cachet.

- Do not give a civil servant a gift. This is illegal.

AVOID GIVING

- White or red flowers: White is a symbol of mourning, red is a symbol of blood.

- Clocks, which are associated with death. (Watches are OK.)

- Knives.

DO

- Expect Hong Kong Chinese to ask personal questions.

- Show great respect to and for older people.

- Do compliment Hong Kong Chinese, but expect them to decline. If someone compliments you, politely decline to show humility. Do not say "Thank you."

- Bargain everywhere except in department stores and high-fashion boutiques. Bargain only if you intend to buy an item. Be careful of scams when purchasing

HELPFUL HINTS

Bargain only if you intend to buy an item.

merchandise from street vendors or stalls.

- If store staff is rude, ignore their behavior and walk away.

DO NOT
- Never cause a Chinese to lose face. This will surely end a relationship.

- Do not talk loudly.

Do not talk about failure, poverty or death.

- Avoid using triangular shapes in Hong Kong, as the triangle is considered negative.

- Don't take it personally if you are referred to as a *guei lou* (foreign devil). It reflects a centuries-old belief in the superiority of Chinese culture.

- Do not talk about failure, poverty or death. Hong Kong Chinese are very superstitious, and mentioning these possibilities offends them.

PUNCTUALITY

- Punctuality is expected and respected; be on time for all appointments. Never be late for a banquet.

- Allow "courtesy time" (30 minutes) if someone is late for an appointment with you. Heavy traffic may be the reason.

- The business climate in Hong Kong is "wide open," with a free market and limited government involvement. A business can be opened in Hong Kong in one day. A proper three-step Hong Kong business plan:

  1) Register business (morning).

  2) Rent premises (morning).

  3) Make money (afternoon).

- On July 1, 1997, Great Britain turned Hong Kong over to China. Although some see this as a risk, others see it as an opportunity. China has agreed retain Hong Kong's capitalist economy for at least 50 years, but as a practical matter China is likely to do whatever it believes will best serve its interests.

BUSINESS CARDS

- Bring business cards printed in English on one side and Chinese on the other side. Make sure that the Chinese side uses the "classical" characters used in Hong Kong, and not the "simplified" characters used in the People's Republic. If you are planning to visit both Hong Kong and China, you should mark your boxes of business cards in some way to avoid mix-ups.

Make sure that the Chinese side of business cards uses the "classical" characters.

- Upon introduction, present your business card with both hands and with the Chinese side up.

- Be sure to look at a card upon receiving it. Do not write on a business card in front of the person who gave it to you.

CORPORATE CULTURE

Structure: 90 percent of all private businesses are family-owned and -operated. The senior executive is generally the oldest man and the head of the family—and has absolute authority. Decisions are from the top down. The firm's head decides, and it gets done.

Hong Kong's business leaders are well-educated—often in Western schools and universities—well-traveled, highly motivated and bicultural. The Hong Kong economy is the freest in the world, and the labor force is flexible, hard-working and quick to learn. Hong Kong business is highly competitive.

Hong Kong businesspeople share a business network with 55 million overseas Chinese. Every Hong Kong businessperson is preparing in one way or another for 1997, when Hong Kong will revert to China—many by making as much money as possible in the next three years. Others have immigrated to the U.S., Australia, Canada or Singapore, but return regularly to Hong Kong to do business.

Meetings: Meetings generally take place on time. Tea is served; do not drink until your host takes the first sip. A host leaving tea untouched signals the end of the meeting.

Lawyers are not included in negotiations until contracts are drawn up and signed. Never bring a lawyer to the initial meetings.

Negotiations may be slow and detailed, but very efficient. Send senior people with technical and commercial expertise. They should be prepared to function as a team and make decisions on the spot. Be prepared to compromise. Business deals may be sealed with a handshake alone, showing trust.

Banking contacts are very important. Use a bank to set up your meetings.

Communication: Business discussions are conducted in English.

A tradition of politeness, personal relationships, modesty and quiet conduct combined with directness and a primary concern with results characterize business communication in Hong Kong. Hong Kong people get down to business quickly. Etiquette and protocol are not as important as in the rest of Asia; making money is what counts.

Take time to build relationships. It may take several meetings to accomplish goals. Do business face-to-face whenever possible. Courtesy calls and personal selling are vital to success.

"Yes" means "I hear you" rather than "I agree." "No" often means "It will have to wait" or "This may be very difficult."

BE AWARE

- Do not attempt to open an office or factory without consulting a geomancer or *feng shui* person. See "Animism and Feng Shui" in Chapter 5.

ENTERTAINMENT

- Never refuse an invitation to lunch or dinner. If you can't make the date, suggest another one.

- The host may stage an elaborate banquet.

- Lunch and dinner are appropriate for business entertaining, which is usually done in restaurants, on boats or in clubs. Many deals are done over dinner. Businesspeople frequently work and entertain late into the evening. It can be exhausting and expensive.

- Power breakfasts are very popular in Hong Kong.

- Spouses are usually not included in business dining. Do not bring a spouse unless invited to do so. If spouses are present, business is not discussed.

APPOINTMENTS

- Normal business hours are Monday through Friday, 9 a.m. to 5 p.m., and Saturday, 9 a.m. to 1 p.m. A six-day, 48-hour work-week is not uncommon. A 9-to-5, five-day workweek is usual for foreign companies and government officials.

- Make appointments for serious business meetings a month before arrival. It's often possible to arrange a meeting on short notice by phone, but you can't count on it.

Make appointments for serious business meetings a month before arrival.

- October through November and March through June are the best times for business meetings. Avoid the weeks before and after Christmas; the weeks before and after the Chinese New Year (late January or February); and the weeks before and after Easter.

ESPECIALLY FOR WOMEN	• Foreign businesswomen should encounter little resistance to doing business in Hong Kong.

ESPECIALLY FOR WOMEN

- Foreign businesswomen should encounter little resistance to doing business in Hong Kong.

- Hong Kong has no sex-discrimination laws. Businesses can state gender preferences in employment ads, and women are not allowed in some private clubs. This latter situation is changing rapidly.

- Younger women are increasingly entering the workplace. The majority still hold low-paying jobs; however, there are women in the professions, government and business. A small number are entrepreneurs or hold top corporate jobs.

- Chinese women generally do not drink alcohol in public, usually opting for tea or orange juice. However, it is acceptable for Western women to drink alcohol in public.

HEALTH AND SAFETY

- Medical care in Hong Kong is excellent.

- Tap water is safe to drink.

- Crime is not a problem in areas frequented by visitors.

- **Emergency Number: Police/Fire/Ambulance 999.**

January	New Year's Day (1).
January/ February	Chinese New Year (determined by lunar calendar).
Spring	Easter (Friday-Monday).
April	Ching Ming Festival (5).
June	Dragon Boat Festival (24), Queen's Birthday (second Saturday).
August	Tuen Ng (last weekend), Liberation Day (25).
September	Mid-Autumn Festival (30).
October	Chung Yeung Festival (23).
December	Christmas (25-26).

NOTE: Some holidays are based on the lunar calendar. Both Chinese and Western New Year's are celebrated.

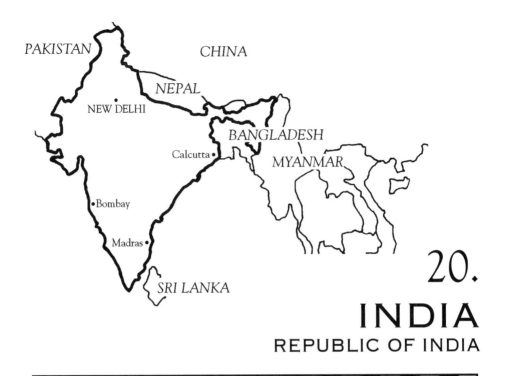

20.
INDIA
REPUBLIC OF INDIA

VITAL STATISTICS

POPULATION: 975.8 million, second-largest in the world.

CAPITAL: New Delhi, with an estimated population of 8.3 million (1991).

MAJOR CITIES: Bombay (12.5 million), Calcutta (10.8 million).

LAND SIZE: 1,269,000 square miles, about one-third the size of the U.S.

GOVERNMENT: Federal republic. Each of the 25 states has its own elected legislature and a governor appointed by the federal president. The federal parliament has a 245-member Council of States elected for six years by the state assemblies and a 543-member House of the People elected for five years from single-member constituencies. The president, who is head of state, is elected by a college of parliament and the state assemblies; he in turn appoints the prime minister, who is chief executive. India is the world's largest democracy.

LIVING STANDARD: GDP = US$360 per capita.

NATURAL
RESOURCES: Coal (fourth-largest reserves in the world), iron ore, manganese, mica, bauxite, titanium ore, chromite, natural gas, diamonds, crude oil, limestone.

AGRICULTURE: Accounts for about 30 percent of GDP and employs 67 percent of the labor force. India is self-sufficient in food grains. Principal crops include rice, wheat, oil seeds, cotton, jute, tea, sugarcane and potatoes.

INDUSTRIES: Textiles, food processing, steel, machinery, transportation equipment, cement, jute products, mining, petroleum, chemicals, pharmaceuticals, electronics, footwear.

CLIMATE: Monsoons are the dominant feature of India's climate, which ranges from tropical in the south to temperate in the north and is characterized by extremes: torrential rains, searing heat, violent winds. The basic seasons are hot (March-June), rainy (July-September) and cool (October-February).

CURRENCY: Indian *rupee* (Rs). Rs1 = 100 *paise* (p). There are notes of Rs 100, 50, 20, 10, 5, 2, 1 and coins of 50, 25, 20, 10, and 5 p.

THE PEOPLE

CORRECT NAME: Indians.

ETHNIC MAKEUP: One of the most diverse in the world. Religion and language separate people; 72 percent are Indo-Aryans, 25 percent Dravidians, 2 percent Mongoloid and Australoid.

VALUE SYSTEM: Indians are religious and philosophical, and such Indian values as humility, self-denial, tolerance, purity, refinement and social harmony are based on religion. The caste system, which once severely limited social mobility, has virtually disappeared in the cities but still exists in rural areas. India has a huge middle class—over 100 million—but there is also a glaring disparity between the relative handful of very wealthy and large numbers of desperately poor. Especially among the poor and undereducated, a traditional fatalism causes people to accept their lot.

FAMILY: The family takes precedence over the individual. Families are generally large, even though the government actively promotes family planning. Extended families generally live together or near each other. Increasing numbers of women work outside the home, especially in urban areas. In villages, most people make their living from small-scale agriculture, and most of the work in the fields is done by women.

RELIGION:	83 percent Hindu, 11 percent Muslim, 3 percent Christian, 2 percent Sikh, 1 percent Buddhist and Jain. Most Indians actively practice a religion. Hinduism, Buddhism, Jainism and Sikhism all developed in India; all believe in reincarnation.
SPORTS:	Cricket, field hockey, football (soccer), tennis and badminton are the most popular sports. Most large cities have golf courses, tennis courts and swimming pools.

India is a country of staggering contrasts and contradictions. It is at once modern and primitive, industrial and agrarian, fabulously wealthy and hopelessly impoverished. Its scale and diversity are overwhelming. Be prepared to accept India on its own terms.

IMPORTANT DATES

2500 B.C.	Earliest known civilization in the Indus Valley.
1500-1200 B.C.	Aryans invade India.
500 B.C.	Siddhartha Gautama founds Buddhism.
326 B.C.	Alexander the Great invades India.
320-185 B.C.	Mauryas rule first Hindu empire.
320 A.D.	Northern India united under the Gupta empire.
1000	Muslim invasions begin.
1206-1526	Delhi sultanate.
1526	Babar founds Muslim Mogul Empire in India.
1556-1605	Akbar the Great, grandson of Babar, rules the Mogul Empire.
1612	British East India Company builds factory at Surat.
1757	British East India Company consolidates its control in India after victory in the Battle of Plassey.
1774	Warren Hastings becomes first governor-general of India.
1858	British Crown assumes administrative control of India.

1920s	Mohandas K. Gandhi leads nonviolent civil disobedience campaign against British rule.
1935	Second Government of India Act grants greater autonomy.
1942-44	Gandhi imprisoned by the British.
1947	India and Pakistan become independent nations. Jawaharlal Nehru becomes first prime minister of India.
1948	Gandhi assassinated.
1966	Indira Gandhi, daughter of Nehru, becomes prime minister.
1971	With India's help, East Pakistan declares its independence from West Pakistan, renaming itself Bangladesh.
1984	Indira Gandhi assassinated by Sikh bodyguards. Rajiv Gandhi, son of Indira, becomes prime minister.
1991	Chandra Shekar resigns as prime minister. Rajiv Gandhi assassinated. P.V. Narasimha Rao elected prime minister.

- Greet Hindus with the phrase *namaste* (nah-mahss-TAY) and the accompanying gesture. Hold your hands chest high with palms pressed together in the prayer position, and make a slight bow.

- In the south, greet Hindus with the phrase *namaskaram* (nah-mahss-CAR), accompanied by the same gesture.

- Greet Muslims with the phrase *salam alaikum* (sah-LAAM a-LIE-come).

- Greet Sikhs with the phrase *sat sri akal* (sut sree ah-kaal).

- Since it may be difficult to determine a person's religion, a Westerner may shake hands and say in English "How do you do?" and "Pleased to meet you."

- Men shake hands with men when meeting or leaving.

- Men do not touch women when meeting or greeting.

- Western women may offer their hand to a Westernized Indian man, but not normally to others.

Men do not touch women when meeting or greeting.

- Traditionally, Indian women shake hands with foreign women but not usually with men. Educated and more modern women may offer their hand to a man.

- Indians ask permission before leaving others.

- When greeting or saying goodbye to Muslims, use only your right hand.

- If you meet Indians around noon, they may ask if you've eaten. Such a remark is usually a straightforward inquiry. If you haven't, you may be invited to join the meal.

NAMES AND TITLES

- Never address Indians by their given names. Use the English courtesy title (Mr., Mrs. or Miss.) or English professional title (doctor, professor) and family name unless you're thoroughly familiar with the Hindu, Muslim or Sikh greeting customs.

Here are some guidelines to Indian name usage:

HINDU

- Given names come first, followed by family names.

  Examples: Jawaharlal Nehru's family name was Nehru; Indira Gandhi's family name was Gandhi.

- When you become friends, Indians might give you a familial nickname. Do not refuse this offer of friendship.

  Examples: "Uncle" or "Mother."

- The proper form for the salutation in correspondence is: Dear (Title) (Surname).

- Common Hindu family names include *Gopal, Krishna, Ram, Lal, Prakash*.

MUSLIM

- Muslims have no surname. Their names are written with their given name + *bin* or *binti* + their father's given name.

  Examples: Ali bin Isa is the son of Isa bin Osman; he should be addressed as Mr. Ali. Zaitun binti Isa is the daughter of Isa bin Osman; she should be addressed as Miss Zaitun or Mrs. Zaitun.

- Common Muslim names include *Khan, Ali, Muhammad, Hussein*.

- Muslim women who marry do not necessarily take their husband's name.

Muslims have no surname. Their names are written with their given name + bin or binti + their father's given name.

SIKH

- All Sikhs use the name *Singh* (but not all Singhs are Sikhs).

- The given name precedes Singh.

Example: Manu Singh is addressed as Mr. Singh or Mr. Manu Singh.

- All Sikh women have the title Kaur after their first name.

- A married woman is addressed as Mrs. + her husband's full name.

Example: Mrs. Manu Singh.

LANGUAGE

No one language is spoken by the majority of people in India.

- Including Hindi and English, India has 16 official languages; altogether, more than 300 languages are spoken.

- No one language (not even Hindi, the main official language and the fifth-most-spoken language in the world) is spoken by the majority of people in India.

- English is the most useful language throughout India. English is the language of national communication and an important business and government language.

- While English is widely understood in India, only a relatively small percentage of people actually speak English. Most businesspeople a foreigner deals with are likely to be English speakers.

- When an Indian answers, "I will try," he or she generally means "No." This is considered a polite "No."

- Public displays of affection are considered improper.

BODY LANGUAGE

- Indians generally allow an arm's length space between themselves and others. Don't stand close to Indians; they value personal space.

- Men do not touch women in public—a sign of respect for a woman's privacy.

- Indian men may engage in friendly back-patting merely as a sign of friendship. Women may hug each other when they meet.

- When Indians smile and jerk their heads backward or move their heads in a figure 8, it means "Yes."

Indians generally allow an arm's length space between themselves and others.

- The Western side-to-side hand wave for "Hello" is frequently interpreted by Indians as meaning "No" or "Go away."

- Use only your right hand to touch someone, eat, pass money or pick up merchandise. The left hand is considered unclean.

- Do not touch anyone's head.

- Indians are very sensitive to being beckoned rudely. To beckon someone politely, extend your arm and hand, palm down, and make a scratching motion with fingers kept together.

- Grasping your earlobe expresses remorse, repentance or sincerity.

Pointing feet or shoes at people is considered an insult.

- Pointing feet or shoes at people is considered an insult.

- Never point with a single finger or two fingers (used only with inferiors). Point with your chin, whole hand or thumb. The chin is not used to point at superiors.

- Never wink at a woman; this is a demeaning gesture.

- Beckon a waiter as described in the "Body Language" section above. Never beckon with your index finger, and never snap your fingers or hiss as Indians sometimes do.

- Better hotels and some restaurants serve Western food.

- Hindus eat no beef (the cow is considered sacred). Many are vegetarians.

- Muslims have strict dietary rules and eat no pork.

- Sikhs eat no beef, and many are vegetarians.

Hindus eat no beef; Muslims eat no pork.

- When first offered tea, coffee or food, it is polite to refuse once before accepting. Obviously, this does not apply if you're already sitting at a restaurant table, a banquet table or your host's dining table. It does apply if you're in someone's office, a conference room or a hotel lobby.

- At a social gathering, a garland of flowers is often placed around a guest's neck. Remove it after a few minutes and carry it in your hand to show humility.

- The guest of honor is seated first and sits where the host indicates.

- Be sure to wash hands before and after meals. Use your own handkerchief to dry your hands. A bowl of hot water with a slice of lemon may be brought to the table for washing your hands.

- In Western-style homes, hotels and restaurants, utensils are provided.

- If utensils are not used, use the tips of the first three fingers and thumb of your right hand only. In the south, people use their entire right hand (which can be very messy for the inexperienced).

- Don't serve yourself. Allow your hosts to serve you. If hosts eat with their hands, assure them you enjoy doing the same.

- Never refuse food, but you do not have to empty your plate. Hindu hosts are never supposed to let their guests suffer empty plates.

- Food and drink should be offered with the right hand only.

- Take food from a communal dish with a spoon, never your fingers. Use *chappati* or *poori* (bread) torn into small chunks to wrap around pieces of meat or scoop up vegetables and sauces from your plate.

- If you can't finish your food, don't offer it to anyone else or return it to the serving dish after it has been on your plate. Once you've touched food, it is considered tainted.

- Do not take food out of the eating area.

- Orthodox Hindus prefer that their food is not touched by people outside their caste or religion.

- At social functions, men usually talk to men and women to women. Don't be surprised if women go off to a separate corner to talk.

- In traditional homes, men, the elderly and children generally eat with guests. Women eat alone later.

- *Namaste* (see "Meeting and Greeting" above) is a polite way to signal you have had enough food. Meals may end with *paan*, a betel nut mixture believed to be an aid to digestion.

Food and drink should be offered with the right hand only.

- In crowded restaurants, you may share a table with other diners. Check your bill for accuracy. If it's incorrect or unclear, question the waiter.

- The host pays for guests in a restaurant. Guests give gifts to the host and the host's children as a thank-you. You should reciprocate with an invitation to a dinner of comparable value. Never invite someone to a far more lavish dinner—it could embarrass them.

DRINKING AND TOASTING

- Strict Muslims don't drink any alcohol.

- Most Hindus, especially women, do not consume alcohol.

- You may offer a Sikh man a drink even though he will probably refuse.

- Beer isn't as popular as in Western countries, but it is widely available. Whiskey, gin, rum and other spirits also are available.

- "Foreign liquor" means Indian-made spirits. It is generally of good quality and inexpensive.

- "Indian liquor" is generally illegal and dangerous to drink.

- Toasts are not required, except at ceremonial banquets and other formal occasions.

- "To your health," "To your country" and "To your prosperity" are acceptable toasts.

TIPPING

- People may offer to help you and expect a tip; or tipping can actually be a bribe necessary to get something done. Don't be surprised if a tip is thrown on the ground: It will be picked up.

- Hotels: 10 percent service charge included in major hotels.

- Restaurants: Tip 10 percent in urban areas and 5 percent in other areas, unless a service charge is included in the bill.

- Taxi drivers: 5 to 10 percent of the fare.

- Hired driver: Rs10 for a half day, Rs20-25 and meals for a full day.

- Porters: Rs5 per piece of luggage.

- Tour guides: Rs5 to 10 per hour.

- Shoe guardian (temple or mosque): Couple of Rs.

- Room waiter: Rs5 per night.

DRESS

- Northern India is cold in the winter, so warm woolen clothing is required for two to three months.

- Light and loose-fitting clothing is best in most parts of India.

Light and loose-fitting clothing is best in most parts of India.

- You will see beautiful, expensively dressed women in the major cities.

- Many Indians do not wear shoes in their homes. Follow your host's example. Make sure your socks are clean and do not have holes.

- Wearing leather might offend strict adherents of some Indian religions; Hindus do not kill cows, and members of other sects do not kill any animals.

- Women should wear modest clothing, especially in Muslim areas. Revealing clothing may cause unflattering remarks and unwanted stares.

- If a Western woman wants to wear a *sari*, she should ask an Indian woman to show her how to wear it correctly; the fabric is draped according to socioeconomic status and/or religious affiliation.

- Bikinis are worn only at pools and beaches. Conservative one-piece swimsuits are a better choice.

BUSINESS

- Men: Suits and ties. In very hot weather, you may omit the jacket.

- Women: Conservative pant suits or dresses.

In very hot weather, men may go without a suit jacket.

RESTAURANT

- Neat, casual attire is usual. Most restaurants do not have dress codes.

CASUAL

- Men: Cotton shirts and pants.

- Women: Dresses, skirts, slacks, blouses.

- Casual wear is normal for the theater.

- Shorts should be avoided except at beaches and for athletic activities.

TEMPLE

- Men: Long pants only, but short-sleeved shirts are OK.

- Women: Cover arms and legs. Wear skirts, dresses or neat pants.

- Remove shoes before entering a temple or mosque.

- Men and women cover their heads when entering a sacred building. When sightseeing, it is advisable to carry a large, clean handkerchief for the purpose.

GIFTS

- Give gifts with both hands.

- Gifts are not normally opened in the presence of the giver.

- Gifts from the visitor's home country are appreciated (perfume, chocolates, small china or crystal objects).

WRAPPING

- Wrap gifts in happy or lucky colors— yellow, red and green.

- Do not wrap in unlucky colors—white or black.

HOSTESS

- Give: Fruit, flowers, candy, small gifts for children, wine or scotch (if your host drinks alcohol), books about your home country.

- Avoid giving: Items unique to any religion.

BUSINESS

- Gifts are not normally expected at the first meeting. Gifts may be given once a relationship develops. Be prepared.

- Give: Whiskey (if the recipient drinks), pens, ties.

- Avoid giving: Alcohol unless you know the recipient drinks. Never give alcohol to a Muslim. Large or very expensive gifts could cause embarrassment.

Gifts are not normally expected at a first business meeting.

DO

- Show great respect for elders.

- Apologize immediately if your feet or shoes touch another person.

- Expect Indians to be vague in conversation.

- Ask permission before smoking. It is considered rude to smoke in the presence of elders or seniors.

HELPFUL HINTS

- Bargain freely with street vendors or in small shops and stalls. Generally make an initial offer of one-half the value and gradually work up to 70 or 75 percent of the original asking price.

DO NOT

- Do not stare, especially at the poor. This is humiliating to them.

- Do not show anger.

- Do not whistle in public.

- Do not wink.

- Do not touch or point at anyone with your feet or shoes. Do not show the soles of your shoes.

- Do not expect Indians to say "No." If invited to an event they cannot attend, they usually will say "I'll try."

- Do not praise children. It is an old belief that praise might draw the attention of the "evil eye." Do not pat children on the head.

- Do not be critical of Indian customs in the presence of Indians.

- Do not offer cigarettes to Indian women or Sikhs. Do not smoke in the presence of Sikhs without permission.

- Do not bargain in government emporiums or large stores.

- Always refuse the offers of "touts" and tour guides to take you to a shop. A commssion for the guide will be added to the price of your purchase. Say, "No, thank you."

TEMPLES AND HOLY PLACES

- Step over, not on, the threshold when entering.

- Wash your feet before entering.

- Never drink alcoholic beverages on temple grounds.

- Ask permission before photographing holy places.

Ask permission before photographing holy places.

- Some Hindu temples do not allow non-Hindus to enter (at least the inner sanctum).

- Walk clockwise around Buddhist structures—inside and out.

- People are separated by gender in some shrines.

- Many Hindu and Sikh temples (gurudwaras) do not allow leather to be worn inside (shoes, belts, purses, camera cases).

- Do not touch statues or paintings.

- Visitors may be offered saffron powder, holy water or food as a blessing from God. Do not refuse these gifts.

- Brahman priests may approach you and touch your forehead with sandalwood paste and vermillion and give a blessing. A few rupees donation to the temple is expected.

PUNCTUALITY

- Punctuality is expected in business, but less strictly so in social situations.

- Arrive 15 to 30 minutes later than the stated time for a dinner party.

STRICTLY BUSINESS

BUSINESS CARDS

- Business cards are exchanged when you are introduced; Indians are very conscious of this protocol. Business cards in English are appropriate.

CORPORATE CULTURE

Structure: Decisions are made at or near the top of an organization, usually by one person.

All decisions are considered major and are made slowly. Middle managers value job security and will check every decision with many people at various levels. This makes the Indian bureaucracy very cumbersome.

Attempt to deal initially with the highest-level person possible, even if details will be worked out with middle managers.

Meetings: Many meetings are necessary to get through multiple layers of management.

It is considered rude to plunge into business discussions immediately. Ask about your counterparts' families, interests and hobbies before the meeting begins. You also may ask for opinions on current economic and political issues, but do not offer your comments— especially if they are negative.

Make presentations in a reserved, controlled manner. In negotiating, Indians generally stick pretty close to the original proposals; however, never make your best offer at the outset.

Communication: In business, English is the most commonly used language. Contracts will be written in a local language and English.

Do not get angry if you are told something "can't be done." Instead, restate your request firmly but with a smile. Ask for suggestions on

Attempt to deal initially with the highest-level person possible, even if details will be worked out with middle managers.

You may ask for opinions on current economic and political issues, but do not offer your comments— especially if they are negative.

how to get it done, how to get around restrictions. Express the conviction that your Indian counterpart can help you. In a friendly and polite manner emphasize the urgency and importance of your task and your appreciation for any assistance and support.

BE AWARE

- During meetings or negotiations, you may be offered sugary or milky tea, coffee or soft drinks. Never refuse. Your glass or cup may be refilled as soon as it is empty.

- Knowing the right family is vital to success. Get an agent to help you make necessary contacts.

- Indian businessmen touch and back-slap a great deal. This is a sign of friendship.

ENTERTAINMENT

- Initial business entertainment is usually done in the restaurants of prestigious hotels.

- Never flatly refuse an invitation to the home of or dinner with a business counterpart; make a plausible excuse if necessary.

- Invite spouses to a social function. Let them decide whether or not to attend.

Spouses often attend unless they are Muslims.

- Business can be discussed during meals. Allow your host to initiate business conversation. Business meals are generally in the evening.

APPOINTMENTS

- Requesting an appointment in advance is suggested; 10 a.m. to 5 p.m. are the normal hours for meetings. You may stop at someone's office and request an appointment.

- October through March are the best months for business trips. Avoid May-June (very hot) and July-August (monsoon rains).

- Indian counterparts may not show up for scheduled meetings. Be prepared to reschedule.

- Try to get your business in banks and government offices done early in the day. Lunch hours can extend well into the afternoon, especially in government offices.

ESPECIALLY FOR WOMEN

India is a particularly difficult place for women to do business. To be accepted, establish your position and credentials immediately.

- India is a difficult place to do business, but particularly tough for women. India is a male-dominated society.

- To be accepted, Western women must establish their position and credentials immediately.

- Women may not be included in social events or conversation.

- Western women may invite an Indian man to a business lunch and pay the tab without embarrassment.

- Men rule the roost, especially in the countryside. Couples still desire sons, and girls are regarded as a burden. In rural India, boys generally get better food, education and medical care than girls. The life expectancy of women is shorter than men's.

- Although relatively few Indian women work outside the home, women are making steady advances in medicine, education, law, science, commerce and politics.

- Traditional Muslim women usually keep out of the view of strange men.

- Women can eat alone in restaurants without being bothered.

- Women never wink or whistle.

- Medical care is adequate in major cities but limited in rural areas. Many doctors speak English and some have been trained in the West. Dental care is not up to Western standards. Check your medical insurance coverage before you travel.

- If possible, drink only bottled water or other bottled drinks; make sure tamper-proof seals are intact. Use bottled water even for brushing your teeth.

- If bottled water is not available, drink only water that has been boiled and filtered.

- For emergency use, carry your own water purification tablets and a plastic glass.

- It is not rude to turn down a drink of tap water. If you must drink water from a communal container, do so without your lips touching the container.

- Don't use ice in your drinks—even in good hotels.

- Eat only thoroughly cooked meats and fruits or vegetables that have been cooked, peeled or washed in diluted permanganate solution.

- Wear shoes to avoid hookworm and other parasites; take precautions against

If possible, drink only bottled water or other bottled drinks; use bottled water even for brushing your teeth.

insect bites; and avoid swimming in fresh water.

- Wear rubber thongs in showers, bathrooms and kitchens—wiring and plumbing problems could combine to cause a shock.

- Most international brand-name pharmaceuticals are available over the counter without a prescription.

- Petty crime is common, especially the theft of personal property. Take precautions on public transportation, in crowds, and around airports and train or bus terminals; watch your pockets and handbag, and wear a security belt inside your clothing to hold your valuables.

- The potential exists for violence in most major cities. While foreigners have not been the targets of violence in India, they could inadvertently become victims.

- Travelers are invited to contribute to worthy Indian charities but asked by the government to resist beggars. Begging is considered a racket and the government is attempting to wipe it out. If you give money to a beggar, you'll become an immediate target and will be surrounded by other beggars. Some may be professionals.

Begging is considered a racket and the government is attempting to wipe it out.

Try not to be rude, but appear indifferent, if possible.

- You may be approached by street people as if they wish to shake your hand. They then fasten a religious bracelet on your arm and demand money.

- **Emergency numbers: Police 100, Fire 101, Ambulance 102.**

		HOLIDAYS AND FESTIVALS
January	International New Year's Day (1), Republic Day (26).	
February/ March	Ramadan (dates change annually).	
March	Hindu Fire Festival (7), Eid Al-Fitr (breaking of the fast of Ramadan—date changes annually).	
March/ April	Good Friday (date changes annually).	
May	Buddha Puvima (5), Hajj season (approx. May 11-19), Eid Al-Adba (culmination of the Hajj season).	
June	Sacrifice Feast (1, 2, 3), Islamic New Year (approx. 21).	

August	Jonashtami (10), Independence Day (15).
October	Mohandas K. Gandhi's Birthday (2), Dasheva (24).
November	Festival of Lights (13), Guru Nanak's Birthday (29).
December	Christmas (25).

21.

INDONESIA
REPUBLIC OF INDONESIA

VITAL STATISTICS

POPULATION: 203.3 million.

CAPITAL: Jakarta, with a population of more than 8 million.

LAND SIZE: 740,000 square miles, comprising 14,000 islands in the world's largest archipelago. Slightly less than three times the size of Texas.

GOVERNMENT: Military-dominated republic, independent since 1945. The president, who is both chief executive and head of state, is elected for a five-year term by the Consultative Assembly, whose members are partly elected and partly chosen through a variety of other processes.

LIVING STANDARD:	GDP = US$1,210 per capita.
NATURAL RESOURCES:	Crude oil, tin, natural gas, nickel, timber, bauxite, copper, fertile soils, coal, gold, silver.
AGRICULTURE:	Accounts for 23 percent of GDP; subsistence food production; small-holder and plantation production for export; main products include rice, cassava (tapioca), peanuts, rubber, cocoa, tea, coffee, palm oil and copra.
INDUSTRIES:	Petroleum refining, textiles, mining, cement, chemical fertilizers, plywood, food, rubber.
CLIMATE:	Maritime equitorial, with high temperatures and lots of rain year round. Two seasons: the rainy season runs from November to April, the dry (or, more accurately, less wet) season from May to October. Temperatures range from 75°F (23°C) to 95°F (33°C), humidity from 69 to 95 percent.
CURRENCY:	*Rupiah* (Rp) = 100 *sen*. Notes come in 10,000, 5,000, 1,000, 500 and 100 Rp denominations, coins in 100, 50 and 25 Rp.

THE PEOPLE

CORRECT NAME: Indonesians.

ETHNIC MAKEUP: 60 percent Javanese; there are more than 360 tribal and ethnic groups, many with their own customs and languages.

VALUE SYSTEM: Unity, conformity to society's rules, personal honor and respect for the individual are the basis of the culture. Indonesians value loyalty to family and friends above all else. They try never to disagree in public or otherwise to cause another to lose face. Patience is the key to personal relationships.

FAMILY: Families traditionally have been large, with several generations often living under one roof. The extended family offers a complicated system of alliances and friendships as well as a supportive environment for children and the elderly. Indonesia as a whole is viewed by its people as an extended family with the president as father.

RELIGION: 88 percent Muslim, 9 percent Christian, 2 percent Hindu. Indonesia has the largest Muslim population in the world.

SPORTS: Golf, soccer, badminton and basketball.

IMPORTANT DATES

600-1200 A.D.	The Buddhist kingdom of Srivijaya rules much of Indonesia.
1200	Muslim invasions begin; during next two centuries most Indonesians convert to Islam.
1500s	Portuguese, British and Dutch fight for control of Indonesian trade.
1595	Portuguese driven out of Indonesia by the Dutch.
1602	Dutch East India Company formed.
1620s	Dutch drive British out of Indonesia.
1799	Dutch East India Company cedes lands to the Dutch government.
1811-16	Britain takes the islands of Indonesia during the Napoleonic Wars, but returns them to The Netherlands in 1816.
1922	Indonesia officially joins the Kingdom of the Netherlands.
1927	Sukarno leads formation of Indonesia National Party (PNI).
1942-45	Japanese troops occupy Indonesia, are viewed by many Indonesians as liberators from the Dutch.

1945	Indonesia declares independence; Sukarno becomes president.
1949	Netherlands recognizes Indonesian independence. United States of Indonesia formed.
1959	Sukarno consolidates power with ratification of 1945 Constitution.
1963	West New Guinea (now Irian Jaya) becomes part of Indonesia. Sukarno declared president-for-life.
1965	Attempted coup linked to Communists crushed by Suharto.
1966-68	Tens of thousands of Communists die in massive purge; Suharto becomes president.
1971	First national elections since 1955 take place.
1975	Indonesia invades former Portuguese possession of East Timor.
1991	Many new pro-democracy groups formed; government reform program continues.

MEETING AND GREETING

- Shake hands and give a slight nod when meeting a man or woman for the first time. After the first meeting, a slight bow or nod of the head is sufficient—a handshake is not necessary. Handshakes are customary only on first introduction or when someone leaves on a long journey or returns from one. Shake an Indonesian woman's hand only if she initiates the greeting.

- Elders are revered; give them a slight bow. When bowing, a person of lower rank needs to bow lower than the superior.

- Greet people by saying *Selamat* (S'lah-maht), which means "peace." It is polite to introduce yourself to strangers.

- "Hello" is used generally to get someone's attention.

NAMES AND TITLES

- Most Indonesians have two names, with the given name first and the family name last. Because family names are often very long and complicated, most Indonesians are addressed using the appropriate courtesy title and first name.

- To address an Indonesian man, use *Bapak* (Bah-pahk) + first name.

  Example: Ismail Saleh would be addressed as Bapak Ismail.

- To address an Indonesian woman, use *Ibu* (Ee-boo) + first name.

- Bapak and Ibu mean "sir" and "madam." If you don't know someone's name, you can address them with just Bapak or Ibu.

- Titles are customarily used: professor, doctor, noble titles, political titles, military ranks, president director or vice president director in companies.

- Introduce a person using Bapak or Ibu, any noble or academic title, given name, family name, and business or social position.

- Rural women often keep their maiden names when married. Middle-class urban women usually take their husbands' names.

- In correspondence, never use the family name in the salutation.

  Examples: "To the most respected Bapak Ismail" or "Dear Bapak Ismail."

LANGUAGE

- Bahasa Indonesian (a form of Malay) is the official language, although more than 300 other languages are spoken. Javanese is the second language. Dutch is still spoken by older adults, but has been replaced by English as the leading international language.

- Indonesians say *Belum*, "Not yet," rather than "No."

BODY LANGUAGE

- Good relationships involve a great deal of physical contact and touching. Foreigners must allow time before they're accepted on this level; Indonesians loathe those who feign friendship.

The head is considered sacred. Do not touch anyone, including children, on the head.

- Men and women do not touch in public, except to shake hands. Avoid public displays of affection.

- The head, where the spirit is thought to reside, is considered sacred. Do not touch anyone, including children, on the head.

- When sitting, do not cross your legs, especially not with an ankle over the knee. Sitting erect with both feet on the floor is a sign of respect—be sure to do so with superiors or elders. Never let the soles of your shoes face or point at another person.

- Point with your thumb, not your index finger. Never beckon with one finger.

- The left hand is considered unclean. Do not touch food, pass or receive anything, touch anyone or point with your left hand.

- Approval is sometimes shown with a pat on the shoulder, but American-style back-slapping is very bad form.

- Thumbs up (extending your right thumb while making a fist) means "Please go first."

- Try not to yawn. If you can't avoid it, at least cover your mouth.

- Standing with your hands on your hips or in your pockets or with your arms crossed over your chest is a sign of defiance or arrogance and can be quite insulting.

Sitting erect with both feet on the floor is a sign of respect—be sure to do so with superiors or elders.

The left hand is considered unclean. Do not touch food, pass or receive anything, touch anyone or point with your left hand.

PHRASES

English	Indonesian	Pronunciation
Good morning	*Selamat pagi*	S'lahmaht pahghee
Good afternoon	*Selamat sore*	S'lahmaht sawrreh
Good evening	*Selamat malam*	S'lahmaht mahlahm
Please	*Silahkan*	Seelakahn
Thank you	*Terima kasih (man)* *Terima kembali (woman)*	T'rreema kasseehh T'rreema kembahlee
You're welcome	*Kembali/Sama*	Kembahlee/Sahmah
Yes	*Ya*	Yah
No	*Tidak*	Teedah'
Excuse me	*Maaf*	Mahahf
How are you?	*Apa kabar?*	Ahpah kahbahr
Goodbye	*Selamat tinggal*	S'lahmaht teenggal

MANNERS

- To summon a waiter or waitress, raise your hand. Address them as *mas* (waiter) or "miss" (waitress). Do not whistle or beckon with your index finger.

- A fork and spoon are used for dining. The fork is held in the left hand and the spoon in the right. Use the fork to push food onto the spoon.

- Many Indonesian foods are quite hot and spicy. Rice is included in almost every meal. Rice and spicy mixtures of vegetables, chicken, seafood and meat are staples of the Indonesian diet.

- Most Indonesians are Muslim and consume no liquor or pork.

- Indonesians are known for their hospitality; to refuse their hospitality is to reject them personally. Never refuse food or drink, but never finish either completely. Compliments about the food are appreciated.

Most Indonesians are Muslim and consume no liquor or pork.

- Strangers may share a table in a crowded restaurant. Women traveling alone don't need to worry about being hassled.

- In a mixed group, the male guest of honor sits next to the host and the female guest of honor sits next to the hostess.

- Pass and accept food and drinks with your right hand only. If you eat anything with your hand, use only your right hand. It is considered unclean to touch food with your left hand.

Fingers are used instead of fork and spoon in some places. Eat only with the right hand.

- Fingers are used instead of fork and spoon in some places. Eat only with the right hand, but keep both hands above the table. In Java, finger bowls and napkins are used throughout the meal when eating with fingers.

- A request for salt, pepper, soy sauce or spices is an insult to the cook. Try not to make special requests for food or drink.

- Do not talk with food in your mouth.

- Avoid using a toothpick in public, but if one must be used, cover your mouth. (Indonesians believe only animals show their fangs.)

- When finished with your meal, place the fork (tines down) on your plate with your spoon (face down) crossed over the fork.

- The person who invites is expected to pay the bill in a restaurant. Request the bill by making a scribbling gesture on palm of hand.

- Eating while standing or walking in the street is inappropriate.

DRINKING AND TOASTING

- Do not drink until invited to do so by your host. A finished drink signals the desire for a refill. Leave a little in your glass if you don't care for more.

- Although many Indonesians drink alcohol, you should never offer a practicing Muslim an alcoholic beverage. When in doubt, don't.

- Toasts are not commonly made, but a general toast "to friendship" is OK.

MOSQUE/TEMPLE

- Quiet behavior is required. Don't walk in front of anyone praying; keep your head lower than a priest's.

- Ask permission before taking photos inside a mosque or temple. Don't climb on or touch anything.

- Be careful where you sit. Some seats are reserved for the gods. Keep to the rear in a room where people are kneeling in prayer.

TIPPING

- Restaurants: A 10 percent service charge is usually included in the bill at better restaurants; small change can be left as an additional gratuity. If the service charge is not included, leave a 10 percent tip in better restaurants.

- Hotels: No tip necessary; a 10 percent service charge is generally added to the bill.

- Taxis: It's important to negotiate the fare *before* you get in a cab. A tip of Rp 500 is optional, but common.

- Porters: Rp 500 per bag.

- Barbers and beauty shops: Rp 1,000.

- Washroom attendants: Rp 100-500.

- Dress for the climate—hot and humid. Lightweight, absorbent fabrics are recommended. Sweaters or jackets are necessary for travel to mountain areas.

- If your host goes shoeless, do likewise. Do not wear shoes on carpeted floors.

- *Batik* is a traditional, pattern-dyed cotton fabric and one of Indonesia's most famous exports. In Java, batik clothing is traditional for both men and women. Javanese appreciate foreigners wearing batik (but not for business meetings!).

- Traditional dress for Indonesian women is a sarong, a long wrap-around dress with an intricate batik pattern.

Dress for the climate— hot and humid.

BUSINESS

- Men: Jackets and ties, dress trousers. Wear a suit for the first meeting. Suits are generally not worn by Indonesians except for formal occasions or meetings with senior government officials.

- Women: Skirts and blouses (never sleeveless) or dresses. Avoid bright colors and flamboyant fashions. The Muslim rules of modesty should be honored.

HOME/RESTAURANT

- Men: Batik shirts, cotton shirts; coats and ties for better restaurants.

- Women: Dresses, or skirts and blouses (short sleeves).

CASUAL

- Men: Shirts and pants.

- Women: Cotton dresses, skirts or slacks and blouses.

- Shorts, halter tops, tank tops and thongs are appropriate only at the beach or at sporting events. Bikinis are acceptable at beaches and hotel pools.

FORMAL

- Men: Coats and ties. A long-sleeved batik shirt and dress trousers are acceptable for formal occasions.

- Women: Dresses, cotton shirts, batik blouses or skirts.

- Gifts are generally not expected. Compliments and notes of appreciation are welcome. Always give or receive a gift with the right hand.

- Receive a gift appreciatively. It is impolite to refuse. Gifts are not opened in the giver's presence except at a ceremony, where the gift is opened in front of an assembled group.

HOSTESS

- Always bring a small gift for the hostess when invited to someone's home.

- Give: Flowers, candy, cakes, pens and notebooks for children, stationery, heavy-duty cotton towels. Women appreciate scarves.

- Do not give: Alcoholic beverages, or gifts in any way associated with dogs or pigs.

BUSINESS

- Business gifts are generally not exchanged. A small token of appreciation may be given to the secretary. Gifts to colleagues should be given after most business has been concluded.

- Give: Fruit, candy, lighters or tie pins (discreet company logos are OK).

- Do not give: Alcoholic beverages.

Business gifts are generally not exchanged.

HELPFUL HINTS

DO

- Allow Indonesians to talk about their families.

- Treat civil servants with great respect. They are highly honored.

- Allow all to save face.

Show respect for elders, superiors and civil servants.

- Show respect for elders, superiors and civil servants.

- Be prepared to hear open discussion and questions about birth control. Feel free to give a humorous answer if you don't wish to discuss this subject.

- Understand that Indonesian Muslims do not adhere to the rigorous codes of conduct that exist in Arab countries. Indonesians are tolerant of all religions.

- Barter when purchasing goods, except in large stores where prices are fixed.

- On public transport, always give your seat to the elderly. Men should give their seats to women. Offer to hold packages for anyone standing. Feel free to ask someone seated to hold your packages.

DO NOT

- Never sit on a table or desk.

- Never use the term "Indo"—this is an insulting name for a person of mixed parentage.

- Don't assume tomorrow means tomorrow. Tomorrow may mean sometime in the future.

- Never use your left hand to shake hands, touch others, point, eat or give or receive objects.

- Never laugh at someone's mistakes or embarrass anyone in public. It is a terrible insult. Never mimic or make fun of someone's behavior—even someone you know well. Don't disagree, correct or criticize anyone in public.

Don't disagree, correct or criticize anyone in public.

- Don't force anyone to say "No" or admit error. In fact, don't expect "No" for an answer; Indonesians seldom say "No."

- Do not chew gum or yawn in public.

PUNCTUALITY

- Westerners are expected to be punctual for business appointments. Call if you are delayed. However, don't be surprised if your Indonesian counterpart is late.

  - To Indonesians, punctuality is secondary to personal relationships. Never get angry if someone arrives late.

  - Don't rush or fret over lost time. Haste is considered rude.

- Social events generally start late. Indonesians usually arrive 30 minutes after the stated time. A guest should arrive at an Indonesian home 10 to 20 minutes late.

STRICTLY BUSINESS

Business cards in English are acceptable.

BUSINESS CARDS

- Present your business card to the receptionist immediately upon arrival; otherwise there could be a long delay.

- Exchange business cards when being introduced. Present and receive the card slowly and with much interest. Cards in English are acceptable.

CORPORATE CULTURE

Structure: Many major industries are state-owned and -operated. Other major industries are directly or indirectly controlled by generals—and thus by the army. Ethnic Chinese dominate the business sector.

Decisions in an Indonesian firm are made at the top and, as a general rule, senior executives of foreign companies are the only ones who can gain access to their Indonesian counterparts.

For this reason, it's a good idea to initiate negotiations at the top level of a corporation, then move down to the operating level to discuss technical matters—after which discussions will be concluded at the top level.

Meetings: Businesspeople enter a room according to rank and don't sit until invited to do so. Initial conversation tends to be casual, friendly, and to revolve around families, personal interests and other nonbusiness subjects. Business matters will be mixed in slowly and gently. An initial meeting may last 45 to 60 minutes without any substantial accomplishment. At this point, the visitor should initiate the process of setting the next meeting and departing.

Business relationships must be allowed to develop over time; several visits are usually necessary to agree on, draft and sign a contract. Meetings are formal and proper, and negotiations are slow and calculated. Patience is absolutely essential if you're to succeed in Indonesia.

Summarize and clarify the main points at every stage of a negotiation. State disagreement diplomatically and avoid argument. Indonesians love to bargain, so making concessions too quickly will be viewed as naivete or weakness. To Indonesians, insisting on a written agreement is a breach of trust— but they also have accepted the Western need for written agreements. A formal meeting is generally held to announce agreement.

Communication: English is the most widely used business language in Indonesia. Indonesians in Jakarta generally provide an interpreter, but the visitor should assume responsibility for an interpreter elsewhere in the country.

English is the most widely used business language in Indonesia.

Presentations should be authoritative and highly detailed, backed up with charts, graphs and other exhibits. A foreign company's offer will be evaluated based on the company's reputation, experience and service (especially in the local market), as well as on price, quality, delivery time and reliability. Make sure your presentations cover all these points clearly.

Personal visits are important to Indonesians. They do not respond well to faxes, telephone calls or letters. Show up in person whenever possible.

Indonesians very much want to please; an untruthful answer may be given so as not to disappoint anyone. Try not to ask questions that can be answered "Yes" or "No," because the answers are hard to interpret. *Belum* (not yet) is the Indonesian way of saying "No"; *Mungkin* means "probably"; "Yes" means "I understand" or "I hear you."

Do not use red ink in correspondence.

BE AWARE

- To Indonesians, facts are degrees of probability. A contract should be viewed as a guideline rather than a statement of duties and responsibilities.

- Indonesians bargain in daily life and are proud of their bargaining abilities.

- Never pressure or try to hurry Indonesians. Time is viewed as a limitless pool; time is flexible.

- Taking a photograph is a way of honoring someone. Indonesians may ask to take your picture.

To Indonesians, facts are degrees of probability. A contract should be viewed as a guideline rather than a statement of duties and responsibilities.

ENTERTAINMENT

- Indonesian businesspeople like to entertain. Business lunches are common. However, most business entertaining is done in a restaurant at dinner. Since social life is important to developing relationships, spouses are often included in dinners. Make an effort to invite your Indonesian counterpart's spouse.

- If you've been a dinner guest, reciprocate before you leave the country if possible. Lavishness may be criticized—be generous and hospitable, but don't overdo it.

- It is a special honor to be invited to an Indonesian's home.

- Do not invite practicing Muslims to lunch during Ramadan, when they fast from dawn to dusk.

- Any business discussions at social events should be initiated by Indonesians.

APPOINTMENTS

- When discussing evening dates and times, be sure to specify both the calendar date and the day of the week; the way Indonesians refer to the time after sunset can be confusing to foreigners.

Do not invite practicing Muslims to lunch during Ramadan, when they fast from dawn to dusk.

- When making appointments, be sure to take into account the heavy traffic, unpredictable phone service, heavy travel schedules of Indonesian executives, numerous public holidays and the different pace.

- Business and government offices close on Friday at midday for worship. Try to avoid planning meetings for Friday. Many businesses also close on Saturday and Sunday.

- It is best to schedule appointments in the morning. Afternoons should be used for personally reconfirming future appointments by going to the office concerned.

- September through June is the best time to schedule business visits to Indonesia; July and August are very popular vacation months.

- Indonesia is a Muslim society and very male-oriented. The concept of feminism seems strange to most Indonesians.

- Women visitors to Indonesia are seldom hassled, although blond-haired, blue-eyed women may be somewhat more vulnerable than dark women. It helps if you dress modestly.

- Foreign women will have few problems doing business in Indonesia. Unlike their counterparts in other Muslim nations,

ESPECIALLY FOR WOMEN

Although Indonesia is a Muslim society and very male-oriented, foreign women will have few problems doing business there.

Indonesian women have played a role in business and government for many years. Few, however, are in top-level positions.

- Indonesian women have good maternity leaves and many rights, including inheritances, divorce, property settlements and the right to vote.

- In Indonesia, Muslim women do not usually wear veils.

- A woman is expected to initiate a handshake.

- A woman should not invite an Indonesian man to dine at her hotel. This could cause embarrassment.

- Businesswomen may invite an Indonesian businessman and his wife to dinner. Do not insist if he prefers not to bring his spouse. Arrange payment in advance to avoid embarrassment to the male guest.

- A woman may eat alone in a restaurant; most Indonesian men respect the privacy of a women dining alone. In Java, some men may be more aggressive. Local bars are not safe for unaccompanied women.

- Drink only boiled (20 minutes) or bottled water. Avoid ice cubes, unless you know the water was boiled before freezing. Use bottled water even for brushing your teeth. Carry a bottle of water with you as a precaution against dehydration.

- Food should be thoroughly cooked. Salads and unpeeled fruit can cause dysentery. Avoid milk (which is usually unpasteurized), ice cream and other dairy products; fish may be a problem if it's not freshly caught (and it's usually hard to be sure).

- For medical treatment, Catholic or missionary hospitals are usually good and many have English-speaking staff. If you are seriously ill, go to Jakarta, Semarang, Bandung, Surabaya, Medan or Singapore; these cities have the best-equipped hospitals, many with 24-hour emergency service. Your embassy or consulate may be able to refer you to a good medical facility.

- Hospitals are reluctant to bill. They like cash or at least partial payment in advance.

- Indonesian "health clinics" often reuse needles without properly sterilizing them first. If you need injections or must have

Hospitals are reluctant to bill. They like cash or at least partial payment in advance.

blood samples taken, bring your own
needles and syringes.

- Bali's medical services should be avoided.
  They are very substandard and there is
  widespread malpractice.

- There isn't much violent crime in
  Indonesia, but pickpockets are very
  common. Crowded buses and trains are the
  most common places to get your pockets
  picked. Take precautions, especially before
  and during busy holiday periods.

- Some youths hang around trying to irritate
  foreigners. They may make jokes, try to
  pinch you or make obscene gestures. Don't
  get angry—that's what they want. Just
  leave.

- **Emergency numbers: Jakarta Police 110,
  Ambulance 119; Solo and Yogyakarta
  Police 110, Ambulance 118, Fire 113.**

January	New Year's Day (1, Birth of Muhammad (18).
January/ February	Chinese New Year (varies according to lunar calendar).
February	Ascension of Muhammad.
March	Buddhist Saka New Year (22), Ramadan Feast.
March/ April	Wafat Isa Almasih (Christian Good Friday).
May	Idul Fitri, Buddha's birthday, Ascension Day, Waisak Hariraya (The Great Day of Waisak).
July	Islamic New Year.
August	Independence Day (17).
November	Muhammad's Birthday (25).
December	Batara Turunkabeh (23—temple ceremonies in Bali), Christmas (25).

- The dates for many of these Islamic holidays are set by the lunar calendar and change from year to year.

CHINA

RUSSIA

NORTH KOREA

SOUTH KOREA

Sapporo

TOKYO
Kyoto
Osaka Nagoya

22.
JAPAN

POPULATION:	126.3 million, making it one of the most densely populated countries in the world.
CAPITAL:	Tokyo, with a population of 8.1 million (1990), one of the world's largest metropolitan areas.
LAND SIZE:	143,700 square miles, slightly smaller than California.
GOVERNMENT:	Constitutional monarchy with the emperor as head of state. Executive power is vested in a cabinet and prime minister. Legislative power is held in the Diet, consisting of the 512-member House of Representatives (Lower House) and the 252-member House of Councillors (Upper House).

LIVING STANDARD:	GDP = US$38,120 per capita.
NATURAL RESOURCES:	Forests and fisheries; almost total lack of petroleum, natural gas, iron ore and other minerals. Virtually all industrial raw materials are imported.
AGRICULTURE:	Accounts for only two percent of GDP; a highly subsidized and protected sector, with crop yields among the highest in world; principal crops include rice, sugar beets, vegetables, fruit; animal products include fish and other seafood, pork, poultry, dairy products and eggs. Japan is about 50 percent self-sufficient in food production, with shortages of wheat, corn and soybeans.
INDUSTRIES:	Metallurgy, engineering, electrical and electronic equipment, textiles, chemicals, automobiles, telecommunications, machine tools, construction equipment, shipbuilding, paper, pulp and rubber.
CLIMATE:	Pacific coast has hot, humid summers, with August temperatures exceeding 79°F (26°C), and cold, dry winters. Sea of Japan coast has heavy winter snowfalls. North of 38° latitude, average temperatures in January (the coldest month) are less than 32°F (0°C). In the south, January temperatures average 39-43°F (4-6°C).
CURRENCY:	The Yen (¥) is one of the strongest currencies in the world. Notes are in denominations of ¥10,000, 5,000, and 1,000. Coins are in denominations of ¥500, 100, 50, 10, 5 and 1.

THE PEOPLE

CORRECT
NAME: Japanese.

ETHNIC
MAKEUP: More than 99 percent Japanese, making it one of
                         the world's most homogeneous societies. The
                         only significant minority is a community of about
                         700,000 Koreans, mostly descendants of laborers
                         imported during World War II.

VALUE
SYSTEM: *Wa* (harmony) is the key value in Japanese
                         society. Great importance is placed on loyalty,
                         politeness, personal responsibility and on
                         everyone working together for the good of the
                         larger group. Japanese respect age and tradition
                         and promote modest and reserved behavior. The
                         welfare of the group—family, clan, work group,
                         company, country—always takes precedence over
                         the welfare of the individual.

                         Education, ambition, hard work, patience and
                         determination are held in the highest regard.

                         Because Japanese live in a highly structured society
                         where everyone knows and understands the rules,
                         Japanese may be uncomfortable in the company of
                         gaijin (foreigners). Learning a few rules of Japanese
                         etiquette will help relax everybody.

                         The crime rate is one of the lowest in the world.

FAMILY:

The family is viewed as the foundation of Japanese society. Families are small, few with more than two children. More and more women are working outside the home—in part because of the high cost of living; women now make up 40 percent of the work force in Japan. It's becoming less common for older people to live with their children and grandchildren.

RELIGION:

Shinto 87 percent, Buddhist 73 percent (most Japanese practice elements of both).

SPORTS:

Baseball, golf, sumo wrestling, judo, karate and *aikido* are the most popular sports in Japan. *Pachinko*, or pinball, also is a very popular form of recreation.

IMPORTANT DATES

660 B.C.	According to Japanese legend, Jimmu Tenno becomes the first emperor of Japan.
300 B.C. - 300 A.D.	Immigration from mainland Asia.
300 A.D.	Yamato clan achieves dominance.
550	Buddhism introduced.
794-1885	Heian period; imperial capital established at Kyoto
1192	The first shogun, Yoritomo, initiates military system of feudal rule that lasts for almost seven centuries.
1543	Portuguese are the first Westerners to arrive in Japan.
1603	Tokugawa family begins its 264-year rule of Japan.
1630	Japan isolates itself from rest of world.
1853-54	Commodore Perry arrives in Japan, negotiates U.S.-Japan trade treaty.
1868	Emperor Meiji announces policy of industrial and military modernization. Capital moved from Kyoto to Edo, which is renamed Tokyo ("eastern capital").
1904-05	Japan defeats Russia in Russo-Japanese War. Japan recognized as a world power.
1910	Japan annexes Korea.
1931	Japanese invade Manchuria.

1937	Japan goes to war with China.
1941	Japan attacks U.S. fleet at Pearl Harbor.
1945	Atom bombs dropped on Hiroshima and Nagasaki. Japan surrenders; Allied occupation begins.
1947	New constitution abolishes armed forces and transfers power from the emperor to the people.
1952	Allied occupation ends.
1955	Liberal-Democratic Party formed, initiating single-party rule of Japan that lasts more than three decades.
1960s	Japanese economy grows at an average rate of 10 percent annually.
1980s	Japan runs up massive trade surpluses with the United States and Europe. Criticism of its restrictive trade practices grows.
1987	U.S. slaps 100 percent tariffs on Japanese electronics parts in retaliation for what it considers unfair trade practices.
1989	Akihito becomes emperor of Japan following the death of his father, Emperor Hirohito. Influence-peddling scandal leads to resignation of Premier Noboru Takeshita.
1993	One-party control of Japanese government ends after voters force the Liberal-Democratic Party to form a coalition government.

- A handshake is appropriate upon meeting. The Japanese handshake is limp, with little or no eye contact.

- Some Japanese bow and shake hands.

- The bow is a highly regarded way of showing respect.

- A bow is appreciated by the Japanese. However, be aware that a bow between Japanese is a complicated ritual, in which the degree of inclination depends on the relationship between people involved and the situation in which bows are exchanged. Foreigners should not attempt more than a slight bow to show courtesy.

- Never bow in jest.

- When introduced say: "How do you do?" (not "Hello"), your name, your title and your relationship to the person making introductions.

  Example: "How do you do? I am John Moore, chief executive officer of Accent Co., and a business colleague of Mr. Hata."

Faux Pas

Foreigners should not attempt more than a slight bow to show courtesy.

NAMES
AND
TITLES

- Use family names and appropriate titles until specifically invited by your Japanese hosts or colleagues to use their given names. Many close friends use family names rather than given names.

- Never address an older Japanese person by his or her given name.

- Younger Japanese and those educated in the U.S. may ask to be or even insist upon being addressed by their given name.

- Japanese traditionally say and write their family name first, followed by their given names. However, today many Japanese who deal with Western businesspeople use the Western name order. When in doubt, ask.

- The best way to address Japanese is to use the family name + *san*, a suffix showing honor.

Examples: Mr. Mijoshi is addressed as Mijoshi-san.
Mrs. Mijoshi is addressed as Mijoshi-san.
Miss Mijoshi is addressed as Mijoshi-san.

There is no distinction between gender and marital status with the *san* suffix. Specify to whom you are referring by saying, "I would like to introduce you to Mr. Mijoshi's wife,

Mijoshi-san," or "This is Mr. (or Mrs.) Mijoshi's daughter, Mijoshi-san."

- Never use *san* with your own name or when referring to yourself. This is very impolite; use *san* only when referring to someone else.

- It is also acceptable (though less desirable) to address Japanese people in English using Mr., Mrs. or Miss + family name. For example, Yohei Mijoshi could be addressed either as Mijoshi-san or as Mr. Mijoshi.

- Corporate titles and ranks are very important.

- For very senior executives, titles are used instead of the family name.

    Example: Yohei Mijoshi, company president, is *Shacho-san* (Mr. President). Yohei Mijoshi, company general manager, is *Bucho-san* (Mr. General Manager).

- When introducing a Japanese person, say: This is (name), title and company, relationship to introducer.

    Example: "This is Mijoshi-san, systems analyst of Sony Corporation and a colleague of Mr. Rice."

- If you are introducing a very senior person, it is not necessary to use his or her name.

  Example: The president of Sony Corporation would be introduced by saying, "This is Shacho-san of Sony Corporation, a colleague of Mr. Smith."

LANGUAGE

- Japanese is the official language.

- Many Japanese can read but not speak English. Young people speak more English than older people.

Rule of Thumb

- If trying to communicate in English, speak slowly and clearly in short sentences. Writing down what you want to say may help.

When trying to communicate in English, speak slowly and clearly in short sentences.

- Learning a little Japanese is the best way to make friends in Japan.

- Most taxi drivers do not speak English. Ask your hotel concierge to write your destination in Japanese for the cabdriver, and carry a hotel card with your hotel's name and address written in Japanese for your return trip.

- Japanese do not express opinions and desires openly. What they say and what they mean may be very different.

Example: "I'll think about it and let you know" may mean "Please make an alternative suggestion." "Yes" may mean "I hear you" or "I understand"—*not* "I agree."

- Rather than saying "thank you" and accepting a compliment, Japanese may take great pains to disclaim any achievement or give the credit to others. It is very important for Japanese to show modesty and humility.

- *Nodding is very important!* When listening to Japanese speak, especially in English, you should nod to show you are listening and understanding the speaker. If you don't, the speaker will fear you do not understand.

- Quiet, dignified and modest behavior is essential to fit in with your Japanese hosts. Always keep in mind that the group, not the individual, is the basis of Japanese society. Harmony and consensus are essential to acceptable social and business behavior. Cooperation is necessary to accomplish anything.

- The Japanese place great worth on nonverbal communication and consider a person's inability to interpret feelings as a lack of sensitivity.

BODY LANGUAGE

The group, not the individual, is the basis of Japanese society. Harmony and consensus are essential to social and business behavior.

- Silence is a natural and expected form of nonverbal communication. Do not feel a need to chatter.

- Do not stand close to a Japanese person.

- A smile could mean happiness, amusement, confusion, embarrassment, anger, sadness— or nothing. Interpret it in context.

- Prolonged eye contact or staring is considered rude.

- Avoid touching.

- Avoid public displays of affection, such as hugging or shoulder-slapping.

- An open mouth (when yawning, laughing or using a toothpick) should always be covered.

- Never beckon someone with your forefinger. Japanese beckon someone by extending their right arm to the front, bending the wrist down and waving the fingers in and out. Do not beckon older people.

- Sit erect with both feet on the floor. Never sit with your ankle crossed over your knee.

- The "OK" symbol (thumb and index finger connected to make a circle) means "money" or "all right."

- When a woman waves her hand from side to side in front of her face, palm out, it means "No" or "I don't know." This is a polite response to a compliment.

- Never touch or push anything with your feet.

PHRASES

English	Japanese	Pronunciation
Hello (telephone)	*Moshi-moshi*	MOE-shee MOE-shee
Good morning	*Ohaiyo gozaimasu*	o-HIGH-yoh go-ZIGH-ee-mahss
Good afternoon	*Konnichi wa*	KONE-nee-chee-wah
Good evening	*Konban wa*	KONE-bahn-wah
Please	*Kudasai/Dozo*	kuu-DAH-sigh/DOE-zoe
Thank you	*Arigato*	ah-REE-gah-tow
You're welcome	*Doitashimashite*	doe-ee-TAHSSH-mahssh-tay
Yes	*Hai*	HIGH
No	*Iie*	ee-EH
Excuse me	*Gomen nasai*	go-MEHN na-SIGH
Goodbye	*Sayonara*	sigh-YOH-nah-ra
Pleased to meet you	*Hajimemashite*	hah-JEE-may-mahssh-tay
How are you?	*O genki desu ka?*	oh-GEN-kee dess KAH?
I'm fine	*Genki desu*	GEN-kee dess

- *Domo* (DOE-moe): Polite all-purpose expression meaning hello, goodbye, please, thanks.

- *Sumimasen* (su-MEE-ma-sen): Excuse me, I apologize for my offense; please or thank you when giving or receiving anything.

- There may be little distinction between *hai* (yes) and *iie* (no). Because the Japanese are extremely polite and avoid conflicts, they often respond with hai when they really mean iie.

MANNERS

- Japanese are very accommodating and understanding of foreigners. They appreciate courteous behavior, especially when guests show some knowledge of and respect for their customs.

- Japanese are curious about and very polite to foreigners. They will go out of their way to make you feel welcome.

- Allow Japanese hosts to initiate conversation. There may be several minutes without conversation. This is normal and appreciated.

Asking personal questions is considered a polite way to show interest.

- Japanese may ask personal questions. This is not considered rude but rather a polite way to show interest. You may give vague or general answers if you feel a question is too personal.

DINING

- *Hashi* (HAH-shee), or Japanese-style chopsticks, are shorter than the Chinese version.

- Eating out is a favorite pastime in Japan. There are more restaurants per capita in Japan than anywhere else in the world.

- To beckon a waiter or waitress, raise your hand, make eye contact and say *onegaishimasu* (oh-NAY-guy-shee-mahss)—a strong but polite "please."

- Shapes, textures, flavors and colors of food are balanced for the delight of all senses. Harmony and presentation of food are very important.

- If you prefer not to eat Japanese style, there are many Western-style restaurants in Japan serving complete Western menus.

- Menus are generally not in English. Realistic plastic replicas of the dishes available are often displayed at the entrance of a restaurant. It is acceptable to point at a desired item.

- The guest of honor at a meal is seated in the *kamiza* area in front of the *takonoma* (alcove). The more important other guests, the nearer they are seated to the *kamiza* area.

- The highest-ranking guest is seated to the host's right.

- The highest-ranking host is seated at the center of the table.

- The least-important guest is seated in the *shimoza* area (near the door).

- Ladies are not served first. The guest with the highest status is served first, the eldest is served second.

- Wait for the most important person (honored guest) to begin eating.

- If you are the honored guest, wait until all the food is on the table and everyone is ready before you eat.

- It is polite to say before a meal, *Itadakimasu* (ee-TAH-dah-kee-MAH-soo), "Thanks to the hostess (or cook)."

- Taste all food served. You do not have to eat much, but it is rude not to taste each dish.

Rule of Thumb

Taste all food served. You do not have to eat much, but it is rude not to try each dish.

- Show respect for the eldest or most senior person at the table. Pour their drinks, serve their food and pay special attention to them.

- It is polite to slurp your noodles. Japanese believe that it makes them taste better.

- Do not finish your soup before eating other foods. It should accompany your meal. Replace the lid of the soup bowl when finished eating.

- Remember an empty plate signals a desire for more food. Leave a little food on your plate and your glass half full when you are finished eating.

- If you get up from the table, it is polite to keep your head and shoulders slightly lower than people who are seated by bending at the waist until you are away from the table.

- Brown or green tea is served at the end of a meal. This indicates all the dishes have been served.

- It is polite to say after a meal, *Gochisosama-deshita* (go-chee-so-sa-ma-desh-ta), "The dishes were delicious and enjoyed."

- An evening generally ends about 10 p.m.

- Write a thank-you note to the hostess.

DRINKING/TOASTING

- Drinking is a group activity. Do not say "no" when offered a drink.

- Japanese may drink excessively. This is generally accepted.

- An empty glass is equivalent to asking for another drink. Keep your glass at least half full if you do not want more. If Japanese attempt to pour more and you do not want it, put your hand over your glass or fill it with water if necessary.

> An empty glass is equivalent to asking for another drink.

- When drinking with a Japanese person, fill his or her glass or cup after he or she has filled yours. While your companion is pouring, hold your cup or glass up so that it's easer to fill. Never pour your own drink and always pour your companion's.

- Japanese lack experience with wine, and most wine available in Japan is either very expensive or of poor quality.

- *Hashigozake* (pub crawling or bar hopping) is a favorite Japanese activity, generally reputed to build teamwork among bosses, subordinates and colleagues.

> Pub crawling is a favorite Japanese activity.

- There are 200,000 alcohol (mostly beer) vending machines in Japan.

- *Sake* (sah-kay) is the national drink of Japan. Sake is a rice wine that may contain as much as 17 percent alcohol; served both hot and chilled.

- *Biru* (beer) and whiskey are popular drinks.

TOASTS

- Toasting is very important in Japan and many toasts are offered during the course of the evening.

- *Kampai*: (kahm-PIE) "Bottoms up" or "Cheers." Hold your drink in your hand, raise it in front of you, make eye contact, and say *Kampai!* Sometimes everyone shouts *kampai* together, clinks glasses and downs their drinks.

- *Banzai*: (bahn-ZAI) "Three cheers"/"Ten thousand years." Raise both your hands straight above your head and shout *Banzai!* three times. This is done at the high point or the end of the evening; the main host may give a speech to celebrate cooperation between companies; take your lead from your host.

- At dinner, wait for the toast before you drink your beer—and keep your neighbor's glass full.

- Respond to each toast with a toast.

HOME

- Japanese rarely entertain at home.
  Consider it a great honor if you are invited
  to a Japanese home.

- Take your coat off before entering a home.

- Take your shoes off before stepping into a
  home. You will see an obvious place for
  your shoes at the entrance. Place your
  shoes together facing back the way you
  came. Observe and follow the example
  of others.

- Slippers are provided by the host. Wear
  only slippers inside.

- Take slippers off when entering a room with
  tatami mats.

- In a carpeted home, do as the family does.

- Toilets in homes may not lock. Leave your
  slippers outside the door to show the toilet
  is occupied. Wear the special slippers
  provided for toilet rooms. If someone
  knocks, knock back to indicate the toilet is
  occupied. Be sure you don't walk outside
  the toilet with the toilet slippers on or
  you'll cause yourself considerable
  embarrassment.

- When taking a bath in a Japanese home, you are expected to wash and rinse yourself completely before entering the tub. The hot bath water is for soaking and may be used by several people in turn.

- Doors may be low. Watch your head when entering or leaving.

- Doors are often paper. Don't touch, push or knock on doors. This could soil or damage them.

- Do not sit until you are invited to do so.

- A legless chair may be offered.

- If possible, sit with your legs tucked under you when first seated. When invited to relax, men may sit cross-legged and women should sit with their legs together to one side (if possible).

- Try not to step on doorsills or borders of *tatami* mats.

- Do not ask to see other rooms in a home.

- Do not wander into the kitchen. It is considered impolite.

- Do not excessively compliment an item of decor. Japanese may feel obligated to give it to you.

- Do not play games or walk off paths onto the grass in gardens.

PUBLIC BATH

Expect to be stared at in a public bath.

- *Sento* (public baths) and *onsen* (hot spring baths) are popular with Japanese.

- As a Westerner, expect to be stared at.

- Before entering the tub, sit on one of the little plastic stools and wash yourself. Then rinse thoroughly. Soap suds floating in the bath water are abhorrent to Japanese.

TIPPING

- Japan is a no-tipping country. In general, if a gratuity is expected, a service charge is automatically added to the bill. However, in hotels and restaurants catering primarily to foreigners, tipping is becoming more customary. The following gratuities are optional:

- Taxis: Tip the driver if he helps with your luggage.

- Hotel maids: Leave tip in an envelope on the desk in your room.

- Porters: ¥200 per bag.

- Chauffeurs: ¥500 for a half-day excursion, ¥1,000 for a full-day excursion.

DRESS

- Squat toilets are very common in Japan. Dress appropriately.

- Dress is modern and conservative. Japanese dress well at all times.

- Dress smartly for parties, even if an invitation says "casual" or "come as you are."

- Don't wear bright colors, dangling jewelry, low-cut dresses or heavy makeup.

Faux Pas

Generally, the kimono should not be worn by foreigners.

- The *kimono* is a traditional garment and wearing it involves many subtleties. Generally, it should not be worn by foreigners. Most modern Japanese reserve the wearing of kimonos for special occasions.

- Shoes that slip on and off easily are very helpful. Never wear shoes into Japanese homes.

- Because shoes are often removed, be careful not to wear socks with holes.

- Restaurants and office buildings may have Japanese-style toilets that require you to squat. Dress accordingly.

BUSINESS

- Men: Dark suits and ties (subtle colors).

- Women: Dresses, suits, heels. Younger Japanese women enjoy wearing red, but subtle colors and conservative styles are best for business.

RESTAURANT

- Men: Jackets and ties (in better restaurants).

- Women: Dresses or dressy pants. Avoid tight skirts as you may be sitting on the floor.

- Dress varies depending upon the type of restaurant. Inquire before going.

CASUAL

- Men: Shirts and pants, sport coats.

- Women: Skirts or nice pants.

- Clean and neat clothing is most important; jeans, tennis shoes and T-shirts are OK.

GIFTS

- Give and receive a gift with both hands and a slight bow.

- Present a gift in a modest fashion, saying something like, "This is just a small token of my esteem."

- Japanese may refuse a gift once or twice before accepting it.

- Do not expect a gift to be opened in front of you. If you would like it to be opened, say, "Please open it."

- Do not open your gift unless asked to by the giver, or you may ask the giver, "May I open it?"

- When opening a gift, never rip open the wrapping. Wrapping paper is often selected for its design, elegance and significance, and it is considered good form to undo a package with care in order to preserve the paper.

- If possible, deliver a gift personally.

- Do not give a gift unless you have one for everyone present.

- Avoid gifts that are either dramatically extravagant or obviously inferior.

- A small, high-quality gift is better than a large, cheap one.

Rule of Thumb

Give and receive gifts with both hands and a slight bow.

- Where a gift is purchased is very important. A prestigious department store is always a safe bet.

- Thank the giver immediately for any gift received and follow up with a thank-you note.

- You should give a return gift that is equal to a third or half of the value of the original gift.

- Don't get into a gift-giving contest with Japanese colleagues; you will always lose, and it will be embarrassing to everyone.

WRAPPING

- Correct wrapping is very important. Appearance counts for as much or more than the contents.

- It is better to have a gift wrapped in Japan. Tell the clerk the occasion.

- Pastel-colored wrapping paper is preferred.

- Never use black paper.

- Formal gifts are usually wrapped in a heavy white paper called *noshi-gami*, tied with stiff strings called *mizuhiki* and decorated with a folded paper called *noshi*.

HOSTESS

- Always bring a small gift for the hostess when invited to someone's home.

- Give: Expensive or high-quality gifts, brand names, white precious metal (preferred over gold), box cakes, candy, flowers (check with florist for wrapping and appropriate type), fruit cake, wine, a gift from Tiffany's, Lenox china, fine whiskey.

- Do not give: Flowers that are symbolic of courtship or death (check with your concierge or the florist); gifts in even numbers, fours or nines (the pronunciation of the word "four" sounds like "death", and the word for "nine" is associated with suffering); or intimate items.

BUSINESS

- Allow Japanese to initiate the gift-giving ceremony.

Be prepared to give and receive a gift at the first business meeting.

- Be prepared to give and receive a gift at the first business meeting. Gifts are frequently given at the end of the first meeting. Not giving a proper gift could ruin the business relationship.

- It is very important to receive a gift properly (see "Gifts" section above).

- Give: Top-quality, brand-name whiskey or cognac, recorded music, books, office attire, golf balls, objets d'art, practical items of high quality and design, something from your home country.

- Do not give: Anything with your company name printed in large letters, gifts in even numbers, fours or nines, or intimate items.

- *Oseibo* in December and *Ochugen* in late June to mid-July are gift-giving seasons celebrated by the Japanese. If you are negotiating with the Japanese at this time, you should present a gift to your counterpart and be prepared to accept a gift in return. This is also a good time to send a gift to a colleague, business associate, customer or anyone to whom you have an obligation.

DO

- Be prepared for a dramatic difference between public and private behavior. Privately, Japanese are graceful and courteous. In public, pushing and shoving are common, especially on crowded trains during rush hour (sometimes filled to three times seating capacity). *Oshiya* are official pushers who force people in so the doors can close.

HELPFUL HINTS

- Take time to learn and respect Japanese ways. This is the easiest way to ingratiate yourself with the Japanese.

- Avoid conflict and direct confrontation.

- Speak in a quiet voice.

- At a Shinto shrine or Buddhist temple, take off your shoes, hat or scarf before entering.

- At a Shinto shrine, splash your hands and mouth with water from the water container near the entrance to purify yourself before entering the shrine. Do not splash over or into the water container. Do not drink the water.

DO NOT

- Do not expect Japanese to say "no." "Maybe" generally means "no."

- Do not comment on someone's appearance, although they may comment on yours.

- Do not stare at people.

- Do not litter.

- Do not smile and greet strangers. Strangers usually ignore each other.

Do not expect Japanese to say "no." "Maybe" generally means "no."

- Do not eat while walking in the street.

- Do not compliment Japanese publicly.

- Do not chew gum, especially while conducting business. It is very rude.

- Do not blow your nose in public or at the dinner table; go to the restroom.

- Do not lose your temper. It is considered childish.

- Avoid bragging about your country, your company, your home or yourself.

PUNCTUALITY

- Japanese consider it rude to be late for a business meeting, but acceptable, even fashionable, to be late for a social occasion. However, as a visiting foreigner, err on the side of courtesy: Always be punctual.

- Allow ample time to get to meetings in Tokyo. Traffic delays are often lengthy, and even taxi drivers sometimes have difficulty finding an address.

STRICTLY
BUSINESS

- The Japanese take literally the old Confucian maxim," The nail that sticks up gets hammered down." That means conformity is expected. Or as we might put it, "If you want to get along, you have to go along."

- The Japanese do not expect foreigners to have any knowledge of their social or business culture. Any knowledge of Japanese culture is greatly appreciated and highly rewarding, personally as well as professionally.

- Japan is one of the most productive industrial nations, with close to 10 percent of the world's GNP though less than a fortieth of its population.

BUSINESS CARDS

- In Japan, first impressions are generally made with the presentation of business cards. Japanese may exchange business cards even before they shake hands or bow. Be certain your business card clearly states your rank. This will determine your negotiating counterpart.

- Present business cards correctly. See the "Business Card" section of chapter 15.

CORPORATE CULTURE

Structure: Both business and personal relationships are hierarchical. Older people have higher status than younger, men higher than women, buyers higher than sellers, big companies higher than small ones, and executives higher than managers.

It is very important to send an executive or manager with rank equivalent to that of the Japanese you want access to. You can't send sales reps or middle managers and expect them to meet with a Japanese vice president; it just doesn't work that way.

Equally important, the Japanese do business based on relationships, and you'll have to establish that you are trustworthy before you can sell your company's products or services.

Business in Japan is a group activity. The work group is strongly united with no internal competition—all succeed or all fail. Decision-making is by consensus; everyone on the team must be consulted. This is a very slow process, but once decisions are made, implementation is swift.

Business in Japan is a group activity.

Japanese business planners and top executives, unlike many of their American counterparts, are more concerned with long-term results than earnings in the current quarter or fiscal year.

Meetings: The first meeting may be to establish an atmosphere of friendliness, harmony and trust. Business meetings are conducted formally, so leave your humor behind. Japanese meetings are all business, but developing personal relationships is very important; always allow for 10 minutes of polite conversation before the meeting begins.

Presentations should stress the group, not the individual. Send materials to the Japanese team well in advance of your meeting. Include several copies to demonstrate your respect for the team approach. Proposals should be factual, technical and detailed. Proposals translated into correct Japanese make a good impression. Proposals, presentations and reports with lots of visual aids are good tools for communicating. Presentation is very important. A sloppy presentation assumes a sloppy product.

Initial negotiations generally begin with middle managers. Do not attempt to go over their heads to senior executives, who will be brought into the process when the Japanese think it's appropriate. A Japanese company may be represented by one or more teams of negotiators.

Business meetings may have periods of silence. Don't worry about it; silence is considered part

Faux Pas

Initial negotiations generally begin with middle managers. Do not attempt to go over their heads to senior executives.

of conversation and communication. Sit quietly without talking.

It usually takes several meetings to reach an agreement. When the time comes, be content to close the deal with a handshake and leave signing of the written contract to a later meeting.

Refreshments (tea or coffee) are always served at meetings.

Communication: You may need to hire a qualified interpreter. Remember when Japanese speak English, it is their second language. Speak slowly, softly and clearly, and repeat often. Watch for understanding. It is acceptable to use the Japanese company interpreter in the first meeting. Once negotiations begin, hire your own interpreter.

Use standard English, avoiding colloquialisms, jargon and sports analogies. Respect silence. It is the Japanese way of pondering a question. When your Japanese counterparts are speaking, nod your head to show you are listening attentively.

Be yourself, but not to the point of disrupting the local rhythm. The Japanese may ask about your family, your age, the university you attended and degrees you have received. Ask the same questions of your counterparts. Many customs are based on the traditions of respect for age and status.

Faux Pas

Avoid colloquialisms, jargon and sports analogies.

Try to avoid saying flat-out "No." Instead, say something like, "This could be very difficult, but we'll certainly explore the possibility"— allowing your Japanese counterparts to save face. Also, keep in mind that the spokesperson for the Japanese team may be the one who speaks English best, not the team leader.

Don't change deadlines or schedules. Japanese respect those who stick with the original dates.

BE AWARE

- Proper introduction to business contacts is a must. The introducer becomes guarantor for the person being introduced. The introducer should know both your company and the Japanese organization with which you want to do business.

- Do not bring your lawyer. The important thing is to build a business relationship based on trust. Japanese do not like complicated legal documents. Write a contract that covers essential points.

- Once a solid relationship with a Japanese person is established, you can count on him or her for anything.

ENTERTAINMENT

- Restaurant entertaining is crucial to business. A person is judged by his or her behavior both during and after business hours. Seldom is a business deal completed without dinner in a restaurant. Most entertaining is done in restaurants or on the golf course.

- Banquets with many courses, toasts and gifts are the usual business entertainment.

- Foreign guests should reciprocate in kind.

- A ceremony with a party or dinner will follow the signing of a contract.

- Japanese spouses are generally not included in business dinners, but the spouse of a Western businessman may be invited.

- The host picks the topics of conversation at a business dinner. A safe topic is your family, but be careful not too brag too much, even about your children.

- There are no business breakfasts.

- It is an insult not to accept an invitation from a Japanese counterpart to go drinking. This is important to develop personal relationships. Karaoke bars with group singing are popular for business entertainment. Join in with the group and sing a solo when it's your turn.

Banquets with many courses, toasts and gifts are the usual business entertainment.

- Make appointments at least two weeks in advance.

- Avoid planning business meetings from mid-December to mid-January; Golden Week, April 29 through May 5; and Obon, a week in mid-August when families visit the graves of their ancestors.

- Note: Businesspeople are often in their offices from 8 a.m. to 8 p.m.

ESPECIALLY FOR WOMEN

- Non-Japanese women are treated very politely in business and it is understood that Western women hold high-level positions in business. Western women must establish credibility and a position of authority immediately. Japanese value competence and professionalism above all else when dealing with foreign executives—including women.

- A non-Japanese woman is viewed first as a foreigner and then as a woman, and is treated accordingly. Acceptance of Japanese women in business is increasing, but the environment is still difficult. Japanese men and women are bound by rigid roles that define their behavior in all aspects of life. Japanese society is male-dominated, and men may not be comfortable working with women in positions of power or socializing with them as equals. Be patient. Reassure

Rule of Thumb

Western women must establish credibility and a position of authority immediately.

them that you are in a position of authority in your company.

- Japanese judge capability by your dress. Don't wear loud colors, dangling jewelry or heavy makeup. Try not to stand out in dress or behavior. Conform! Conform! Conform!

- Japanese women, referred to as "OL" or office ladies, are often hired as temporary workers despite the fact that they are well-educated. Some Japanese companies still require women to resign if they get married.

- If a woman is accompanying her spouse on a business trip, it is generally acceptable for her to participate in social events.

- Extend an invitation to a Japanese businessman and his wife, but if his wife doesn't come, don't mention it or be insulted.

- It is important to participate socially. You may be the center of attention. Enjoy the experience. Remember, you are an honored foreign guest and social events are an aspect of business.

- More young women are choosing a career instead of marriage; it's difficult to do both in Japan. Child-care facilities are scarce.

- Many marriages in Japan are still arranged by families.

- Most Japanese cities are safe for a woman alone—much more so than American or European cities. However, very occasionally a foreign woman can have a strange effect on a Japanese man—usually a drunken one. He might make a lewd proposition or expose his private parts in a public place. Usually, the best course of action is to calmly ignore the behavior and leave the area as quickly as possible. If you're threatened, you might yell *chikan* (pervert) or *omawari-san* (police).

HEALTH AND SAFETY

- Japanese are among the only people in the world more concerned about hygiene and sanitation than Americans. The water purification system is one of the best in the world, and tap water is safe to drink everywhere in Japan. Food is of high quality and milk is pasteurized.

- Swimming in lakes, streams or harbors near populated areas is not recommended because of water pollution. Air pollution is a problem in Tokyo and, to a lesser degree, in other major cities.

- Health-care facilities are good in Japan. Many doctors speak English. In larger cities, there are some Western doctors. Dental care is also excellent.

- Hospitals and clinics insist upon payment in full at the time of treatment. Foreigners may be required to show proof of ability to pay prior to treatment. Be certain to have supplemental medical insurance that covers treatment in Japan.

Be certain to have supplemental medical insurance that covers treatment in Japan.

- Overall, Japan is one of the safest countries in the world. Crime against foreigners is rare and usually limited to petty theft.

- **Emergency numbers: Police 110; Fire/Ambulance 119.**

HOLIDAYS AND FESTIVALS

January	New Year's Day (1), Coming of Age Day (15).
February	Founding of the Nation (11).
March	Vernal Equinox (20 or 21).
April/May	Golden Week (April 29-May 5), including Greenery Day (29), Constitution Day (3), Children's Day (5).
June	Summer solstice (22).
August	Obon, the Buddhist Festival of the Lanterns (week in mid-August).
September	Respect for the Aged Day (15), Autumn Equinox Day (about 23).
October	Health and Sports Day (10).
November	Culture Day (3), Labor-Thanksgiving Day (23).
December	Emperor's Birthday (23), New Year's Eve (31).

NOTE: Holidays are subject to change.

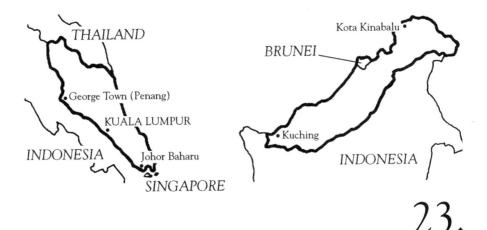

THAILAND

George Town (Penang)

KUALA LUMPUR

INDONESIA

Johor Baharu

SINGAPORE

Kota Kinabalu

BRUNEI

Kuching

INDONESIA

23.

MALAYSIA
FEDERATION OF MALAYSIA

VITAL STATISTICS

POPULATION: 21.2 million.

CAPITAL: Kuala Lumpur, with a population of 1 million.

LAND SIZE: 127,320 square miles, with two distinct land
                     regions. Peninsular Malaysia is approximately
                     the size of Alabama; East Malaysia, on the island
                     of Borneo, is about the size of Louisiana.

GOVERNMENT: Malaysia is a federation of 13 states and one
                     federal territory (Kuala Lumpur). Executive
                     power is held by the prime minister and cabinet,
                     who are responsible to the bicameral legislature.
                     The hereditary monarchs of nine states meet
                     every five years to elect one of their number as

king of the country; the king is referred to as the Supreme Head of State, but holds little real power.

LIVING STANDARD: GDP = US$4,543 per capita.

NATURAL
RESOURCES: Tin, crude oil, timber, copper, iron ore, natural gas, bauxite.

AGRICULTURE: Peninsular Malaysia produces natural rubber, palm oil and rice; East Malaysia produces rubber, timber and pepper. There is a deficit of rice in all areas.

INDUSTRIES: The industrial sector of Peninsular Malaysia includes rubber and palm oil processing, light manufacturing, electronics, tin mining and smelting, logging and timber processing; in East Malaysia there is logging, food processing, and petroleum production and refining.

CLIMATE: Tropical, with lowland temperatures ranging from 70°F (21°C) to 90°F (32°C); highland resorts can have temperatures as low as 61°F (16°C). Relative humidity averages 80 percent year-round. Annual precipitation averages 114 inches (254 cm); monsoon season is October to March.

CURRENCY: Malaysian *ringgit* (M$). M$1 = 100 *sen*. Notes in circulation are M$ 1,000, 500, 100, 50, 20, 10, 5 and 1. Coins in use are 50, 20, 10, 5 and 1 sen.

THE PEOPLE

CORRECT NAME: Malaysians or Malays.

ETHNIC MAKEUP: 60 percent Malay, 31 percent Chinese, 8 percent Indian/Pakistani/Bangladeshi. There are tensions between Malays and Chinese over so-called "preferential quotas": The Chinese feel these policies make them second-class citizens, while the majority Malays support quotas as their only way to overcome traditional Chinese dominance.

VALUE SYSTEM: Many Malaysians identify primarily with an ethnic group, island or region, and only secondarily with the country. They are proud of both their traditional cultures and their modern economy. *Berbudi* is a fundamental concept of Malaysian society that espouses respect and courtesy toward elders, love of parents, a pleasant disposition and harmony in the family, the neighborhood and society as a whole.

FAMILY: The family is the most important unit in Malaysian society. Two, three or more generations may live in the same house in rural areas. Elders are respected by young people.

RELIGION: 53 percent Muslim, 17 percent Buddhist, 12 percent other Chinese religions, 7 percent Hindu, 6 percent Christian.

SPORTS: Soccer, sepak takrah (volleyball with no hands), badminton.

IMPORTANT DATES

2000 B.C.	Ancestors of modern Malays move into area.
1400 A.D.	Islam introduced; Melaka becomes major trading center.
1511	Portugal seizes Melaka.
1641	Dutch take Melaka from Portuguese.
1826	British form "Colony of the Straits Settlements."
1942-45	Japanese occupation.
1948	Federation of Malaya, a partially independent British territory, is formed.
1957	Federation of Malaya gains complete independence.
1963	New, independent nation of Malaysia formed, including Singapore and the states of East Malaysia (Sarawak and Sabah).
1965	Singapore leaves Malaysia and declares independence.
1966	Hostilities with Indonesia end.
1978	"Boat people" from Vietnam begin to arrive.

1981	Mahathir bin Muhammad succeeds Hussein Onn as prime minister.
1990	General elections won by Mahathir and his Barisan national coalition.

NOTE: See chapters on China, Hong Kong, Taiwan and India for additional background information on the Chinese and Indian minorities in Malaysia and their customs and cultures.

MEETING AND GREETING

- Shake hands with men at a business meeting or social occasion. Shake hands again when leaving. Malay men customarily shake hands with one another; close male friends may use both hands to grasp the hand of the other man. Malay women and elderly people generally do not shake hands; they may offer verbal greetings instead.

- Nod or give a slight bow when greeting a woman or an older person. Introduce higher-ranking and older people before others, and women before men. Western women should greet a Malay man with a nod of her head and a smile.

- Traditional Malays may greet each other with the *Salaam*, which involves bowing while touching the forehead with the right hand. This is not recommended for foreigners.

- Common greetings include *selamat pagi* (s'lah-maht pah-ghee), which means "good morning"; *selamat petang* (s'lah-maht pay-tahng), which means "good afternoon"; and halo (hah-low) which means "hello."

- Malays have no surname. Their names are written with their given name + *bin* (son of) or *binti* (daughter of) + their father's given name.

- Address Malays with the proper courtesy title in English or Malay + given name.

  -Mr. = *Encik* (In-seek)

  -Mrs. = *Puan* (Poo-ahn)

  -Miss = *Cik* (Seek)

  Examples: Ali bin Isa is the son of Isa bin Osman; he should be addressed as Mr. Ali or Encik Ali.

  Zaitun binti Isa is the daughter of Isa bin Osman; she should be addressed as Miss Zaitun (Cik Zaitun) or Mrs. Zaitun (Puan Zaitun).

- Some (but not all) married Malay women drop their father's name and take their husband's name.

- English is used in commercial correspondence. The form of the salutation is Dear + Mr., Mrs. or Miss + given name.

  Example: Dear Mr. Ali.

LANGUAGE

- There is continuing controversy in multi-ethnic Malaysia over whether the national language should be called *Bahasa Malaysia* (the Malaysian language) or *Bahasa Malayu* (the Malay language).

- Malaysians also are torn between maintaining the Malay language as a vehicle for cultural homogeneity and emphasizing English for economic reasons.

- English is taught in schools and is widely spoken and understood.

- Chinese, Tamil and numerous tribal languages and local dialects also are spoken.

BODY LANGUAGE

Faux Pas

Never touch anyone—especially a child—on the top of the head.

- Never touch anyone—especially a child—on the top of the head, which is believed to be the home of the soul.

- Avoid touching anyone of the opposite sex.

- Public displays of affection are inappropriate.

- Use only your right hand to eat or pass things.

- Do not move objects with your feet or point at another person with your foot.

- Giving a slight bow when entering or leaving a room or when passing people means "excuse me."

- A smile or laugh can mean surprise, anger, shock, embarrassment or happiness.

- Cover your mouth when yawning or using a toothpick.

- It is impolite to beckon adults, especially with the index finger.

- Single fingers are not used for gesturing.

- Hitting your fist into a cupped hand is an obscene gesture.

- Hands in pockets signify anger.

A smile or laugh can mean surprise, anger, shock, embarrassment or happiness.

PHRASES:

English	Malay	Pronunciation
Good morning	*Selamat pagi*	Seh-lah-maht pah-ghee
Good afternoon	*Selamat petang*	Seh-lah-maht peh-tahng
Good evening	*Selamat malam*	Seh-lah-maht mah-lahm
Please	*Minta*	Min-tah
Thank you	*Terima kasih*	Tree-mah kay-say
You're welcome	*Sama sama*	Sah-mah sah-mah
Yes	*Ya*	Yah
No	*Tidak*	Tee-dahk
Excuse me	*Minta maafkan*	Min-tah mah-ahfkan
Goodbye	*Selamat tinggal*	Seh-lah-maht ting-gahl
Hello/ How are you?	*Apa Khabar?*	Ah-pah kah-bahr

- Dining customs vary among ethnic groups. Most Malays and Indians eat with spoons and hands; some use forks and spoons, and some use no utensils. Chinese eat with chopsticks and spoons.

- If using a fork and spoon, hold the spoon in your right hand and the fork in your left. Food is cut in bite-size pieces, making a knife unnecessary. Push your food onto the spoon with the fork and eat from the spoon. When finished, put the fork and the spoon on your plate.

- When eating with their hands, Malays and Indians use only their right hand. Never use your left hand to touch, eat or pass food.

- When eating satay, use a skewer to spear and eat rice cakes.

- Malays who are strict Muslims don't eat pork or drink alcohol. Hindus and Buddhists don't eat beef. Pork is a staple of the Chinese diet.

- Do not blow your nose or clear your throat while eating; leave the room if necessary.

- Malaysians enjoy eating at restaurants.

Malays who are strict Muslims don't eat pork or drink alcohol.

- It is OK to ask someone if you may share their table in a crowded restaurant; you are not expected to talk to them.

- Inviting an even number of guests to a dinner is thought to bring good luck.

- Allow your host to order all dishes.

- Alcoholic drinks are generally not served before dinner.

- To beckon a waiter raise your whole hand—not just one finger.

DRINKING AND TOASTING

- The serving of alcoholic beverages is much less common than in some other Asian countries.

- Tea—often with milk added—and coffee are usually offered after dinner or with dessert.

- Fruit juices are widely drunk.

- Beverages are offered and accepted with both hands.

- There are no common toasts or toasting etiquette in Malaysia.

HOME

- If it's not mealtime, guests are usually offered tea, coffee or a soft drink when visiting a Malaysian home.

- Be on time for a dinner in a Malaysian home. Remove your shoes and sunglasses before entering.

- There is no "cocktail hour" before dinner. The meal is served as soon as guests have arrived.

- The guest of honor is seated to the host's right or at the head of the table.

- A towel and small bowl of water are given to guests to wash their hands before dinner.

- It is impolite to refuse any food or drink offered. Take at least a small amount and taste it. To refuse additional helpings, put your hand above your plate and say, "No, thank you."

- In many homes, the women eat after the men finish.

- Malaysians do visit others' homes unannounced.

A towel and small bowl of water are given to guests to wash their hands before dinner.

- Muslim families pray between 6 and 7:30 p.m. Respect their privacy during these hours.

- Do not touch the Koran (Muslim holy book) in someone's home.

- You may be invited to sit on mats on the floor. Men sit cross-legged. Women tuck their feet to the left if possible.

- Do not stand or sit on a prayer rug.

- Do not request a tour of your host's home or wander through private areas alone.

- Ask permission to smoke.

- When you leave a home, never say "Goodbye." Say, "I'll go and come back." When someone else leaves, say "Go, and come back."

MOSQUE/TEMPLE

- Chinese temple: Remove your hat, enter through the right door, and exit through the left door, do not step on the threshold. Dress and behavior are formal.

- Hindu temple: Do not touch statues or smoke.

- Muslim mosque: Get permission before entering, put on a robe supplied at the entrance, put shoes in the shoe rack. Women must cover their heads and never touch a man on mosque premises (he would have to re-wash). Do not walk in front of people praying or stand on a prayer rug. Never smoke.

Rule of Thumb

Get permission before entering a mosque.

TIPPING

- Tipping is not customary in Malaysia.

- Restaurants: A service charge of 4 percent is usually included in the bill; an additional gratuity may be expected in restaurants patronized by tourists.

- Taxi drivers: Round the fare up or tip with coin change.

- Gas station attendants: Round up to nearest ringgit.

- Bellboys and porters: 1 ringgit per bag.

- Toilet attendants: 50 sen to 1 ringgit.

DRESS

Rule of Thumb

Dress for a hot, humid climate; wear natural fabrics and bring an umbrella.

- Western style clothing is worn by most people. Batik prints are popular.

- Dress for a hot, humid climate; wear natural fabrics and bring an umbrella.

- Women should wear conservative skirts and pants; avoid shorts, short skirts and other revealing clothes.

- Yellow is traditionally reserved for royalty. Avoid wearing yellow to a palace or to formal events.

- Veiled Muslim women with their heads covered and wearing long dresses are seen in some areas.

BUSINESS

- Men: White shirts, dress trousers, ties for executives. Conservative suits should be worn when meeting with government officials or for a first meeting with business colleagues.

- Women: Sleeved blouses with skirts or dressy pants.

RESTAURANT

- Men: Inquire about dress ahead of time. Some better restaurants require jackets.

- Women: Pants or skirt and blouse.

CASUAL

- Men: Smart casual, clean and neat.

- Women: Skirts or slacks, designer jeans, shirt or blouse.

GIFTS

- Giving or receiving gifts with both hands shows respect. Never use only your left hand to give or receive a gift. Never open a gift in the presence of the giver.

- Reciprocate with a gift of equal value. A dinner invitation can substitute for a gift.

- Bring gifts for children (but no dog images).

WRAPPING

- Yellow wrapping is for royalty.

- Don't use white paper (white is a funeral color for Malays and Chinese).

HOSTESS

- Always bring a small gift for the hostess when invited to someone's home.

- Give: Fruit, sweets, perfume, crafts from home.

- Do not give: Money, liquor, knives, scissors or images of dogs.

BUSINESS

Gifts generally are not exchanged at the first meeting, but be prepared to reciprocate if one is given to you.

- Gifts are not exchanged at the first meeting, or in general among business associates, but be prepared to reciprocate if one is given to you.

- Give: Company products with logo, gifts made in the U.S., pens, books, desk accessories.

- Do not give: Money, liquor, knives, scissors or images of dogs.

HELPFUL HINTS

DO

- Give sincere compliments, but expect Malays to decline out of modesty.

- Respect the elderly.

- Keep the soles of your shoes on the floor. It is rude to expose the soles of your shoes or feet to anyone.

- Cover your mouth when you yawn or use a toothpick.

- Understand that Malays believe that successes, failures, opportunities and misfortunes result from fate or the will of God.

- Understand that ethnic tensions exist between Malays and Chinese over preferential quotas.

- Expect to bargain in street markets, flea markets and antique stores. Prices in most shops and larger stores are fixed, but you can discreetly ask for a discount.

DO NOT

- Do not bring illicit drugs into Malaysia. The penalty for sale or possession of illegal drugs is death!

- Never use your left hand to eat, shake hands, touch others, point, or give or receive objects.

- Never whistle, hiss or shout.

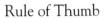

Rule of Thumb

Keep the soles of your shoes on the floor. It is rude to expose the soles of your shoes to anyone.

Rule of Thumb

Do not bring illicit drugs into Malaysia. The penalty for sale or possession of illegal drugs is death!

- Don't be surprised if Malays ask personal questions about your marital status, income or religion. Such questions are part of customary smalltalk. You're under no obligation to answer, and you can feel free to ask similar questions in return.

- Never step over anyone resting on the floor. This is extremely rude.

- Don't cross your legs in front of elderly people, and never cross your ankle over your knee. Don't use your feet to touch or move objects.

- Never smoke in front of elderly people.

- Do not wait to queue for buses. Rush to a seat, holding tight to your bags and purse.

- Never offer a bribe.

- Westerners are expected to be punctual for social occasions and business meetings. Call if you are delayed.

- On the other hand, punctuality is not important to Malays. People are considered more important than schedules. Don't get frustrated if a Malay is late or your business meeting does not start on time.

STRICTLY BUSINESS

BUSINESS CARDS

- After you are introduced, exchange business cards. Business cards may be printed in English.

CORPORATE CULTURE

Structure: Decisionmaking is authoritative, subjective, intuitive and concerned with preserving existing interpersonal relationships. A promotion is based on a superior's respect and personal regard for an employee rather than on performance.

Rapport and trust are the keys to a business relationship.

For Malaysians, rapport and trust are the keys to a business relationship. Your counterparts will want to get to know you personally before doing business with you. Malaysians also are cautious in forming opinions and making decisions. Patience is required.

Meetings: A letter of introduction from a bank or a mutual acquaintance will help start a business relationship. Without an introduction, your request for a meeting might be ignored. Malaysians probably will engage in polite conversation for a lengthy period before getting down to business. Discussions will be long and detailed. Presentations should be very informative.

Once an agreement is reached—even written down and signed—don't be surprised if your counterparts try to renegotiate. Malaysians regard the future as vague and unpredictable, and written contracts as less important than personal trust. Expect a request for an escape clause.

Your Malaysian counterparts will try to apply pressure for concessions by their foreign partners. They won't give up much in the beginning, but the longer the negotiations continue, the more concessions Malaysians are likely to make. Plan on several trips.

Communication: English is the language of business. It is generally understood, and is often used for communication among different ethnic groups.

Never publicly criticize a person, a company, a proposal or a report. If it must be done, do it

Rule of Thumb

If you must criticize a person, do it privately and tactfully.

privately and tactfully. Harmony is important, and loss of face is never forgiven.

Malaysians don't appreciate bluntness, and sometimes avoid saying things directly—especially things the listener probably doesn't want to hear. Learn to listen carefully and to read between the verbal lines.

BE AWARE

- Malaysians tend to judge people by who they are rather than what they do. Family background, education, social position and professional status all are important.

- Malaysians generally do not pursue wealth for its own sake.

- Never smoke around royal family members. Many are in business and may attend meetings with foreigners.

ENTERTAINMENT

- Entertaining is an important part of doing business. Most business entertaining is done in restaurants.

- Most important meetings are followed by lunch or dinner. Be sure to reciprocate with a meal of equal value (i.e., neither more nor less expensive).

- Ask your guests if they have dietary restrictions.

- Spouses may be invited to dinner if the dinner will not include business discussions. Do not bring spouses to a business lunch.

APPOINTMENTS

- Employees in Islamic offices work a half day on Thursday, with Thursday afternoon and Friday as their weekend rather than Saturday and Sunday.

- March to July is the best time for a business trip; November to February is vacation time.

- Make appointments at least a month in advance.

- Avoid the Chinese New Year (January/February) and the Muslim holy month of Ramadan (dates vary from year to year).

- Women are generally accepted in business in Malaysia and hold many influential positions in government and business.

- Although it's unlikely, Western women may encounter a few hassles while doing business in Malaysia. In the Muslim East Coast area, men might harass a single woman.

- It is perfectly acceptable for a woman to invite a Malaysian businessman to dinner. She may or may not invite his wife.

- Women alone should eat in hotel restaurants or hotel lounges.

Although it's unlikely, Western women may encounter a few hassles while doing business in Malaysia.

HEALTH AND SAFETY

- Although tap water is considered potable in major cities, it's recommended that foreigners drink only boiled or bottled water as a precaution—especially in rural areas.

- Most expatriates in Peninsular Malaysia use private hospitals in Kuala Lumpur, Ipoh, Penang and Petaling Jaya; those living in East Malaysia seek treatment in Kuala Lumpur or Singapore. Fees are low, but doctors and hospitals often expect immediate cash payment for health services. Supplemental medical insurance with specific overseas coverage is recommended.

- Malaysia is a relatively safe country. Major crimes against tourists are uncommon, but beware of pickpockets. Transvestites in Kuala Lumpur are often pickpockets targeting tourists. Also be aware that Malaysia has one of the highest rates of credit card fraud in the world.

- **Emergency numbers: Police/Fire/Ambulance 999.**

January	New Year's Day (1).	
January/ February	Chinese New Year.*	
February	Federal Territory Day (1, only in Kuala Lumpur).	
March	Hari Raya Puasa (Ramadan feast).*	
May	Labor Day (1), Wesak Day.*	
June	Birthday of His Majesty the Yang Di Pertuan Agong (5), Hari Raya Haji*.	
July	Maal Hijrah.*	
August	National Day (31).	
September	Birthday of the Prophet Muhammad.*	
November	Deepavali.*	
December	Christmas (25).	

* These Malaysian holidays are determined by the lunar calendar; the dates change yearly.

24.

PHILIPPINES
REPUBLIC OF THE PHILIPPINES

VITAL STATISTICS

POPULATION: 71.2 million.

CAPITAL: Manila, with more than 7 million people in the
                metro area.

LAND SIZE: 116,000 square miles comprising more than 7,000
                islands, of which 880 are inhabited; the two
                largest, Luzon and Mindanao, account for more
                than 64 percent of the entire land area, which is
                slightly larger than Arizona.

GOVERNMENT: Republic since 1946. The 1987 constitution
                provides for a bicameral legislature with a
                president, elected for a single six-year term, as head
                of state and chief executive. The 24 members of

the Senate are elected for five years, and the 200 members of the House of Representatives for three. Up to 50 additional members of the House are appointed by the president to represent various minority groups.

LIVING STANDARD: GDP = US$1,200 per capita.

NATURAL
RESOURCES: Timber, crude oil, nickel, cobalt, silver, gold, salt, copper.

AGRICULTURE: Accounts for about one-third of GNP and 45 percent of employment. Major crops include rice, coconut, corn, sugar cane, bananas, pineapple, mango and animal products.

INDUSTRIES: Textiles, pharmaceuticals, chemicals, wood products, food processing, electronics assembly, petroleum refining, fishing.

CLIMATE: Tropical except highlands. Average high temperature at sea level is 85°F (30°C), with overnight lows around 72°F (22°C). High humidity and heavy rainfall, especially from June to November.

CURRENCY: Philippine *peso* (P). P1 = 100 *centavos*. Notes are in denominations of 500, 100, 50, 20, 10, 5 and 2 pesos; coins in denominations of 5, 2 and 1 pesos as well as 50, 25, 10, 5 and 1 centavos.

THE PEOPLE

CORRECT NAME: Filipinos (the people collectively); Filipinos (men); Filipinas (women).

ETHNIC MAKEUP: More than 95 percent of Malay descent.

VALUE SYSTEM: Filipinos are casual and fun-loving, sensitive and hospitable people. Personal and family honor are stressed, as well as dignity and pride. Filipinos accept what comes their way and bear it with hope and patience. Education is highly valued and families make great sacrifices to educate their children. *Bayanihan* is the communal spirit that enables Filipinos to come together and help each other at a moment's notice in times of need.

FAMILY: The family is more important than the individual, and interdependence is more important than independence. The extended family is the basis of society, with the clan providing security and easing the impact of illness or unemployment. Divorce is illegal, families are large, and the mother's advice is listened to and followed.

RELIGION: 85 percent Roman Catholic, 8 percent other Christian, 4 percent Muslim.

SPORTS: Basketball, baseball, softball, soccer, tennis, horse racing, cockfighting.

IMPORTANT DATES

1521	Ferdinand Magellan lands in the Philippines.
1565	Philippines settled, claimed by Spain.
1898	Spain cedes Philippines to the United States as part of Spanish-American War settlement.
1941	Japanese troops invade on December 8.
1942-44	Japan occupies the Philippines.
1946	Philippines gains full independence on July 4.
1965	Ferdinand Marcos elected president.
1972	Marcos declares martial law, which lasts until 1981.
1981	Opposition leader Benigno Aquino assassinated upon return from exile.
1986	President Marcos resigns amid widespread protests. Corazon Aquino, widow of Benigno Aquino, assumes the presidency.
1992	Gen. Fidel Ramos wins the presidency in a seven-way race.

- English greetings are customary.

- Men and women shake hands with everyone present at a business meeting or social occasion. Shake hands again when leaving. Your handshake should be friendly and informal, but limp. Men may also pat one another on the back. Men should wait for women to extend their hand.

- Show respect for elders by greeting the oldest person present first.

- Children may take a visitor's hand and press it against their forehead as a sign of respect.

NAMES AND TITLES

- For both men and women, the given name comes first, followed by the initial of the mother's family name, then by the father's family name. When introducing someone, give their full name—don't use initials.

- Use Mr., Mrs., Miss or appropriate professional title + family name until specifically invited by your Filipino hosts or colleagues to use their given names. Engineers, architects, lawyers, doctors and others use professional titles.

Engineers, architects, lawyers, doctors and others use professional titles.

- Address elders and superiors as Sir or Ma'am, or by courtesy title + family name, even after familiarity has developed.

- Many women retain their maiden name when they marry. Some women add their husband's family name after a hyphen.

  Example: Mrs. Maria Bacani-Aquino.

- "Vda," written between a woman's maiden name and her husband's family name, means she is a widow.

  Example: Mrs. Maria Bacani vda Aquino.

- In correspondence, Mrs. Maria Bacani-Aquino would be addressed as "Dear Mrs. Aquino." She should be addressed in conversation as "Mrs. Aquino."

- Most Filipino families have Hispanic names due to more than three centuries of Spanish rule.

Mrs. Maria Bacani-Aquino should be addressed as "Mrs. Aquino."

- English and Filipino (based on Tagalog) are the official languages. English is spoken by most people and used in business, government and education. Tagalog phrases are often mixed with English. The result can sound like a different language to foreign English-speakers.

- The people are smiling, open, warm and friendly. There is more touching than in most other Asian countries. People of the same gender may hold hands in public as a sign of friendship.

- If Filipinos don't understand a question, they open their mouths. Raised eyebrows signify recognition and agreement. Laughter may convey pleasure or embarrassment; it is commonly used to relieve tension or in emotional situations.

There is more touching than in most other Asian countries.

- In social situations, Filipinos extend their hands and stoop when passing in front of people.

- "Yes" is signified by a jerk of the head upward. "No" is signified by a jerk of the head down. Since Filipinos rarely say "no," the sign for "no" is sometimes accompanied by a verbal "yes"—which still should be understood as "no."

- Avoid prolonged eye contact or staring. It could be misinterpreted as a challenge. Although staring is considered rude, Filipinos may stare at or even touch foreigners, especially in areas where foreigners are rarely seen.

- Standing with your hands on your hips means you are angry.

- Never beckon with your index finger; this is an insult. Instead, extend your arm and hand, palm down, and make a scratching motion with your fingers.

- To indicate two of something, raise your ring and pinkie fingers.

- Touch someone's elbow lightly to attract attention. Do not tap people on the shoulder.

- The "eyebrow flash"—a quick lifting of the eyebrows—is a Filipino greeting.

- Filipinos don't point at an object or a person. Instead, they shift their eyes toward an object or purse their lips and point with their mouth.

- Filipinos are familiar with American gestures.

The "eyebrow flash"—a quick lifting of the eyebrows—is a Filipino greeting.

PHRASES

English	Filipino	Pronunciation
Good morning	*Magandang umaga*	Mahg-ndahng oo-mah-ga
Good afternoon	*Magandang hapon*	Mahg-ndahng hah-pon
Good evening	*Magandang gabi*	Mahg-ndahng ga-bee
Goodbye	*Paalam na po*	Pa-ah-lam nah poh
Please	*Paki*	Pa-kee
Thank you	*Salamat*	Sah-lah-maht
You're welcome	*Walang anuman*	Wah-lahng ah-noo-mahn
Yes	*Oo*	Aw aw
No	*Hindi*	Hin-dee
Excuse me	*Ipagpaumanhin*	Eepahk-pawman-hin
Hello/ How are you?	*Kumustá?*	Kuh-moos-tah?

MANNERS

DINING

- Western utensils are used. The fork is often held in the left hand and used to push food onto the spoon, which is held in the right hand.

- Food generally is served all at once rather than in courses.

- Filipinos love to eat; most social actitivities revolve around food.

- The cuisine is diverse, influenced by many cultures. A typical meal includes boiled rice, fried fish, vegetables and fruit.

- Filipinos may view a dinner or party invitation as just a passing thought. They may answer "yes," but not take the invitation seriously. Phone to reinvite and remind your guests; an invitation must be repeated to be taken seriously. Similarly, don't accept an invitation unless it's repeated at least three times.

- Don't sit until your host seats you. The guest of honor generally is seated at the head of the table. It is polite to decline the first offer of seating, food or drink. Accept the second offer.

An invitation must be repeated three times to be taken seriously.

- The host generally gives the first serving to guests. After that, serve yourself. Keep your hands above the table during dinner.

- Compliment the host on the good food; eating heartily is the sincerest compliment.

- Leave a small amount of food on your plate when you are finished eating; place your fork and spoon on your plate.

- Leave a weekend dinner party at approximately midnight, a weekday party at 10 p.m.

RESTAURANT

- It is common to have a drink before ordering dinner.

- There is no "going Dutch." The person who makes the invitation pays the bill.

- To beckon a waiter or waitress, raise your hand with the fingers together. Waitresses are addressed as "Miss."

DRINKING AND TOASTING

- Do not get drunk—it is considered "greedy."

- Filipino women rarely drink alcohol in public. Do not offer them liquor. Women generally drink soft drinks, orange juice or *calamansi* (a local citrus fruit drink).

- Toasts are common in the Philippines, especially at business meetings. Usually the host or senior visitor initiates a toast.

- Toasts in English are appropriate.

HOME

- Some Filipinos remove shoes in their homes; follow your host's example.

- Filipinos are very hospitable and strive to make their guests feel comfortable and at home. Eating a lot is the best compliment to your host.

- Do not take a peek into the kitchen or wander unguided around a home. Ask permission to use the bathroom.

- Do not refer to the woman of the house as the "hostess." The term is often used to refer to prostitutes.

- Tipping is not a Filipino tradition, but it is becoming common in hotels and restaurants frequented by foreigners.

- Always carry some small-denomination bills. Taxis may not have change for large notes, and in remote areas it can be difficult to change even P100 notes.

- U.S. dollars are accepted and appreciated.

- Restaurants: A service charge of 15 percent is usually included in the bill. Small change can be left as an additional gratuity for good service. If the service charge is not included, leave a 15 percent tip.

- Taxi drivers: Don't tip unless the driver performs a special service.

- Porters, barbers, hairdressers: Small tip.

DRESS

- Western attire is the norm, and Filipinos are some of the smartest dressers in Asia. Dress well unless the occasion specifically calls for casual attire.

- April and May are the hottest months, and the rainy season extends from June to November. A suit coat is seldom needed during this period.

- Women should dress modestly despite the heat.

Filipinos are some of the smartest dressers in Asia.

BUSINESS

- Men: Wear a jacket and tie for initial meetings. Some Filipino men wear the *barong Tagalog*—a loose shirt worn outside the trousers.

- Women: Dress or skirt and blouse.

RESTAURANT

- Men: Suit, barong, or shirt, tie and dress trousers.

- Women: Dress; skirt or pants with blouse.

CASUAL

- Men: Open-collar cotton shirts and pants. Don't wear shorts on the street.

- Women: Slacks or jeans; shorts only at the beach, pool or resort.

GIFTS

- Gifts are not expected but appreciated. It's the thought that counts—not the cost.

- Gifts are not opened in the giver's presence. Thank the giver and set the gift aside.

WRAPPING

- Gifts should be elegantly wrapped; there are no special guidelines for the color of wrapping paper.

HOSTESS

- Take a small gift or send a gift to the hostess following a dinner.

- Suggested gifts: Fruit or fruit baskets.

- Do not give flowers (they are given for funerals).

BUSINESS

- Bring a small gift to your first meeting. Something with your company logo is acceptable.

- Suggested gifts: Crafts, liquor (Chivas Regal, Johnny Walker Black Label), pen sets.

- Avoid giving gifts from the Philippines. Filipinos appreciate gifts from their guest's country.

Bring a small gift to your first meeting. Something with your company logo is acceptable.

DO

- Show respect for the elderly. Greet them first. Offer your seat if none is available.

- Always ask permission before photographing anyone.

- Expect to be asked personal questions. Don't be offended. These questions show

HELPFUL HINTS

interest. Feel free to ask the same questions in return, especially about family.

- Understand that Filipinos seldom form a line or queue.

- Speak softly and control your emotions in public. Make requests, not demands.

- Bargain everywhere except in large department stores.

- Offer to share food with anyone around you.

- Understand that Filipinos feel obligated to return a favor.

DO NOT

- Never bring disgrace or dishonor on a person. This is a disaster not only for the individual, but also for his or her family.

- Never criticize anyone, especially in public. Don't criticize a person's family, the country or the culture.

- Don't express personal opinions if they could offend someone.

- Don't offer insincere compliments.

- Don't speak with a loud voice; it's considered ill-mannered.

- Don't expect Filipinos to say "no." They express the negative in a subtle or ambiguous manner.

- Don't be angry if a Filipino laughs at a sad or unfortunate event. Laughter relieves tension and embarrassment.

- Do not immediately accept a verbal invitation. Wait to be invited two or three times before you accept.

- Never disagree with the elderly.

- Filipinos have a relaxed attitude toward time. Meetings often begin late—but foreigners are supposed to be on time.

- Punctuality is appreciated but not required when attending social affairs.

BUSINESS CARDS

- Exchange business cards when introduced. Cards in English are acceptable.

CORPORATE CULTURE

Structure: Philippine business culture has been strongly influenced by Spain, China and the United States. Many Filipino business and

Rule of Thumb

Don't expect Filipinos to say "no." They express the negative in a subtle or ambiguous manner.

PUNCTUALITY

STRICTLY BUSINESS

government leaders were educated in the United States, and American business practices are common.

Because age and experience are equated with wisdom and authority, the management style is what might be described as "benevolent autocracy." Companies are expected to care for their employees.

Companies have a sense of loyalty to their customers and suppliers. This can be an obstacle for outsiders.

Filipinos identify with the group—clan, community or company—because it gives them a sense of belonging. By extension, companies have a sense of loyalty to their customers and suppliers. This can be an obstacle for outsiders.

A personal introduction by a mutual friend or business associate makes it easier to initiate business contacts. It's important to develop a personal relationship as the foundation on which successful business dealings can be built. Trust, loyalty and sincerity are the building blocks, and patience is the essential cement.

A third-party go-between can help achieve compromise on particularly sticky issues.

Meetings: Casual conversation usually precedes serious business discussions. Negotiations proceed at a much slower pace than in the U.S. A third-party go-between can help achieve compromise on particularly sticky issues. Proposals should be practical and conservative. Filipinos often have a "take it or leave it" attitude on price when they're the sellers; concessions evolve only over an extended period. Don't allow meetings to last too long; Filipinos love to eat and their enthusiasm wanes when they are hungry.

Communication: English is the language of commerce, but it's a gentler English than some Westerners are used to. The truth is diplomatically presented, controversial matters may be alluded to only vaguely, and the listener's perception is always taken into account. All communication is courteous, regardless of its content; excessive candor is sometimes viewed as a lack of culture. Criticize Filipino counterparts only in private. Don't be pushy or back anyone into a corner.

Filipinos find it difficult to say "no," disagree, reject, or be confrontational, especially when a superior is involved. Expect an ambiguous or indirect answer—not to deceive, but rather to please and avoid confrontation. This desire to please may result in apparent agreements that never produce results, or in projects started but never finished.

Be sure to phrase your questions simply and avoid those that can be answered "yes" or "no." Especially avoid negatively phrased questions, such as "Won't you join me for dinner?" The answer may be "Yes!" but the meaning may be "Yes, I won't join you for dinner."

Rule of Thumb

Avoid negatively phrased questions, such as "Won't you join me for dinner?"

Face-to-face meetings are preferred. Communication by mail or telephone is unreliable at best, and letters may go unanswered.

BE AWARE

- Ethnic Chinese are a tiny minority of the population but major players in the business community.

- Traditionally, nepotism, cronyism and favoritism are more important than ability and performance, but the importance of competence is growing as a new generation of Western-trained managers takes charge.

- The Filipino sense of time and pace may cause them to ignore deadlines—things get done, but perhaps not as quickly as a foreigner would hope.

- Filipinos consider innovation, change and competition risky, because failure could bring shame. Success is attributed to fate as much as to ability and effort.

ENTERTAINMENT

- Most business entertaining is done in restaurants or clubs, preferably a good restaurant in an international hotel. During business entertaining, you may be asked to sing. Try to join in.

- A dinner invitation to counterparts and their spouses is appreciated before you leave the country. Don't bring your spouse to a business lunch. Lunches are generally for business discussions.

- Arrange lunch and dinner engagements personally. Remember to invite someone at least three times to a dinner.

- Business is generally not discussed during meals, but it is discussed at other social occasions. Filipinos mix business and pleasure.

- People who have not been invited may turn up at a dinner. They should be included graciously.

- If you've been invited to dinner, reciprocate with a meal of equal lavishness.

APPOINTMENTS

- Make appointments at least a month before your trip.

- October, November and January to March are the best times for business travel. Avoid the Christmas and Easter periods, when many Filipinos are on vacation.

Rule of Thumb

A foreign women should not pay the bill when dining with a Filipino businessman. It would embarrass him and harm the business relationship.

- Foreign women will have little problem doing business in the Philippines.

- Women in the Philippines are active in government, business and the professions. Women are doctors, lawyers, and bankers, and dominate the fields of education, pharmacy and dentistry. Women manage households and often run companies in which a man is the figurehead. Filipina women are often in charge of financial and business operations.

- Men may make comments to women walking on the street. These should be ignored.

- It is not unusual for a Filipina woman to travel alone, but Western women alone need to be very careful. A woman should not walk alone after dark—take a taxi with a friend or someone you know well.

- Filipina women rarely smoke in public.

- A foreign woman should not pay the bill when dining with a Filipino businessman. It would embarrass him and harm the business relationship.

- Although tap and well water are considered generally safe, as a precaution foreigners should drink boiled or bottled water, or *serbésa* (beer) and soft drinks served with caps on.

- Be wary of ice, raw produce, unpasteurized dairy products and food served in unsanitary conditions.

- Travelers should take malaria prevention measures, follow precautions against insect bites, make sure vaccinations are up to date and consider tetanus and polio booster shots.

- Avoid swimming in freshwater lakes or streams.

- The Philippines has a fairly good health care system. If you have a serious ailment or injury, go to Manila if possible, or to the nearest large city. The bigger the place, the better the care.

- Most hospitals provide 24-hour emergency care and have pharmacies. Many deluxe hotels have medical and dental services for their guests.

- Most common medicines are available, but bring unusual prescriptions with you. Be aware that new drugs may be prescribed in the Philippines with little knowledge of long-term side effects.

- Crime is a serious concern in the Philippines. Homicide, kidnapping, other violent crimes, con games, and theft are common. If you are ever held up, don't try to defend yourself. Foreigners are often victims of petty crimes. Travel by public transportation may be risky. Don't reveal the name of your hotel to strangers. Check with authorities before traveling to remote areas.

- Avoid showing anger, shouting and being rude to people, even if you have cause. Back away from trouble to avoid an attack with a knife, bottle or other weapon.

- **Emergency numbers: Police 166; Fire 581-176 (Manila), 816-2553 (Makati); Emergency 911; Crisis Line 872-284.**

January	New Year's Day (1).	
March/April	Easter (Thursday-Sunday).	
April	Araw Ng Kagitingan (9).	
May	Labor Day (1).	
June	Independence Day (12).	
July	Philippine-American Friendship Day (4).	
September	Thanksgiving Day (21).	
November	All-Saints' Day (1), Bonifacio Day (30).	
December	Christmas (25), Rizal Day (30).	

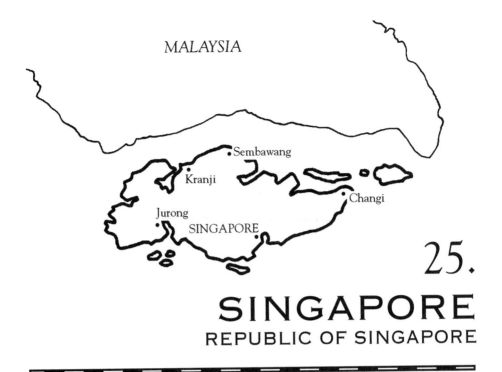

MALAYSIA

Sembawang
Kranji
Changi
Jurong
SINGAPORE

25.

SINGAPORE
REPUBLIC OF SINGAPORE

VITAL STATISTICS

POPULATION: 3.1 million, making it one of the most densely populated countries in the world.

CAPITAL: Singapore.

LAND SIZE: 225 square miles, approximately the size of Chicago.

GOVERNMENT: Republic since 1965. Parliament elects a president as head of state every four years. Executive power is vested in a cabinet headed by a prime minister. The 81 members of parliament are elected from single and multi-member constituencies for five years; the People's Action Party has won almost every seat since 1972. Voting is compulsory for all over 21. Males must serve two years in the military.

LIVING STANDARD:	GDP = US$32,878 per capita, one of the highest in Asia.
NATURAL RESOURCES:	Fisheries, deepwater ports on major global shipping routes.
AGRICULTURE:	Occupies a position of minor importance in the economy; self-sufficient in poultry and eggs, but must import much of other food. Crops include rubber, copra, fruit and vegetables.
INDUSTRIES:	Petroleum refining, electronics, oil drilling equipment, rubber processing and rubber products, processed food and beverages, ship building and repair, entrepôt trade, financial services, biotechnology.
Climate:	Tropical. Hot and rainy throughout the year, with temperatures ranging from 75°F (24°C) at night to 95°F (35°C) in the daytime.
CURRENCY:	Singapore dollar (S$). S$1 = 100 cents. Notes are in denominations of S$10,000, 1000, 100, 50, 10, 5 and 2, and coins in denominations of S$1 and 50, 20, 10, 5 and 1 cents.

THE PEOPLE

CORRECT NAME: Singaporeans.

ETHNIC MAKEUP: 77 percent Chinese, 15 percent Malay, 6 percent Indian, 2 percent European. This racial mixture has produced some conflict in the past, but today Singapore is characterized by racial harmony and national unity. Each ethnic group works hard to maintain its own cultural traditions while building a modern, cohesive society. Younger people think of themselves as Singaporean first, and as Chinese, Malay or Indian second.

VALUE SYSTEM: With its roots in the Confucian tradition, Singapore is a highly disciplined society. Singaporeans love to make money and enjoy life.

FAMILY: The family is central to all ethnic groups, with great emphasis on unity, loyalty and respect for elders. Although three generations traditionally live under one roof, this is often impossible in the high-rise apartments of modern Singapore.

RELIGION: 29 percent Taoist, 27 percent Buddhist, 16 percent Muslim, 10 percent Christian, 4 percent Hindu.

SPORTS: Soccer, cycling, running.

IMPORTANT DATES

1200	Temasek ("Sea Town") is renamed Singapore ("Lion City" in Sanskrit).
1819	Sir Thomas Stamford Raffles establishes trading post for the East India Company.
1826	Singapore, Penang and Malacca are joined to form the Straits Settlements.
1867	Straits Settlements become a Crown Colony.
1942	Japanese invade Singapore.
1945	British retake Singapore from the Japanese.
1946	Straits Settlements dissolved; Singapore becomes separate British Colony.
1959	State of Singapore announced. Singapore granted internal self-rule. Lee Kuan Yew becomes prime minister.
1963	Singapore joins Federation of Malaysia.
1965	Singapore leaves Federation of Malaysia and becomes a separate, independent nation.
1990	Lee resigns as prime minister, but remains head of People's Action Party. Goh Chok Tong becomes new prime minister.

- Shake hands with everyone present at a business meeting or social occasion. Shake hands again when leaving. Your handshake should be firm.

- Singaporeans may bow slightly as they shake your hand. A slight reciprocal bow to Chinese or older people is particularly appreciated.

- Introduce the more important person first, or the older person. Rank comes before age or gender. Mention a woman before a man. It is best for a man to wait for a woman to extend her hand.

- You can address all Singaporeans in English, using the courtesy titles Mr., Mrs., Miss or Ms. and the appropriate name. Here's a brief guide to name usage in each of the three cultures.

MALAY

- Malays have no surname. Their names are written with their given name + *bin* or *binti* + their father's given name.

  Examples: Ali bin Isa is the son of Isa bin Osman; he should be addressed as Mr. Ali. Zaitun binti Isa is the daughter of Isa

You can address all Singaporeans in English, using the courtesy titles Mr., Mrs., Miss or Ms. and the appropriate name.

bin Osman; she should be addressed as
Miss Zaitun or Mrs. Zaitun.

- Women who marry do not necessarily take their husband's name.

CHINESE

- Chinese names have three parts—the family name followed by the given name, which often has two parts.

  Example: Lee King Feng's family name is Lee; he should be addressed as Mr. Lee.

INDIAN

- Most Indians in Singapore are of Tamil ancestry and don't have surnames. They place their father's initial before their given name.

  Example: T. Manickavas. T. is the father's initial and Manickavas is the person's given name. He should be addressed as Mr. Manickavas.

- An Indian woman usually drops her father's initial and takes her husband's name.

- Malay is the official language. English, Chinese and Tamil also are taught in the schools and are part of the main language stream. The government encourages use of all these languages to maintain traditional cultures and values. Most people are bilingual or multilingual. Trilingual taxi drivers are not unusual.

- English is the working language of commerce, industry and government. All Singaporeans are expected to learn English.

- At least a half-dozen Chinese dialects are spoken in Singapore, but the government has mounted a campaign encouraging all Chinese to learn and speak Mandarin.

Most people are bilingual or multilingual. Trilingual taxi drivers are not unusual.

BODY LANGUAGE

- A woman may hold hands with another woman. This is simply a show of friendship.

- Never touch a person's head—even a child's. The head is considered sacred.

- The foot is considered the lowest part of the body, and is thought to be unclean. Never point your foot or the sole of your shoe at anyone. Tapping your foot or swinging your leg while sitting is thought to indicate nervousness and/or lack of interest. Cross your legs only at the knee; better yet, keep your feet flat on the floor.

Never point your foot or the sole of your shoe at anyone.

- A slight bow when entering or leaving a room or passing a group of people is courteous.

- Raise your hand to get someone's attention.

- Never signal or point at someone with your forefinger.

- Do not pound your fist on an open palm; this is obscene.

PHRASES

- See chapters on China and Malaysia for useful phrases.

- Be aware that the Indian dialect spoken in Singapore is primarily Tamil rather than Hindi.

MANNERS

DINING

- Style: Primarily Oriental, with chopsticks. See "Chopstick Etiquette" in Chapter 10.

- Western-style utensils can be found quite easily.

- Most entertaining is done in restaurants. To beckon a waiter, raise your entire hand. Do not raise one finger. Never whistle, hiss or shout.

- Almost every meal includes rice or noodles.

- You may share a table with strangers in a crowded restaurant. You're not expected to talk with them.

- If you must clear your throat or blow your nose at the table, be very discreet. Cover your mouth when using a toothpick.

- All dishes are usually served at once and shared by all. Cocktails and appetizers are uncommon, though they are available in Western restaurants.

- Allow the host to order all the dishes. Compliments are appreciated by the host, but will probably be declined for modesty's sake.

- An even number of people at the table ensures good fortune.

- Etiquette and eating habits vary according to the style of food being eaten and the nationality of the people eating it. Hindus

All dishes are usually served at once and shared by all.

and Buddhists do not eat beef; Muslims do not eat pork.

- When eating at food stalls in an outdoor market, take care not to mix utensils from a Muslim stall with those from a Chinese stall. Muslims do not use utensils that have touched pork.

CHINESE

- Chinese may offer a banquet. A Westerner should always reciprocate with a banquet of equal value before departing.

- Chinese use chopsticks for most food and porcelain spoons for liquids such as soup. Western-style utensils are sometimes used, but less frequently than chopsticks.

- Host and hostess usually sit opposite one another at a round table. Guests of honor sit facing the entrance, to the host's left.

- The host will invite you to begin the meal; however, allow the host to start first.

- Most Chinese remove bones from their mouths with chopsticks and then set them on the tablecloth. It is impolite to put your fingers in your mouth to pull out a piece of bone.

- When finished with your meal, place chopsticks on the chopstick rest (putting them on your plate means you are not finished).

- A Chinese host usually apologizes for the unacceptable meal you've eaten. Reply that the meal was excellent and appreciated.

MALAY/INDIAN

- Be on time for dinner in a Malay home. The dinner is usually served immediately with no drinks or appetizers beforehand. The guest of honor in a Malay home is seated either to the host's right or at the head of the table.

- Indians always wash their hands before and after a meal. In a Malay home, you will be given a small bowl of water and a towel. Use the water to wash your hands.

- Malays and Indians use a spoon along with their fingers to eat. Never use your left hand to eat; it's considered unclean. You will have no need to use a knife, because the food is cut into bite-size portions. If you're given a spoon and fork, hold the spoon in your right hand and the fork in your left; use the fork to push food onto the spoon.

Malays and Indians use a spoon along with their fingers to eat. Never use your left hand to eat; it's considered unclean.

- Wait for host to start eating and invite you to do so before you begin. Traditionally, women start eating after the men.

- Never let the serving spoon touch your plate and never share your leftovers. Indians believe that anything that touches someone's plate is tainted.

- It is impolite to refuse initial offers of food or drink. To refuse seconds, place your hand above your plate and say, "No, thank you." When finished, place spoon and fork together on your plate. If they are not placed together, you will be offered more food. When eating Indian food served on a banana leaf, fold the leaf in two with the fold toward you to indicate that you are finished.

- Don't offer Indian women an alcoholic beverage; they rarely drink.

- After a meal with Indians, expect to stay for approximately an hour of conversation.

DRINKING AND TOASTING

- In a strict Muslim home, no alcoholic beverages are served.

- In a home or at a business meeting, pass or accept a drink with both hands. This is a sign of respect. With a waiter or waitress (or someone of obviously lower rank), it is acceptable to use your right hand only to pass or receive a drink.

- Toasts are not very common in Singapore. Ethnic toasts are occasionally heard. See the chapters on China, India and Malaysia for examples.

- An exception is the Chinese banquet, at which the toast may be *Yam Seng*, meaning "to your continuing success."

- Stand up if you are proposing a toast. Stand up and respond with a thank you if you are the recipient of a toast.

- The toast is made while holding the glass with both hands and looking the other person directly in the eye. Drink with one hand.

- Tipping is generally not expected and is often discouraged.

TIPPING

- Restaurant: A service charge is usually included in the bill. No extra tip is expected.

- Taxi drivers: Round up to the nearest dollar.

- Bellmen: S$1 or 2.

DRESS

- Due to Singapore's modernity and ethnic diversity, many different kinds of attire are acceptable. Western clothing is most common, and dress is relatively casual.

- Dress for the tropical climate—lightweight cottons are advised. Do not wear safari suits; they are not chic in Singapore.

- When being entertained, wear a jacket and tie or jacket and open-necked shirt.

BUSINESS

- Men: White shirts, ties and trousers. Jackets are usually not required.

- Women: Skirts and blouses with sleeves, or pant suits.

- When meeting a government official, it is customary to dress more formally.

RESTAURANT

- Men: White shirts, ties and trousers; jackets are necessary in some expensive restaurants.

- Women: Skirts and blouses with sleeves, or pant suits.

- Suits and evening dresses are common in nightspots.

HOME

- Men: White shirts, ties and trousers.

- Women: Skirts and blouses with sleeves, or pant suits.

- Most families remove their shoes before entering the house or apartment.

GIFTS

- Each ethnic group has different gift-giving traditions.

- Use both hands to give someone a gift. A gift given to guest or host is not opened in the presence of the giver.

- Always bring the hosts a gift when invited to someone's home.

- Business gifts are generally not exchanged.

- Be careful that a gift—even a small one— isn't misinterpreted as a bribe. Never give a government official a gift.

- Wrap gifts elegantly.

- Give: Brand-names, high-quality gifts.

Each ethnic group in Singapore has different gift-giving traditions.

CHINESE

- Single items or pairs—odd numbers signify separation.

- Wrap the gift, but never in blue or black paper. Red is a good color, signifying prosperity.

- Give: Candy, cakes, fruit, scotch whiskey, brandy, something from your home region.

- Do not give: Clocks, handkerchiefs, 13 of anything, flowers, anything white.

INDIAN

- Present your gift with your right hand.

- Never give anything wrapped in white or black.

- Suggested gifts: Fruit or candy.

- Do not give: Beef.

MALAY

- Use green, red or yellow wrapping paper.

- Give: Perfume (women), shirts or clothing (men), candy.

- Do not give: Gifts wrapped in black or white, knives, liquor, anything connected with or derived from dogs or pigs.

DO

- Haggle for prices in small shops—but not in large department stores. Pay in cash; credit card purchases often carry a surcharge.

- Be aware of strictly enforced laws regarding littering, jaywalking and other public behavior.

- Carry prescriptions for all medications to avoid difficulties. Singapore strictly enforces drug possession laws.

- Respect elders.

- Recognize that a smile or laugh may be used to cover embarrassment.

- Get a haircut before arrival; males with hair that extends below their collars may be denied entry or required to get a haircut.

DO NOT

You can be detained without trial in Singapore, and you are not read any rights when arrested. Police can use force without fear of being charged with brutality. Singapore imposes strict penalties for what Westerners think of as relatively minor offenses, such as littering, spitting and jaywalking; an American teenager recently was sentenced to public flogging for

Haggle for prices in small shops—but not in large department stores.

spraying paint on cars. Possession of illegal drugs can bring a death sentence.

With these facts in mind:

Do not, under any circumstances, bring illegal drugs into the country.

- Do not, under any circumstances, bring illegal drugs into the country.

- Do not jaywalk.

- Do not smoke in air-conditioned public buildings.

- Do not spit on the sidewalk.

- Do not litter.

- Do not import, sell or use chewing gum.

- Do not bring into Singapore pornographic materials; reproductions of copyrighted publications, videotapes, disks, records or cassettes; or firearms.

And a few less strident cautions:

- Avoid public displays of affection.

- Do not step over anyone resting on a floor.

- Do not show anger or raise your voice. Remain disciplined and in control.

- Avoid discussing religion or politics.

- Avoid jokes until you know someone well. Few Western jokes will be understood or appreciated.

PUNCTUALITY

- Westerners are expected to be punctual for both business meetings and social occasions. Call if you are delayed. Tardiness is viewed as a sign of disrespect.

STRICTLY BUSINESS

BUSINESS CARDS

- Business cards are exchanged during introductions. After you are introduced, exchange business cards with both hands.

- Business cards printed only in English are acceptable.

- Include your business card in correspondence.

CORPORATE CULTURE

Structure: Ethnic Chinese dominate business in Singapore. See the chapters on Hong Kong and Taiwan for additional information on the Chinese business culture.

The government finances many large corporations in Singapore. This bureaucratic system is highly efficient and largely corruption-free. Western-style management is the rule in most large firms; traditional, Chinese-style management, with a looser structure and centralized decisionmaking, is common in smaller firms.

Singpore's per capita GNP now exceeds that of its former colonizer, Great Britain.

Personal contacts are important in business. It takes several years to develop business relationships. Take time to get acquainted before discussing business; it will pay off in the long run.

Meetings: Groups enter meeting rooms according to rank—senior person first. Singaporeans tend to get right down to business in meetings. Singaporeans have excellent entrepreneurial instincts and make decisions quickly. They drive a hard bargain on costs and deadlines. You are expected to deliver reports, correspondence, products and services when promised.

Communication: English is the language of business. Always talk straight and get right to the point with Singaporeans. You can be direct when dealing with money matters. Don't correct anyone in the presence of colleagues or counterparts—this could cause embarrassment and loss of face.

Singapore has one of the world's most modern and efficient telecommunications systems.

BE AWARE

- Corruption is very unusual in Singapore.

- Most prominent businesspeople are of Chinese ancestry.

ENTERTAINMENT

- Business breakfasts are not common. Business lunches are popular.

- Dinner is the most common form of business entertainment, but it is a time to socialize and build relationships rather than discuss business details. Don't be surprised if business dinners are scheduled every night of the week.

- Spouses are not included in a dinner invitation.

APPOINTMENTS

- March through July is the best time to do business. November through February are vacation months.

- Arrange appointments well in advance of your visit.

ESPECIALLY FOR WOMEN

- Western women may encounter minor bias when doing business in Singapore, but should generally be well accepted.

- Sexual harassment is very rare, and women can safely travel alone.

- Singaporean women enjoy much more freedom and equality than in much of Asia.

Singapore has an official policy against gender discrimination.

- Singapore has an official policy against gender discrimination, and Singaporean women are gaining wider acceptance in business.

- Women should always cover their shoulders when entering a temple.

- Wear a skirt and blouse with sleeves, or a pant suit, for business. Avoid shorts, short skirts and revealing clothing.

- Singapore's medical facilities are among the finest in the world, with well-qualified doctors and dentists, many of them trained overseas. Doctors and hospitals are listed in the Yellow Pages and most hotels have their own doctor on 24-hour call. Medical and dental services are reasonably priced.

- Pharmaceuticals are available at supermarkets, department stores, hotels and shopping centers. Registered pharmacists work 9 a.m. to 6 p.m., with some pharmacies in major shopping centers open until 10 p.m. Hospitals can fill prescriptions 24 hours a day. Prescriptions must be written by locally registered doctors.

- Supplemental overseas medical insurance is recommended.

- Singapore is one of the safest countries in the world.

- **Emergency numbers: Police 999, Fire/Ambulance 995.**

Singapore is one of the safest countries in the world.

HOLIDAYS AND FESTIVALS	January	New Year's Day (1).
	January/ February	Chinese New Year (set according to the lunar calendar).
	March/ April	Easter (Friday through Sunday).
	April	Hari Raya Puasa (16).
	May	Labour Day (1), Vesak Day (28—Buddha's Birthday).
	June	Hari Raya Haji (24).
	August	National Day (9).
	November	Deepavali (5).
	December	Christmas (25).

When a holiday falls on a Sunday, the following Monday is a public holiday. During the Chinese New Year, many Chinese firms close for the week.

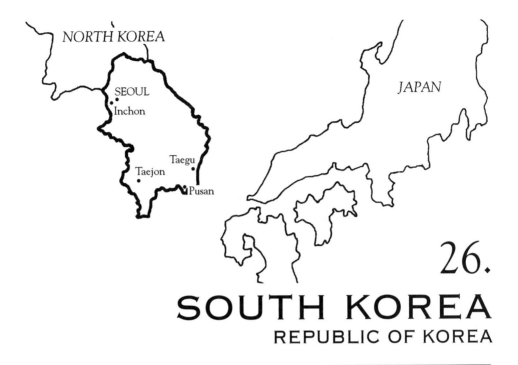

NORTH KOREA

SEOUL
Inchon

Taegu
Taejon
Pusan

JAPAN

26.

SOUTH KOREA
REPUBLIC OF KOREA

VITAL STATISTICS

POPULATION: 45.6 million.

CAPITAL: Seoul, with a population of 10.7 million.

LAND SIZE: 38,310 square miles, slightly larger than Indiana.

GOVERNMENT: Republic since 1948. The 1987 constitution gives executive power to the president, who is directly elected for a single term of five years. Members of the Kuk Hoe, or National Assembly, are elected for four years. The president appoints a prime minister who is technically the head of government; in practice, the president makes all decisions, which are routinely approved by the National Assembly.

LIVING STANDARD:	GDP = US$11,910 per capita.
NATURAL RESOURCES:	Coal, tungsten, graphite, molybdenum, lead, hydropower.
AGRICULTURE:	Accounts for 8 percent of GNP and employs 21 percent of the work force (including fishing and forestry); principal crops include rice, barley, vegetables, fruit, livestock and livestock products.
INDUSTRIES:	Textiles, clothing, footwear, food processing, chemicals, steel, electronics, telecommunications, automobile production, shipbuilding.
CLIMATE:	Continental, with an average temperature range from 23°F (-5°C) in winter to 81°F (27°C) in summer, more extreme in the interior. Winters are cold and dry and summers are hot and humid; spring and autumn are genrally pleasant. Annual precipitation is 67.5 inches (150 cm).
CURRENCY:	Korean *won* (KW). Notes are in denominations of KW10,000, 5000, and 1000. There are coins of KW500, 100, 50, 10, 5 and 1.

THE PEOPLE

CORRECT NAME: Koreans (South Koreans).

ETHNIC MAKEUP: Almost entirely Korean—racially and
                   linguistically one of the most homogeneous
                   countries in the world.

VALUE SYSTEM: Hard work, filial piety, modesty and respect for
                   others are qualities esteemed by Koreans.
                   Confucianism plays a pivotal role in
                   interpersonal relationships and in ordering social
                   behavior, but its importance is slowly being
                   eroded. Friendship is highly valued and friends
                   rely on each other in both their personal and
                   business lives. Koreans are proud of both their
                   traditional culture and their modern economy.
                   Education is seen as the path to status, money
                   and success.

FAMILY: Duty and obligation bind members of the family,
                   which is the foundation of society in Korea.
                   Average family size is 4.5 people. The father is
                   the head of the family. He and the oldest son
                   receive the greatest respect. Sons are expected to
                   care for elderly parents.

RELIGION: 37 percent Buddhist, 30 percent Christian.

SPORTS: Baseball, boxing, golf, soccer, table tennis, tennis,
                   wrestling, speed skating, judo, tae kwon do.

IMPORTANT DATES

1895	Peace treaty ending the Sino-Japanese War recognizes the independence of Korea.
1910	Japan annexes Korea.
1945	Following the defeat of Japan, Korea is divided at the 38th parallel.
1948	Republic of Korea established.
1950-53	Korean War.
1961	Military coup brings General Park Chung Hee to power.
1979	President Park assassinated.
1980	General Chun Doo Hwan reinstates martial law.
1987	Student protests compel Chun to call elections. New constitution ratified. Roh Tae Woo elected president.
1988	Summer Olympics held in Seoul.
1993	International tensions mount over North Korea's nuclear program.

- The bow is the traditional Korean greeting, though it is often accompanied by a handshake among men. To show respect when shaking hands, support your right forearm with your left hand.

- Professionals meeting for the first time usually exchange business cards. Present your card and receive your colleague's card with both hands.

- Korean women usually nod slightly. They generally do not shake hands, and Korean men do not offer to shake hands with Korean women. Korean women will not shake hands with Western men.

- Western women can offer their hand to a Korean man.

- A younger person greets an older person first.

- A senior person offers his or her hand first to a junior person; a junior person bows first to a senior person. Direct eye contact between junior and senior businesspeople should be avoided. This is seen as impolite or even as a challenge.

- Bow when departing. Younger people wave (move arm side to side).

To show respect when shaking hands, support your right forearm with your left hand.

NAMES
AND
TITLES

- Koreans regard names very differently than Westerners. According to Confucian tradition, a name has properties of its own.

- It is considered very impolite to address a Korean by his or her given name. Address Koreans using professional or courtesy titles and family names unless specifically invited by your Korean hosts or colleagues to do otherwise.

- In Korean names, the family name comes first, followed by the two-part given name. The first of the two given names is shared by everyone in the family of the same generation, and the second is the individual's name.

  Example: Lee Dong Sung. Lee is the family name, Dong the generational name and Sung the individual's name.

- The most common Korean family names are Kim, Lee and Park.

- When Koreans address other Koreans, they use the honorific *sonsaengnim*, which means "teacher." It can be used alone or following the family name. However, foreigners should avoid using this form unless they speak Korean.

- In most cases, Westerners should address Koreans as Mr., Mrs., Ms. or Miss + family name.

  Examples: Mr. Lee, Mrs. Kim, Miss Park.

- When addressing a high-ranking person, such as a senior corporate executive, use the person's corporate or professional title + family name.

  Examples: Vice President Lee, Doctor Kim, Professor Park.

- It may be difficult for Westerners to distinguish Korean male names from female names. Common female names include *Soon*, *Sook* and *Ja*, which also may be spelled *Sun*, *Suk* and *Ya*.

  Examples: Park Kyong Soon, Kim Hye Sook, Lee Myong Ja.

- Korean women keep their maiden names after marriage.

- Some Koreans may mistake your given name for your family name (or find your family name unpronounceable) and address you by first name and appropriate courtesy title. For instance, John Murray may be addressed as "Mr. John."

- In correspondence with Koreans, the correct salutation is, "To my respected (title) + (full name)."

  Examples: "To my respected Mr. Lee Dong Sung," "To my respected Vice President Lee Dong Sung," "To my respected Professor Lee Dong Sung."

LANGUAGE

- Korean is the official language. Although it belongs to the Ural-Altaic family of languages, it is unlike any other in the world.

- The written language is called *Hangul*, and it has a phonetic alphabet that makes it much easier for Westerners to learn than Chinese or Japanese.

- Written Korean uses some Chinese characters mixed with Hangul script, but they are pronounced differently than in Chinese.

Korean translates into English with a seemingly endless variety of spellings.

- Korean translates into English with a seemingly endless variety of spellings. In general, words that sound the same probably are the same. Some Korean consonants are midway between two English ones in sound, so P and B, K and G, T and D, and to some extent CH and J are used interchangeably when spelling in English. The vowels U and OO also are interchangeable.

- A Korean who says "Yes" isn't necessarily indicating agreement. He or she may mean "I hear you" or "I understand you."

- English is taught in high schools and colleges, and is spoken and understood by many people. Speak clearly and precisely, but avoid speaking with exaggerated slowness—you may appear patronizing. Don't bring your face too close to a Korean's in an attempt to understand his or her English.

- Never use words like "fellow," "guy," "this man" or "that man." These are considered demeaning.

BODY LANGUAGE

- No touching! Koreans consider it distasteful to be touched by someone who is not a relative or close friend. Avoid hugging, back-slapping and a hand on the shoulder. Touching older people and people of the opposite sex is particularly inappropriate.

- When Koreans are embarrassed, they generally laugh. Laughter can also mean fear, anger or surprise. Korean women cover their mouth when laughing. Men do not.

When Koreans are embarrassed, they generally laugh.

- Close Korean friends of the same gender sometimes hold hands or walk with a hand on the friend's shoulder. Westerners should *not* follow suit.

- Do not cross your legs or stretch them out in front of you. Keep your feet flat on the floor—and certainly never on a desk or chair.

- Always pass and receive objects with your right hand (supported by the left hand at the wrist or forearm) or with two hands.

- Cover your mouth when yawning or using a toothpick.

- People who are acquainted with one another stand and walk very close to each other. It is rude to make someone walk behind you.

- Sit or stand up straight; don't slouch.

- To beckon someone, extend your arm and hand, palm down, and move your fingers in a scratching motion. To say "come here" or to beckon with the index finger is considered rude.

- Tilting your head back and sucking air through your teeth means "no" or "very difficult."

- Never point with your index finger.

PHRASES

English	Korean	Pronunciation
Good morning/		
Good afternoon/	Formal:	
Good evening/	*Annyong hasimnika*	Ahn-yohng hah-shim-nee-kah
How are you?	Informal: *Annyong haseyo*	Ahn-yohng hah-say-o
Please	*Chebal*	chay-bahl
Thank you	*Kamsa hamnida*	Kahm-sah hahm-nee-dah
You're welcome	*Ch'onmaneyo*	Chon-mahn-ah-yo
Yes	*Ye* (or) *Ne*	Yeh (or) Nay
No	*Anio*	Ah-nee-yo
Excuse me	*Silre hamnida*	Sheel-ray hahm-nee-dah
Goodbye (Say to one who is leaving)	*Annyonghi kasipsiyo*	Ahn-yohng-he kae-sip-si-yo
Goodbye (Say as you are leaving others)	*Annyonghi kesipsiyo*	Ahn-yohng-he kae-sip-si-yo
Pleased to meet you	*Mannaso pangosumnida*	Mahn-na-so pahn-gop-soom-nee-dah

MANNERS

All courses of a meal are served at once and food can be eaten in any order.

DINING

- Chopsticks are used for all Korean-style meals. See "Chopstick Etiquette" in Chapter 10.

- Koreans take great pride in their cuisine. It is an essential part of their culture.

- A meal is served before socializing. All courses of a meal are served at once and food can be eaten in any order.

- Elderly are served first and children last. It is very impolite to start eating before the senior person at the table has begun.

- The basic Korean meal is simple—rice, meat or fish soup, *kimchi* (pickled cabbage) and vegetables. Korean food is generally spicy, although some milder dishes are available. Rice and kimchi are the staples of every meal.

- Major hotels serve Western food, but it is difficult to find elsewhere.

- In homes and restaurants, men and women socialize in separate rooms.

- Always allow your host to seat you. The seat of honor is the seat looking at the entrance. If you are given the seat of honor, it is polite to protest slightly.

- You may be given a hot or cold towel before the meal to wash your face and hands.

- Koreans do not like to talk a lot while eating; periods of silence during a meal are common and appreciated. The meal usually precedes socializing at a dinner party.

- Use a spoon to eat soup. Place the spoon in your soup bowl or lay it over your rice bowl when finished. Never place it on the table. Koreans may serve food from a communal dish with the same spoon they are using for their soup.

- It is polite to pass or accept food or drink with your right hand while your left hand supports your right forearm or wrist.

- Never pick up any food with your hands. Use toothpicks to pick up fruit. Never raise a bowl or dish to your mouth.

In homes and restaurants, men and women socialize in separate rooms.

- Pour tea, alcohol and soy sauce in your neighbor's cup, glass or dish. Allow them to do the same for you.

- Never show any sign of distaste for food you're served, regardless of how exotic the dish.

- Leave a dinner party shortly after the entertainment concludes.

- You may be seated with strangers in a crowded restaurant. You are not expected to converse with them.

- To beckon a waiter, say *Yobo seyo*, (yo-bo say-yoh).

- Most entertaining of Westerners is done in a restaurant. The person who invites pays the bill for everyone; however, it is polite for a guest to offer to pay. When two people are dining, usually the younger person pays for the older person.

BANQUET

- In hotels, dishes are served by courses—as many as 12. Appetizers precede the meal. The first course is meat, vegetables and thin pancakes. Roll the meat and vegetables in a pancake and eat. Soup is served before the main course.

- In Korean restaurants, all dishes are served at once. Taste every dish.

DRINKING AND TOASTING

- Drinking alcohol is a popular pastime. Alcohol is usually accompanied by food. Drunkenness is acceptable, but loud and aggressive behavior is not.

- Do not pour your own drink, but do offer to pour for others; it is common to fill each other's cup, and to refuse is an insult. Women pour men's drinks but never pour another woman's drink. A woman may pour her own drink.

Do not pour your own drink, but do offer to pour for others.

- When receiving a drink, lift your glass to a level convenient for the pourer. When pouring a drink for someone, support your forearm with the other hand.

- Leave some of the beverage in your glass if you don't want a refill.

- Be prepared to deliver a solo singing performance while drinking.

- The most common toast is *gonbae* (kahn pay), which means "bottoms up." Raise your drink with your right hand; everybody toasts and clinks glasses.

- Coffee is often served with cream and sugar added.

TIPPING

- Wherever you see a "No Tipping" sign, do not tip. Koreans generally find tipping offensive, although it's now becoming expected in hotels frequented by foreigners.

- A service charge of 10 percent is always included in the bill at Western-style hotels and restaurants. Small change can be left as an additional gratuity for good service.

- Taxis: Tip only if the driver helps with your luggage.

- Airport porters: Pay according to posted schedule.

- Hotel bellmen: Many hotels officially prohibit bellmen from accepting gratuities, but in practice a tip may be expected.

DRESS

- Koreans dress well, and you should dress accordingly to show respect. A sober suit and tie are almost always appropriate. Koreans rarely wear casual outfits. Koreans dress up for city activities, especially in Seoul.

Koreans dress well, and you should dress accordingly to show respect. A sober suit and tie are almost always appropriate.

- Western style clothing is worn.

- Women dress modestly. Never wear tight, short or revealing clothing, shorts, or sleeveless blouses. Prepare to sit on the floor—avoid straight, tight skirts.

- Never go barefoot.

- Bring very warm clothing for the winter. Prepare for distinct seasonal variations.

- Be prepared to use squat toilets; dress accordingly.

BUSINESS

- Men: Dark suits, white or light blue shirts, conservative ties (grey or blue, thin stripes).

- Women: Suits or dresses—no pants. Conservative and modest.

RESTAURANT

- Men: Dark suits, white shirts, ties.

- Women: Evening dresses, suits, or dresses in conservative colors. Dresses are preferred for most social occasions.

CASUAL

- Men: Conservative slacks and shirt.

- Women: Skirts, sweaters and blouses. Slacks are acceptable. Shorts are for the beach only.

GIFTS

- Gift-giving is very common in Korea.

- Offer and receive a gift with both hands. Wrapped gifts are never opened in the presence of the giver.

- If you receive a gift from your Korean colleague, reciprocate with a gift of similar value.

WRAPPING

- Wrap your gift nicely. Bright colors are preferred for wrapping gifts. Yellow with red or green stripes is a traditional Korean wrapping paper design.

- Avoid wrapping gifts in red or dark colors.

HOSTESS

- Always bring a small gift for the hostess when invited to someone's home.

- Give: Candy, cakes, cookies, flowers, fruit.

- Do not give: Liquor to a woman.

BUSINESS

- It is common to exchange gifts at the first meeting. Allow the host to present his or her gift first.

- Give: Liquor (good quality scotch), fruit, desk accessories, items from France or Italy (which confer status), U.S. regional arts and crafts.

- Do not give: Expensive gifts (Koreans will feel obligated to reciprocate with a gift of equal value); knives or scissors (they signify "cutting off" a relationship); green headwear; gifts or cards with red writing (denotes death); or gifts in sets of four (denotes death).

DO

- Recognize that Koreans are distinct from other Asians in food, language and culture. Respect that distinction.

- Remember men are first in Korea. Address an audience as "gentlemen and ladies." Men go through doors first and walk ahead of women. Women help men with their coats.

- At all costs, maintain harmony. Decline a compliment; don't say "thank you"—it shows a lack of humility.

It is common to exchange gifts at the first meeting. Allow the host to present his or her gift first.

HELPFUL HINTS

Recognize that Koreans are distinct from other Asians in food, language and culture.

- Keep to the left on sidewalks and stairs. Expect people to push and shove in crowds. This is not considered impolite. People generally do not form lines. Be aggressive in a line or you will never get anywhere.

- Always stand at attention when the Korean national anthem is played. Show great respect for the elderly—hold doors, give them your seat, stand when they enter a room. Recognize that elderly men are the most important figures in Korea.

- Expect Koreans to ask personal questions. This is viewed as showing a polite interest in your life. An honest answer is not required.

- Expect to be stared at, especially if you have red or blond hair. People may even touch your hair out of curiosity.

- Always knock before entering a room.

- Remove sunglasses when speaking to someone.

- Ask permission before photographing inside a temple.

- Keep a hotel card with you at all times with its name, address and telephone number (in Korean).

- Feel free to bargain except in stores marked "One Price."

DO NOT

- Never confuse Koreans with Chinese or Japanese; this is a grave insult.

- Never upset Koreans or cause them to lose self-esteem. *Kibun* is a feeling of comfort and peace of mind, and it's very important to Koreans to maintain their kibun. Violating this sense of harmony is bad form.

- Never be patronizing or condescending to a Korean; you'll destroy any chance of a business relationship.

- Never embarrass a Korean, especially in front of others. "Face" is extremely important in Korea.

- Don't expect Koreans to admit that they don't know the answer to a question. They may give a wrong answer or the answer they think you would like to hear, either to make you feel good or to save face.

Never confuse Koreans with Chinese or Japanese; this is a grave insult.

Never be patronizing or condescending to a Korean; you'll destroy any chance of a business relationship.

- Never talk about Koreans or their customs or culture within earshot of a Korean, even if you are saying good things. Do not talk about politics. Talk about Korea's remarkable accomplishments over its 5,000-year history.

- Never damage a person's reputation, criticize openly or disagree in public.

- Do not write a living person's name in red (which indicates a deceased person).

- Never laugh or talk loudly; never put your hands in your pockets; never eat while walking on the street.

- Do not blow your nose in public. Never blow your nose and return the tissue to your pocket. Dispose of it immediately.

- Avoid using the number "10," which is considered bad luck.

PUNCTUALITY

- Koreans expect Westerners to be punctual for business meetings and social occasions. Call if you will be delayed.

- You may be kept waiting up to half an hour for business appointments. This is not from disrespect, but reflects the pressure on busy Korean executives.

- Be prepared to see your Korean guests arrive about 30 minutes late for social occasions. They call this "Korean time."

- Korea has one of the longest average workweeks in the world.

BUSINESS CARDS

- Print one side of your business card in Korean and one side in English. Cards can be printed in Hangul (the Korean alphabet) or Chinese characters.

- Never give a Korean a business card in Japanese! The Japanese occupied Korea from 1910 to 1945, and Koreans still harbor considerable animosity toward Japan.

CORPORATE CULTURE

Structure: The founding families still run the huge conglomerates—Chaebal, Samsung, Daewoo, Sungyong and Sanyong Group.

Everyone has a distinctive place in the organizational hierarchy. Korean organizations are generally flat, with middle managers having considerable authority to make decisions. Often, decisions are made by consensus within a department, and then communicated to the senior level for approval. The decision is then implemented by all appropriate units of the company.

Building trust is vital to establishing a successful business relationship. This requires patience. Success depends upon socializing: Koreans prefer to do business with people they know. A Korean businessperson will want to learn all about your company and your position within the company.

Meetings: Without a reference you may be unable to gain an appointment. Seek out a Korean contact and request a formal introduction. The first appointment should be made with a senior executive by a senior executive. Subsequently, be sure to send managers of the same level as the Korean managers whom you expect to meet.

Do not discuss business at the first meeting. This meeting is to establish trust. Be formal in meetings until the Korean delegation loosens up. Be prepared for meetings to extend well beyond normal business hours.

Do not discuss business at a first meeting; this meeting is to establish trust.

The highest-ranking foreigner is usually seated opposite the door. In a business meeting allow Koreans to indicate your seat. You will be seated opposite your Korean counterpart. You will be served tea, coffee or a soft drink before the meeting. A "tea girl" serves tea, kneeling to serve you. Accept your cup or glass with both hands.

Negotiations are generally protracted and may require several trips. A team approach is often used. Koreans generally start negotiations with an unreasonable position and prepare to compromise. Koreans are tough negotiators and admire a firm, persistent opponent—but refrain from being too aggressive. Koreans are very cautious and sometimes will go to great lengths to avoid mistakes.

Communication: English is spoken and understood by many Korean businesspeople, but generally an interpreter will be necessary for clear understanding. If an interpreter is required, your Korean hosts will usually make arrangements in advance of the meeting.

Listen carefully to your Korean counterpart, and maintain eye contact to show attentiveness and sincerity. Look at the person you're speaking to. Koreans consider smiling during negotiations to be frivolous.

Don't be surprised if you are asked the same question several times. It is better to be consistent rather than creative in your answers.

Koreans can be blunt, even aggressive in discussions. A Korean may interrupt you in midsentence to argue. Don't lose your cool.

English is spoken and understood by many Korean businesspeople, but generally an interpreter will be necessary for clear understanding.

"Yes" doesn't necessarily mean agreement; Koreans avoid saying "no." Try to phrase questions in a manner that doesn't require a "yes" or "no" answer. For example, don't ask "Could we sign the agreement by next Friday?" Instead, ask "What's the earliest date by which we could sign this agreement?"

Presentations are generally brief, supported by highly detailed reports. Do your homework. Koreans will be embarrassed if you can't answer a question, and your credibility could be damaged.

Never boast about your company. Professional, written reports can show your company's capabilities and achievements.

Reply promptly to faxes, letters or telexes.

BE AWARE

- Korea is a tough market to crack. It is advisable to get a government-approved agent.

- Legal documents should be flexible with few details. Mutual trust and benefit are much more important than legal documents. Koreans do not like detailed contracts. Who signs a legal document is of vital importance to Koreans. Understand that a written contract is subject to renegotiation.

- Deliver what you promise in a timely manner. Quality, price and service are essential to success. Koreans place great value on after-sale service, and often criticize American companies for not providing after-sale service of very high quality.

Koreans place great value on after-sale service.

- Never sign a contract with red ink.

ENTERTAINMENT

- Business success depends directly on building trust and relationships—and much of this happens after business hours. Sharing a meal or drinks can be essential.

- First meetings often take place over a meal. Business breakfasts are unusual. Business lunches are common, but not as popular as dinners.

- Do not talk business at dinner unless your Korean host initiates the discussion.

- The meal generally precedes any business discussion or other conversation. Show appreciation for the food.

- Koreans are used to drinking large quantities of alcohol at business dinners. They will hold you to your promises, whether or not you are sober when they are made.

- Singing usually follows dinner. Be sure to take your turn (English is acceptable). After dinner, the host generally invites his or her guests to go drinking. Never refuse this invitation.

- Entertainment usually includes a bar or nightclub where a hired hostess sits between you, waiting on you with drinks and snacks. This lets everybody relax and allows a more informal relationship to develop.

- A *kisaeng* house is a very expensive restaurant where beautiful, talented women talk with and play music for guests. You're likely to end the evening in such an establishment regardless of where you dine. Scotch is the favorite drink. Kisaeng girls are *not* prostitutes. They may flirt, sing or talk, but that's all. Western businesswomen usually are not invited to kisaeng houses.

- Generally only the negotiating team or business colleagues are invited to dinner. Spouses are rarely included in business

dinners. Do not invite a Korean to bring
his spouse to dinner.

- Always reciprocate with comparable
  entertainment.

APPOINTMENTS

- General business hours are Monday through
  Friday, 9 a.m. to 5 p.m., and
  Saturday, 9 a.m. to 1 p.m.

- Appointments must be made well in
  advance to give Koreans time to do
  research on your company.

- Avoid scheduling a Korean trip during July,
  August, October and the second half of
  December. February through June are the
  best months for business; September,
  November and early December are OK.

ESPECIALLY FOR WOMEN

Men have priority in Korea. They come first in everything.

- Foreign women may have difficulty doing business in Korea. Although women are becoming more accepted in the Korean businessplace, Korean men prefer to negotiate with men. Foreign women should try to use an impressive title—and be knowledgeable enough to back it up.

- Traditionally, the Korean man has been the decisionmaker. Men have priority in Korea. They come first in everything.

- Women allow men to enter a doorway first. Women help men put their coats on. Women pour drinks for men. Women never pour drinks for other women and never smoke in public.

- Women have not had prominent positions in Korean business and government. Although this is changing, women generally still have low-ranking jobs.

- Korean women seldom shake hands. A Western woman can offer her hand to a Korean man, but should not to a Korean woman.

- Foreign businesswomen should always act elegant, refined and very "feminine." Businesswomen should never act in a "masculine" manner. Laughing and loud talking are frowned on.

- Generally, women wait for Korean men to make the first move.

- Women should dress conservatively.

- Korea is generally safe for women traveling alone, although precautions should be taken in Seoul.

HEALTH AND SAFETY

- Try to eat only fruits and vegetables that have been peeled or cooked.

- Tap water in cities is theoretically safe for drinking, but many Koreans boil their water. Even though major hotels generally have their own filtration systems, it is recommended that Westerners drink boiled or bottled water as a precaution. This is especially true outside the main cities.

Westerners should drink boiled or bottled water, especially outside the main cities.

- Health care facilities in the Republic of Korea are good. Medical and dental clinics with foreign-trained Koreans and the occasional foreign doctor are available. Your hotel can refer you to a suitable physician or clinic. Doctors and hospitals may expect immediate cash payment for health services.

- There are many pharmacies and the range of over-the-counter medicines is enormous. However, labeling is often completely in

Korean and it may be difficult to locate the exact equivalent of Western medicines.

- Korean streets are safe for visitors to wander. The crime rate is low, and police stations on all major streets can be identified by a yellow lighted sign. The Korean National Police (KNP) operate a Central Interpretation Center (CIC) where foreigners can report incidents of crime. The CIC is open 24 hours, seven days a week, telephone 313-0842.

- Student demonstrations, sometimes confrontational, occasionally occur. It is unlikely that violence would be directed against Western travelers.

- **Emergency numbers: Police 112; Fire/Ambulance 119.**

January	New Year's (1-3).
February/ March	Chinese New Year (set according to lunar calendar).
March	Independence Movement Day (1), Labor Day (10).
April	Arbor Day (5).
May	Children's Day (5), Buddha's Birthday (changes annually).
June	Memorial Day (6).
July	Constitution Day (17).
August	Liberation Day (15).
September/ October	Ch'usok (changes annually, Korean Thanksgiving Day).
October	Armed Forces Day (1), National Foundation Day (3), Hangul Day (9—Korean Language Day), United Nations Day (24).
December	Christmas (25).

27.
TAIWAN
REPUBLIC OF CHINA

VITAL STATISTICS

POPULATION: 21.6 million (1994).

CAPITAL: Taipei, with a population of 2.7 million.

LAND SIZE: 13,900 square miles, about the size of Massachusetts and Connecticut combined.

GOVERNMENT: Republic. The head of state and chief executive is a president, elected for a six-year term by the National Assembly. Although the government has been dominated since 1949 by Nationalists who fled the mainland with Chiang Kai Shek, younger native Taiwanese are beginning to hold positions of power.

LIVING STANDARD: GDP = US$14,090 per capita.

NATURAL RESOURCES:	Small deposits of coal, natural gas, limestone, marble and asbestos.
AGRICULTURE:	This heavily subsidized sector accounts for 4 percent of GDP and 16 percent of employment. Major crops include vegetables, rice, fruit, tea and livestock.
INDUSTRIES:	Electronics, textiles, chemicals, clothing, food processing, plywood, sugar milling, cement, shipbuilding, petroleum refining.
CLIMATE:	Subtropical in the north, tropical in the south, with long, warm summers and mild winters. The average temperature is 59°F (15°C) in the winter, 79°F (26°C) in the summer. Monsoons strike the northeast between October and March and pound the south during the summer. Average annual precipitation is a hefty 115 inches (256 cm).
CURRENCY:	New Taiwan dollar (NT$); also known as the *yuan.* NT$ = 100 cents. Notes are in denominations of NT$1,000, 500, 50 and 10. Three coins are in circulation: NT$5 (silver color), NT$1 (silver color) and NT$0.50 (bronze color).

THE PEOPLE

CORRECT NAME: Using the correct name can be a little tricky on Taiwan. Taiwanese is generally applied to those who lived on the island before 1949 and their descendants. The Nationalist Chinese who came to Taiwan in 1949 and after are usually called Chinese or Taiwan Chinese. But because the Taipei regime still considers itself the legitimate government of China, always use the term Chinese when speaking with government officials.

ETHNIC MAKEUP: 84 percent Taiwanese, 14 percent mainland Chinese, 2 percent Polynesian/Malay aborigines. About 80 percent are Taiwan-born; the major distinctions between Taiwanese and mainland Chinese are how long ago their ancestors came from China, and what parts of China they came from.

VALUE SYSTEM: The people of Taiwan are highly motivated, hard-working, patient, friendly and respectful of others. They dislike loud, ostentatious and unrefined behavior. Moral standards are high, based on the Confucian ethic. Causing anyone public embarrassment ("loss of face") is unforgivable.

FAMILY: The family unit is more important than the individual, with each member having a sense of obligation to the others. Children are expected to obey their parents. Extended families still live together, especially in rural areas. Family size, traditionally large, has been reduced through a government program encouraging families to have no more than two children.

RELIGION:

43 percent Buddhist, 21 percent Taoist, 7 percent Christian, small Muslim minority.

SPORTS:

The most popular sports are basketball, soccer and baseball.

The official name of what most Westerners call Taiwan is the Republic of China on Taiwan. The government there considers the capital of China to be Taipei. The government of the People's Republic of China (also called Mainland China by residents of Taiwan) considers the capital of China to be Beijing. Both governments consider Taiwan a province of China. In order to avoid conflicts, Taiwan is sometimes also called (by international sports organizations, for example) Chinese Taipei.

Diplomatic relations between the United States and Taiwan were severed in 1979, when the U.S. officially recognized the People's Republic. Unofficial relations, including trade ties, continue through the American Institute in Taiwan and the Coordination Council for North American Affairs (Taiwan's representative in the United States).

IMPORTANT DATES

1600s	Large-scale immigration from China begins.
1620-62	Dutch rule over Taiwan until driven out by the Chinese.
1683	Manchus assume control of Taiwan.
1895	Japan's rule in Taiwan begins after the defeat of China in the Sino-Japanese war.
1945	China regains control over Taiwan following Japanese defeat in World War II.
1949	Communists assume control in China. Chiang Kai-shek's nationalist Kuomintang establishes itself in Taiwan. Both Beijing and Taipei claim to rule China.
1950	United States promises to protect Taiwan against attack by the People's Republic of China.
1971	Taiwan forced to relinguish its seat at the United Nations after the People's Republic of China becomes a member.
1975	Death of Chiang Kai-shek.
1978-79	United States severs diplomatic relations with Taiwan and establishes relations with China.

1987	State of martial law, first declared in 1949, officially ends.
1988	Death of Chiang Ching-kuo after 10 years as president and 16 years as prime minister. Lee Teng-hui assumes the presidency.
1989	Opposition parties legalized.
1991	Period of emergency rule lifted after 43 years. First multi-party elections held; Nationalists (Kuomintang) remain in control of the government.

- A nod of the head or a slight bow is considered polite for first meeting.

- The handshake is generally only for males who are friends.

- A common greeting in the Mandarin dialect is *ni hao ma* (nee how ma), which means "Are you well?" or "Hello, how are you?" *Hen hao, hsieh hsieh ni* (hen how, syeh syeh nee) is a polite response meaning, "Very well, thank you."

- Always greet the eldest person present first. Stand to greet older or higher-ranking people when they enter the room. Take off your glasses when greeting an elder.

- Introductions are important. If possible, have a third person introduce you. At a party or business meeting, wait to be introduced by the host.

- At a banquet, introduce yourself to everyone else at the table.

A nod of the head or a slight bow is considered polite for first meeting.

NAMES AND TITLES

- Names usually have three parts: the family name, followed by the generational name and the given name. The generational and given names are usually hyphenated.

  Example: Kuo Kwang-shun (Kuo is the family name, Kwang the generational name and shun the given name).

- Use family names + professional or courtesy titles to address people unless specifically invited by your hosts or colleagues to use their given names.

- Courtesy titles in Mandarin include:

  - Mr. = *Xiansheng* (Syen-shung)

  - Mrs. = *Taitai* (Tigh-tigh)

  - Miss = *Xiaojie* (Sheeow-jyeh)

- In Mandarin, courtesy or professional titles follow the family name.

  Example: Kuo Kwang-shun should be addressed as Kuo Xiansheng.

- Alternatively, he could be addressed as using an English courtesy title.

  Example: Kuo Kwang-shun could be addressed as Mr. Kuo.

- Use correct business or professional titles—in English or, better yet, in Mandarin—whenever possible. Titles are extremely important; they indicate rank and status.

  Examples: Director Kuo or Factory Manager Kuo.

- Taiwan Chinese may have an unofficial English name that they like foreigners to use.

  Example: Kuo Kwang-shun may be known to Western colleagues as Dennis Kuo.

- On business cards, the English side is often written with a person's family name last, in the Western style.

  Example: Kuo Kwang-shun's name might read Kwang-shun Kuo.

- Because no standard method of transliteration exists in Taiwan, the same name may be written in different ways by different people.

  Example: Wang could also be written Wong or Wan.

- Chinese women often retain their maiden name after marriage and use it on business

On business cards, the English side is often written with a person's family name last, in the Western style.

cards and socially. If you don't know a woman's maiden name, use Mrs. + her husband's family name until you learn her name.

- Madam (Mdm) is used to indicate a married woman.

LANGUAGE

- Mandarin Chinese is the official language, but Taiwanese is widely spoken as the local dialect. Several Chinese dialects from the nearest mainland province of Fukien also are spoken. The written form of Chinese uses classical Chinese characters rather than the simplified characters used in the People's Republic.

- No standard method of transliteration of Chinese characters exists in Taiwan. I have used the *pinyin* transliteration of the Mandarin dialect in this chapter. Note that spelling and pronunciation of the Chinese words and phrases in this chapter may be slightly different than those you encounter on Taiwan.

English is taught as the primary foreign language starting in seventh grade.

- Many residents of Taiwan speak English. English is taught as the primary foreign language starting in seventh grade. Young people enjoy practicing their English with foreigners.

- Speaking even a few words of Chinese is greatly appreciated.

- "Yes" can signify either understanding or agreement.

- "Maybe" or "not sure" can often mean "no."

- Good posture is admired.

BODY LANGUAGE

- Do not touch anyone, especially a baby, on top of the head.

- Affection for persons of the opposite sex is not shown in public.

- Young women commonly hold hands with each other in public.

- Do not put your arm around another person's shoulder.

- Never use your feet to move an object or to point at an object. Feet are considered dirty.

- Place your hands in your lap when sitting.

- Hand an object to another person with both hands.

- Men should not cross their legs; keep both feet on the floor.

- Point with an open hand. Never point with your index finger—this is a rude gesture.

- The gesture made with hand in front of face, palm out, moving side to side means "no."

- Never wink—it is considered rude.

- People point to their own nose to refer to themselves when speaking.

- To show respect when greeting the elderly, place your right hand over your left fist and raise both hands to your heart.

PHRASES

English	Chinese	Pronunciation
Hello	*Nin hao*	Neen how
Good morning (until 10 a.m.)	*Zao*	Zaow ahn
Good afternoon	*Nin hao*	Neen how
Good evening	*Nin hao*	Neen how
Good night	*Wanan*	Wahn-ahn
Goodbye	*Zaijian*	Dzigh-jyen
Please	*Qing*	Chying
Thank you	*Xie xie*	Syeh syeh
You're welcome/ Not at all	*Bu xie*	Boo syeh
Excuse me (when asking a question)	*Qing wen*	Chying wen
Excuse me (to get by someone)	*Lao jia*	Laow jyee-ah
Excuse me (I'm sorry)	*Duibuqi*	Doo-ee-boo-chyee
Yes	*Dui*	Doo-ee
No	*Bu shi*	Boo shee

MANNERS

DINING

- Most eating is done in the Chinese style, with chopsticks and a ceramic spoon. Attempt to use chopsticks; see "Chopstick Etiquette" in Chapter 10.

- Entertaining is generally done in restaurants.

Dining in Taiwan can be elaborate, with as many as 20 courses in a banquet.

- Be sure to arrive on time or early for a banquet (see "Banquet Etiquette" in Chapter 10).

- Dining in Taiwan can be elaborate, with as many as 20 courses in a banquet. Eat sparingly of the early courses.

- The guest of honor is seated facing the door. The host always sits with his or her back to the door.

- The host serves guests the first course. After that, guests help themselves.

- The guest of honor is first to sample any dish brought to table; everyone else will wait.

- Food is often placed on a revolving tray in the center of the table.

- Each person has an individual rice bowl into which he or she places food from a variety of dishes—not just rice.

- The bowl is held near your mouth. Chopsticks are used to eat the rice and food.

- Each person helps himself or herself to additional food.

- The rice bowl is refilled when empty.

- Place your chopsticks on the chopstick rest when not in use.

- Never place bones or seeds in your rice bowl. If a plate is not provided for this purpose, put them on the table.

- Don't be surprised if Chinese spit bones on the table or floor. This is considered more sanitary than removing them with their fingers.

- Cover your mouth with your hand if you use a toothpick.

- Always leave a little food in your bowl when finished. Place your chopsticks together on the table or on the chopstick rest.

Rule of Thumb

Always leave a little food in your bowl when finished.

- A belch may be considered a compliment at the end of a meal.

- Tea is served at the end of the meal. This signals the end of the party. Leave even if your host, out of politeness, invites you to stay longer.

- Write a thank-you note to your hosts.

- Restaurants in Taiwan serve excellent and relatively inexpensive Chinese food in a staggering variety: Cantonese, Peking, Shanghai, Hunan and Szechuan cuisines all are available. There also are Western-style restaurants, particularly in major hotels.

- To beckon a waiter, extend your arm and hand with palm down and make a scratching motion with your fingers.

- The host (person who invites) always pays the bill. It is polite for the guest to offer to pay—but don't insist.

- You may be seated with strangers in a crowded restaurant, but you are not expected to converse with them.

- Open-air food stalls are abundant, but the standard of cleanliness varies. Visitors may do best to avoid them unless accompanied by a local person.

Rule of Thumb

The host always pays the bill. It is polite for the guest to offer to pay— but don't insist.

DRINKING AND TOASTING

- Cocktails are usually not served before dinner.

- Tea, juice, *Shuihing* (rice wine) and *Shaohsing* (red rice wine) are commonly served.

- Taiwan beer is very good, but imported beer is available.

- Chinese wine, beer and liquor are all locally made and reasonably priced.

- Whiskey and cognac are often drunk during and after dinner.

- Beware of *Gao-ling*, a very potent, 120-proof sorghum liquor (known as *maotai* in the People's Republic)!

- Toasting is common. Toasts are made before and during meals.

- Toasting is done with wine or liquor. The host raises his or her glass with two hands, one hand supporting the bottom of the glass.

- The glass should be drained after the toast.

- *Gan Bei* (gahn bay) means "dry cup" or "bottoms up." Turn your glass upside down to show you have drunk the entire contents. Beware of too many Gan Beis, but try a few to delight your host.

- If your hosts drink a toast to you and pass you an empty glass, it will be filled by one of the hosts. You are expected to toast your hosts and drink the contents of the glass.

- Pace yourself. The drinking and toasting can go on for hours.

- If you prefer not to drink the entire contents of your glass, you can say *Suei yi* (Soo-eh-ee yee).

HOME

- Visitors are usually offered tea, candy, fruit or soft drinks. Take at least a few sips or bites even if you don't like what is served.

- The hostess may spend most of dinner in the kitchen. Don't ask to help or wander into the kitchen.

- Compliment the hostess on the food. Your compliment will be declined but appreciated.

- The host generally walks guests a distance from the house when they leave. Showing

resistance to this effort is polite. Thank the host for this special favor.

- The guest of honor should leave first, shortly after the meal ends.

- Restaurants: A 10 percent service charge is added to most restaurant bills. Leaving small change is appropriate. In small restaurants tipping is unnecessary. A modest gratuity is given at major, expensive Chinese and Western restaurants.

- Taxi drivers: Extra change for good service or for handling of luggage.

- Toilet attendants: NT$5-10.

- Coat check attendants: NT$10-50.

- Bellboys and porters: NT$15 per piece of luggage.

- Hairdressers, barbers, drivers: NT$50-100.

- Maids: NT$10-50.

- Guides and translators: Varies with time and service.

- Ushers and gas station attendants: No tip necessary.

DRESS

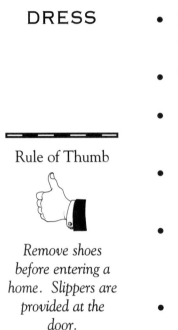

Rule of Thumb

Remove shoes before entering a home. Slippers are provided at the door.

- Remove shoes before entering a home. Slippers are provided at the door.

- Western clothing is common in Taiwan.

- Comfortable, lightweight clothing is best for the hot summer months.

- Clothing should be conservative, clean, neat and modest.

- Medium weight clothing is worn during the winter. Warm clothes are needed in the mountains.

- Do not wear black for a wedding. Do not wear red for a funeral.

- Red is a good-luck color; gold is also popular.

BUSINESS/BANQUETS

- Men: Suits and ties. Men often remove their jackets during meetings.

- Women: Conservative suits in blue or grey, dresses, pant suits, blouses and skirts.

RESTAURANT

- Men: Pants and shirts.

- Women: Pants or dresses.

- No shorts.

CASUAL
- Shorts are acceptable for men and women.

TEMPLE
- Shoes are worn on temple grounds but removed before entering the temple proper.

- Dress modestly.

BEACH
- Bikinis and shorts are acceptable.

- Present and receive a gift with both hands.

GIFTS

- Gifts are not opened in front of the giver.

- Recipients initially may refuse a gift out of politeness. Politely persist until the gift is accepted.

- Custom requires people to reciprocate with a gift of equal value.

WRAPPING

- Gifts—except for flowers and other "unwrappable" items—should be wrapped with great care. The container and wrapping are as important as the gift itself. Red is the preferred color for gift wrapping. White is for funerals only.

HOSTESS

- Bring a small gift for the hostess if invited to someone's home.

- Suggested gifts: Fruit, candy, cookies.

BUSINESS

- Gift-giving is common in business.

- Bring a small gift for your business host. Gifts may be expensive.

- Suggested gifts: Scotch, ginseng, desk accessories.

AVOID GIVING

- Clocks, knives or umbrellas.

DO

- Expect people in Taiwan to be reserved, refined and quiet.

- Give compliments, even though they're likely to be politely declined.

- Revere the elderly: Hold doors for them, rise when they enter a room, give your seat to them.

- Refer to the People's Republic of China as "Mainland China."

- Be prepared to push and shove in lines for buses, trains and taxis.

- Take a hotel card with you to show the taxi driver on the return trip.

DO NOT

- Never imply that the Beijing regime is the legitimate government of China, including or excluding Taiwan. Never suggest that Taiwan is not part of China.

- Never embarrass or cause someone to lose face.

- Never engage in loud, boisterous behavior.

HELPFUL HINTS

Faux Pas

Never imply that the Beijing regime is the legitimate government of China, including or excluding Taiwan. Never suggest that Taiwan is not part of China.

- Don't be too straightforward in conversation; bluntness is not appreciated.

- Don't eat while walking on the street.

- Don't use triangular shapes; the triangle is considered negative.

PUNCTUALITY

- Punctuality is appreciated, but being a few minutes early or late is acceptable.

- You may be kept waiting for a meeting; some Taiwanese businesspeople might even skip a meeting.

STRICTLY BUSINESS

BUSINESS CARDS

- Business cards should be printed in English on one side and Chinese on the other. Make sure that the Chinese side uses classical rather than simplified characters (which are used in the People's Republic). If you are planning to visit both Taiwan and the mainland, mark your boxes of business cards to avoid mix-ups.

Ownership is a tradition in Taiwan. If you don't own your own business, you want to.

CORPORATE CULTURE

Structure: Ownership is a tradition in Taiwan. If you don't own your own business, you want to own it. Businesses in Taiwan are often small to medium-sized. Many businesses are privately owned and managed or controlled by an extended family. Usually the patriarch is the unquestioned decisionmaker. Other family members and relatives will be consulted on major decisions.

Guanxi means "connections." *Guanxi* is developed over a long period of time. It influences social, political and commercial relationships and is essential to business success in Taiwan.

Meetings: Do not enter your host's office or sit until invited to do so. Engage in polite conversation before beginning serious discussions, even though businesspeople in Taiwan get down to business faster than most other Asians.

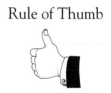

Address comments to and show respect for the group as a whole. Make presentations slowly and clearly, repeating key points. The key decisionmaker may or may not be at the negotiating table. Don't push too hard or too fast in tyring to reach an agreement; allow your counterparts to set the pace. Don't set deadlines; if you do, don't disclose them. Be patient but firm.

Communication: Many businesspeople in Taiwan speak some English. Speak slowly, using simple words and short sentences. Check

---

Rule of Thumb

Address comments to and show respect for the group as a whole.

in advance to see if an interpreter will be needed.

Businesspeople in Taiwan are more open and candid than Japanese or mainland Chinese. They often state their ideas clearly and without hesitation. Nonetheless, people in Taiwan avoid saying "no." They may say "We'll try," or leave it unsaid.

Personal relationships are an essential component of business success in Taiwan. Chinese businesspeople will want to know you personally before they do business with you. Show commitment, sincerity and respect for your Chinese counterparts. Visit often and invite your counterparts to the United States.

Getting approval from a feng shui man or woman before opening an office or factory in Taiwan is common.

BE AWARE

- Getting approval from a feng shui man or woman before opening an office or factory in Taiwan is common. See "Animism and Feng Shui" in Chapter 5.

- Lawyers are *not* part of negotiations. Conflicts are settled by arbitrators and not in the courts.

- The bonus system is the key to motivating people in Taiwan.

- Taiwan is a large, competitive market. Pricing and after-sale service are crucial to success.

ENTERTAINMENT

- The banquet is an important part of business in Taiwan.

- Choosing the right restaurant and entertaining well can greatly enhance your chances of success.

- Chinese take great pride in their cuisine. Show appreciation for the food served.

- Dinners are an opportunity to build trust and rapport. Never regard formal entertaining as a waste of time.

- Business entertainment can last late into the night.

- Do not discuss business during dinner unless your hosts bring it up.

- Reciprocate with a dinner of equivalent value.

- You may invite spouses to a business dinner. They may or may not come.

You may invite spouses to a business dinner. They may or may not come.

APPOINTMENTS

- April to September is the best time to schedule meetings.

- At a minimum, avoid the weeks before and after the Chinese New Year (late January to mid-February).

- 11 a.m. to 4 p.m. is the best time for business meetings.

ESPECIALLY FOR WOMEN

- Western women can do business easily in Taiwan.

- Women in Taiwan play a more traditional role than women in Europe or North America, but this is changing rapidly.

- Although women are becoming more involved in business and government, few yet hold prominent positions.

- Taiwan businesswomen are more likely to hold professional positions in Western companies than Chinese ones.

- Most Taiwan businessmen will invite a visiting businesswoman to dinner but not to the after-dinner entertainment.

- If an American businesswoman invites a Chinese businessman to lunch or dinner, she should pay. The man will offer to pay, even though he would rather not. To avoid misunderstanding, the woman should make payment arrangements in advance.

- Modest and conservative dress with little or no jewelry is best for business.

Taiwan businesswomen are more likely to hold professional positions in Western companies than Chinese ones.

- Health facilities in Taiwan are fully adequate for routine treatment. Doctors and hospitals may require immediate cash payment. Supplemental overseas medical insurance is recommended.

- Water provided for guests at hotels and leading restaurants is either distilled or boiled. Drink only boiled or bottled water and avoid raw vegetables outside of hotels and better restaurants.

- Make sure all vaccinations are up to date, have boosters for tetanus and polio, and get a gamma globulin shot.

- Wear shoes at all times and avoid swimming in fresh water.

- The overall crime rate in Taiwan is low. Residential burglaries, pocket-picking and theft are the main types of crimes affecting foreigners, but other more serious street crimes do occasionally occur.

- Foreigners generally are safe alone at night. Be extra careful when crossing the streets; drivers rarely stop for pedestrians.

- **Emergency numbers: Police 110, Fire 119.**

HOLIDAYS AND FESTIVALS

January	Founding of Republic of China (1-2), Half-year Closing.
January/ February	Chinese New Year (set by lunar calendar).
March	Youth Day (29).
April	Tomb Sweeping Day and Death of Chiang Kai-shek (5).
June	Dragon Boat Festival.
July	Half-year Closing.
September/ October	Mid-autumn Festival.
October	Double Tenth National Day (10), Birthday of Confucius (17), Taiwan Retrocession Day (25), Chiang Kai-shek's Birthday (31).
November	Sun Yat-Sen's Birthday (12).
December	Constitution Day (25).

28.
THAILAND
KINGDOM OF THAILAND

VITAL STATISTICS

POPULATION:	62.1 million.
CAPITAL:	Bangkok, with a population of 6.0 million.
LAND SIZE:	198,115 square miles, approximately the size of Texas.
GOVERNMENT:	Constitutional monarchy. The king is the head of state and the prime minister head of government. The National Assembly consists of 225 members selected by the prime minister with the approval of the monarch; the House of Representatives, with 301 members, is elected by the people to four-year terms. The military continues to have a significant influence on the whole process.

LIVING STANDARD:	GDP = US$3,250 per capita. Although Thailand is one of the most prosperous countries of Southeast Asia, feeding, clothing and sheltering tens of thousands of refugees from Vietnam, Laos and Cambodia has caused considerable strain on the nation's economy.
NATURAL RESOURCES:	Tin, rubber, natural gas, tungsten, tantalum, timber, lead, fisheries, gypsum, lignite, fluorite.
AGRICULTURE:	Accounts for 12 percent of GDP and 60 percent of employment. Thailand is a leading producer and exporter of rice and cassava (tapioca); other crops include rubber, corn, sugar cane, coconuts and soybeans. Except for wheat, Thailand is self-sufficient in food.
INDUSTRIES:	Tourism is the largest source of foreign exchange; other industries include textiles and garment manufacturing, food processing, beverages, tobacco, cement, electric appliances and components, integrated circuits and electronics, furniture, plastics.
CLIMATE:	Hot and humid with three seasons: March to May, hot with temperatures approaching 100°F (38°C); June to October, monsoon rains; and November to February, relatively cool and dry.
CURRENCY:	*Baht* (B); 1 baht = 100 *satang*. Notes are in denominations of 500B (purple), 100B (red), 50B (blue), 20B (green) and 10B (brown). Coins include 10B, 5B and 1B, as well as 50 and 25 satang pieces; 1B and 5B coins come in several sizes.

THE PEOPLE

CORRECT NAME: Thais.

ETHNIC MAKEUP: 54 percent Thai, 28 percent Lao, 11 percent Chinese, 4 percent Malay, 3 percent Khmer.

VALUE SYSTEM: Thais are tolerant of individualism, but find comfort and security in being part of a group. *Mai pen rai* (never mind) is the Thai expression which characterizes their general approach to life—"It is to enjoy." Thais are productive and hard-working, while at the same time happy with who they are and what they have. They are smiling, pleasant, humble and patient people who laugh easily, speak softly, are slow to anger, and try never to cause anyone to lose face.

FAMILY: Thai families are very close, and the family is the primary unit of society. In the countryside, several generations may live under the same roof. Elders have superior status and expect humility, obedience and respect from other family members.

RELIGION: 95 percent Buddhist, 4 percent Muslim. Most Thais are devout Buddhists of the Therevada school. Men over the age of 20 are expected to serve as Buddhist monks for at least a few months, and many do.

SPORTS: Soccer, Thai-style boxing (opponents fight with their hands and feet), *takraw* (players attempt to keep a wicker ball in the air by using hands, legs and feet) and *mak ruk* (a type of chess).

IMPORTANT DATES

1238-1350	Sukothai Period.
1350-1767	Ayutthaya Period.
1782	Nation's name changed to Siam, Bangkok becomes capital.
1851-1868	King Rama IV rules Siam.
1898	Anglo-French accord guarantees Siam's independence.
1932	Revolt against King Rama VII; government becomes a constitutional monarchy.
1939	Siam's name changed to Thailand.
1941-44	Japanese occupy Thailand.
1946	Field Marshal Pibul begins 11-year rule.
1957	Field Marshal Savit Thanavat overthrows Pibul, strengthens ties with the United States.
1967	Thailand becomes a founding member of ASEAN (Association of South East Asian Nations).
1975	Diplomatic relations with China established.

1976	Military coup ends three-year civilian government.
1980	Political parties gain limited freedom. General Prem Tinsulanonda elected prime minister.
1991	General Suchinda Kraprayoon leads nonviolent military coup; state of emergency declared.
1992	Parliamentary elections held. Violent street clashes ensue. Chiam Leekpai elected prime minister.

MEETING AND GREETING

- When being introduced or greeting someone, men say *Sawatdee-krap* (sawt-dee KRAHP) and women say *Sawatdee-kah* (sawt-dee KAHK).

- Thais greet each other with a gesture known as the *wai* (why). Foreigners are not expected to initiate the gesture, but it is an insult not to return it. If a wai is not offered, shake hands with men and smile and nod to women. A Thai businessperson often will shake hands with a foreigner rather than offering a wai.

- To execute the wai, place the palms of your hands together, with fingers together and extended upward, at chest level close to your body and bow slightly. The higher the hands are placed, the more respect is shown. Subordinates might raise their fingers as high as their noses; however, the tips of the fingers should never be above eye level.

A Thai businessperson often will shake hands with a foreigner rather than offering a wai.

- A wai can mean "hello," "thank you," "I'm sorry" or "goodbye." A wai is not used to greet children, servants, street vendors or laborers. Never return a wai to a child, waiter, clerk or other person of lower rank; simply nod and smile in response.

- Monks do not return a wai.

- Thais say "Where are you going?" rather than "hello." A polite response is "Just down the street." (See phrases section.)

- Introductions are common only in formal situations. Introduce yourself by your first name. When introducing your business partner to an important Thai, mention your partner's name first.

- The person of lower rank of status is always introduced first. Thus, a child is introduced before its parents and a secretary is introduced before her boss.

- Thais' given names come before the family name, as in the West.

   Example: Anuwat Wattapongsiri's given name is Anuwat and his family name is Wattapongsiri.

- Thais address one another by titles + given names, reserving family names for very formal occasions and written communications. Last names have been used in Thailand only for the past 50 years and are difficult to pronounce even for Thais. Two people with the same last name are almost certainly related.

- Thai given names are preceded by the courtesy title *Khun*, unless the person has a military, professional or academic title.

NAMES AND TITLES

Last names have been used in Thailand only for the past 50 years and are difficult to pronounce even for Thais.

Khun is used for men and women, married or single. If you don't know a person's name, you can address them simply as Khun.

Example: Anuwat Wattapongsiri should be addressed as Khun Anuwat.

- Titles and ranks are very important. When possible, use rank or title + given name in addressing a Thai.

Example: If Anuwat Wattapongsiri is a physician, he should be addressed as Doctor Anuwat.

- Foreigners are often addressed by courtesy titles + given names because it is easier for Thais; it does not imply familiarity. Thais will probably call you Mr. Joe or Mrs. Mary.

- In correspondence, use Dear + Khun + given name.

Example: Dear Khun Mary.

- Nicknames are common in Thailand.

- Thai is the official language; there are also regional languages and dialects.

- Educated Thais—including international businesspeople—often speak relatively fluent English. With the exception of taxi drivers, Thais employed in the travel industry (especially in Bangkok) usually speak some English.

- Touching between people of the same sex is more common in Thailand than in many other Asian countries. However, touching someone of the opposite sex is taboo. Do not show affection in public.

- Never point your feet at anyone or use your feet to move anything or touch anyone. Feet are regarded as unclean and, both literally and symbolically, as the lowest part of the body.

- Don't put your hands in your pockets while talking to someone, and never put your arm over the back of a chair in which someone is sitting.

- A smile is often used to express many different emotions. It may be an apology, a thank-you, a greeting, or a reaction to embarrassment.

Touching between people of the same sex is more common in Thailand than in many other Asian countries. However, touching someone of the opposite sex is taboo.

Never touch anyone's head, and never pass something over a person's head.

- Never touch anyone's head, and never pass something over a person's head. The head is considered sacred and the seat of the soul.

- A Thai's smiling assurance does not mean you will get what you want, when you want it. It simply reflects the Thai desire for harmony and Thais' "don't worry, be happy" approach to life.

- Don't wave your hands as you talk, giving Thais the impression that you are angry.

- Never pass anything with your left hand. Never point with your hand and never, never with one finger.

- Don't cross your legs in the presence of elderly people or monks.

- To beckon someone, extend your arm and hand, palm down, and flutter your fingers up and down.

PHRASES

- Most expressions spoken by men end in *krap*, those by women in *ka*.

English	Thai	Pronunciation
Hello/Goodbye (said by men)	*Sawatdee krap*	Sawt-dee KRAHP
Hello/Goodbye (said by women)	*Sawatdee ka*	Sawt-dee KAHK

(These expressions are used as a general greeting at any time of day, and also as a farewell when you are the person staying.)

English	Thai	Pronunciation
Hello (literally, "Where are you going?")	*Pai mai*	Piemy
"For a walk" (polite response to above)	*Pai theo*	Pie tay-oh
Goodbye (when you are the person leaving)	*Lah gawn krap* *Lah gawn ka*	Law-gahn KRAHP Law-gahn KAHK
Please	*Garunah*	Ga-roo-nah
Thank you	*Kawp-kun krap* *Kawp-kun ka*	Kawp-koon KRAHP Kawp-koon KAHK
You are welcome	*Mai pen rai krap* *Mai pen rai ka*	MY-pen-rye KRAHP MY-pen-rye KAHK
Yes	*Krap* *Ka*	KRAHP KHAK
No	*Bplahu krap* *Bplahu ka*	Blaw KRAHP Blaw KAHK

MANNERS

Rule of Thumb

Thai food is eaten with a fork and spoon rather than with chopsticks.

Thai food may be sweet, sour, hot, salty or spicy—but never bland.

DINING

- Thai food is eaten with a fork and spoon rather than with chopsticks. The spoon is held in the right hand; the fork is held in the left hand and used to push food onto the spoon.

- The restaurants of better hotels serve Western and continental as well as Thai cuisine.

- Except in first-class hotels and restaurants, avoid eating fruits and vegetables that haven't been cooked or peeled.

- Many Thai dishes use such herbs and spices as lemon grass, coriander and red peppers. They can be among the most piquant in the world, and a bit overwhelming to the Western palate; ask for "medium" spicing rather than "hot." Thai food may be sweet, sour, hot, salty or spicy—but never bland.

- Food is transferred from serving dishes to your individual bowl, where it can be mixed with rice. Rice is eaten with almost every meal.

- Most entertaining is done in restaurants. You may be seated with other diners in a crowded restaurant.

- Thais appreciate visitors who like Thai food. Refusing food is impolite. If you don't like a dish, discreetly avoid it, but don't express displeasure.

- To attract a waiter, extend your hand, palm down, and waggle your fingers. Never snap your fingers or raise your voice to attract a waiter. Address a waiter or waitress as *nong* ("brother" or "sister").

- If a waiter or waitress offers a wai, smile and nod, but don't return the wai.

- Thai banquets usually begin at 8 p.m. At a banquet, dinner is customarily served in a teak-paneled room with Thai dances performed before and during the meal. The guest of honor is seated at a table closest to the dancing. The host may not be seated near the guest of honor.

- Rice will be served, then several dishes will be placed in the center of the table. Serve yourself; dishes are not passed. Don't mix different kinds of food on your plate. Use the side of your spoon to cut your food.

- Wait for the host to invite you to start before you begin eating. The host usually serves the guests a second helping and insists they eat more.

Rule of Thumb

Wait for the host to invite you to start before you begin eating.

- Thai buffets are very informal. You are expected to continue to help yourself.

- Cover your mouth when using a toothpick.

- Leave a small amount of food on your plate when you have finished eating, and place your fork and spoon side-by-side diagonally across the upper right quadrant of your plate.

- The host pays the bill. Never offer to split the bill in a restaurant.

DRINKING

- Soft drinks and beer are widely available. You can ask for "Pep-see" or "Kho-laa" (Coke) and usually get one or the other.

- Singha beer is considered one of the best in Asia. Its slightly bitter taste makes it ideal for a tropical climate and spicy food.

- Restaurants customarily serve a weak tea.

HOME

- It is an honor to be invited to a Thai home.

- Step over the doorsill when entering a home. Remove your shoes if your host isn't wearing any. If the host sits on the floor, do the same; do not expose the soles of your feet or shoes.

Rule of Thumb

Step over the doorsill when entering a Thai home and remove your shoes if your host isn't wearing any

- A hostess may wait until everyone else has eaten to eat her own dinner. Don't eat all the food presented; servants get the leftovers.

- When passing an object or giving a gift to someone, cup your left hand under your right forearm; hold the gift or object with your right hand only.

TEMPLE (WAT)

- Do not step on the doorsill in a temple (wat). According to Thai tradition, souls reside in the doorsill.

- The bot is the central area containing the image of Buddha. This is the most sacred part of the temple. Remove your shoes before entering the bot. Never sit with your head higher than a monk's.

- Always ask permission before taking pictures of Buddha images. Never climb on a statue of Buddha to have your picture taken.

- Women should not touch or offer to shake hands with a Buddhist monk. Do not sit next to a monk on a bus, train or plane. No exceptions.

- To receive an object from a woman, a monk will extend part of his robe onto the table or floor for the object to be placed on.

Rule of Thumb

Always ask permission before taking pictures of Buddha images. Never climb on a statue of Buddha to have your picture taken.

TIPPING

- Never give anyone a one-baht tip; it's considered very insulting.

- Service people expect a tip unless the price has been negotiated in advance.

- Hotels: A 10-15 percent service charge is normally added to the bill.

- Restaurants: Most add a 10-15 percent service charge to the bill. Leave loose change—either more than one baht or nothing at all. Leave a 10 percent tip when no service charge is included.

- Taxis: 10 percent. Bargain for a set fare before entering a taxi.

- Tuk-tuks: Agree on a fare with the driver before climbing into one of these three-wheelers.

- Porters: The charge per bag is fixed at the airport and railway station. Look for signs specifying the current charge.

- Bellmen: 1-2 dollars (25-50 baht).

- Hairdressers and barbers: 10 percent.

- At formal occasions, dress is expected to match one's social station. Wealth is greatly admired, and appearance is very important. Upper-class Thais often overdress, especially considering the hot climate.

- Western clothing is very common. In general, clothing should be stylish and cool, informal but always neat and clean. Shorts are only for beach and resort wear.

- Lightweight cotton clothing is most comfortable in Thailand's hot, humid climate.

At formal occasions, dress is expected to match one's social station.

BUSINESS

- Men: Dressy trousers and shirts, with or without a tie. A lightweight jacket adds status. In the evening, dark business suits or formal Thai shirts are worn. Senior executives wear lightweight suits to work.

- Women: Thai women always dress extremely well. Wear smart suits, Thai silks and designer clothes—never anything revealing.

RESTAURANT

- Men: Top international restaurants and formal banquets may require a dark suit and tie.

- Women: Avoid sheer or low-cut dresses, miniskirts and shorts; these will offend the Buddhist sense of modesty.

- Most restaurants are informal, and smart casual attire is apprpriate. Always take a sweater, shawl or light jacket to air-conditioned restaurants.

CASUAL

- Men: Cotton trousers and shirts without ties. A batik shirt, especially for a home visit, is appreciated.

- Women: Skirts or pants with cotton blouses.

TEMPLE (WAT)

- Modest dress is a must in the vicinity of any temple, including its compound.

Rule of Thumb

Modest dress is a must in the vicinity of any temple, including its compound.

- Gift-giving in Thailand is Westernized, with less formality than elsewhere in Asia.

- Bring a small gift for anyone who works for you regularly. Items such as books, special food items and pens are appropriate.

- Wrap a gift in the paper of your choice.

- Give and receive gifts with your right hand. You should also offer a wai.

- Do not open a gift you've been given unless invited to do so. Thais generally do not open a gift in front of the giver.

Rule of Thumb

Do not open a gift you've been given unless invited to do so.

HOSTESS

- Give: Fruit, flowers, cakes, brandy/liquors, candy.

- Do not give: Carnations, marigolds.

BUSINESS

- Small business gifts may be exchanged.

- Brandy, liquors, American crafts, books and desk accessories are appropriate gifts.

RELIGIOUS CEREMONY

- You may be invited to a religious ceremony, perhaps in conjunction with the opening of an office or factory. Bring an envelope with money (100-200 baht). This gift is presented to the host at the ceremony to please the spirits.

HELPFUL HINTS

Rule of Thumb

Show great respect for the royal family, and stand in respect when the Thai national anthem is played.

DO

- Show great respect for the royal family. Stand in respect when the Thai national anthem is played.

- Take off your shoes before entering a home, wat or building that has a Buddha image in it.

- Use only your right hand for passing, eating, touching and gesturing.

- Show interest in a colleague's family, but don't compliment babies or children; some Thais believe praise attracts evil spirits.

- Bargain everywhere except in major department stores. A merchant's first price is often two to three times the fair price. Cajoling and other forms of friendly persuasion are expected.

- Enjoy the Thai sense of humor. Laugh and be pleasant. Smile.

- Be prepared to have people stare at you, especially if you have fair skin, blond hair and blue eyes. No offense is intended; it's just friendly curiosity.

DO NOT

- Do not be surprised if a Thai asks your age or your income. These are not considered rude questions in Thailand.

- Never step over someone lying on the floor or sidewalk.

- Never criticize the Buddhist religion or its practitioners.

- Do not attempt to take out of the country images of Buddha, other religious articles or antiquities.

- Never discuss personal problems.

- Do not speak in a loud voice or show your temper. Never criticize anyone publicly.

- Do not bathe nude on the beach.

Faux Pas

Never criticize the Buddhist religion or its practitioners.

PUNCTUALITY

- No one in Thailand is in a hurry. Waiting is inevitable in a country where personal relationships are more highly valued than time. While punctuality (especially by foreigners) is appreciated, it is not uncommon for a Thai to be late. Don't show disapproval.

- Two times exist in Thailand: *nat farang*, or "foreigner time," implying punctuality; and *nat Thai*, or "Thai time," implying a more relaxed attitude toward appointments.

- Always allow ample time for travel to appointments. Traffic is a major problem in Bangkok, and it can literally take hours to travel across the city at rush hour. Try to stay as close as possible to where you'll be doing business.

STRICTLY BUSINESS

BUSINESS CARDS

- Business cards are important. A receptionist may ask a visitor for a card.

- When being introduced, hand your business card to the most senior Thai person first.

- Cards should be printed in Thai on one side and English on the other; present your card with the Thai side facing the recipient.

CORPORATE CULTURE

Structure: Status is important in Thai companies, and a more prestigious title may be more avidly sought than a salary increase. Many companies are privately held, and top executives are members of the owning family. Decisions are made slowly and cautiously, with issues filtered through layers of bureaucracy before the final decision is made at the top.

Who you know may play a significant role in reaching a business agreement. If possible, arrange to be introduced to your potential business partner by a well-connected Thai.

Meetings: First meetings generally produce good humor, smiles, polite conversation and few concrete results. The second meeting usually includes an invitation to a meal. Meetings begin with small talk, and discussing business before becoming acquainted is considered impolite. Obviously, you need to be prepared for extended negotiations. Be patient.

In your presentations, modestly explain your firm's successes. Use charts, graphs, photos, blueprints, audio-visual aids and all data necessary to establish credibility.

Don't ever underestimate your Thai counterparts. Thais are very savvy businesspeople, and Thai negotiators have long experience at getting what they want while appearing shy, retiring and hospitable. Contracts should be written in both Thai and English.

A prestigious title may be more avidly sought than a raise.

Rule of Thumb

Don't ever underestimate your Thai counterparts. Thais have long experience at getting what they want while appearing shy, retiring and hospitable.

Communication: Thai is the official language, but many businesspeople speak English. Check in advance to see if an interpreter is needed for a meeting. If important issues are involved, it's advisable to have an interpreter involved to avoid confusion.

Don't expect a direct answer if you ask a Thai for an opinion. "Maybe" or "It might be difficult" generally means "no." Personal contact is essential in developing a relationship, and it's advantageous to hire a reliable local agent who can represent you in your absence.

BE AWARE

Business is kept separate from personal life, and family comes before business.

- Thais prefer to work later in the evening rather than early in the morning. Business is kept separate from personal life, and family comes before business.

- Bluntness is not appreciated. Be subtle in giving a negative response.

- Although ethnic Chinese make up only about 10 percent of the population, they dominate the business community as owners of banks and industrial companies. Chinese money is also a very powerful influence in politics.

- Thailand encourages foreign investment. The foreign investment board grants preferential licenses and permits, provides guarantees against expropriation, bars competition and offers tax incentives to foreign investors.

ENTERTAINMENT

- Entertaining is essential to doing business. Spouses are seldom included in business entertaining.

- Initial lunches may be for getting to know your counterpart personally. Don't discuss business.

- Business dinners are popular. Minimize business talk while eating; dinner is a sociable activity.

- After a dinner in Bangkok, visiting businesspeople are likely to be taken to a bar in the Patpong Road district. Don't decline an invitation.

APPOINTMENTS

- Normal business hours are Monday to Friday, 8 a.m. to 5 p.m. Many businesses are open Saturday until noon.

- Try to schedule meetings between 10 a.m. and 3 p.m. Do not propose a very early or late appointment, or you'll have to contend with the nightmarish rush hour traffic.

- Vacations typically are in April and May. Try not to schedule a business trip during these months, during the Songkran Festival in April or around Christmas.

- November to March is the best time for a business trip to Thailand.

- Large companies prefer or insist on prior appointments. Propose several dates for an initial meeting.

ESPECIALLY FOR WOMEN

Traditional gender barriers are falling, and more Thai women are holding managerial and executive positions.

- A Western businesswoman can succeed in Thailand. However, she should be prepared to defer to men and allow them to feel and appear superior. That may be hard to swallow, but it's a fact of life that's only beginning to change.

- Men conduct most business. However, traditional gender barriers are falling, and more Thai women are holding managerial and executive positions.

- In smaller, family-owned companies, especially among ethnic Chinese, women hold important positions and are shrewd negotiators and decisionmakers.

- Traditional Thais believe a woman can lose face if a man touches her in public.

- The practice of husbands having an unofficial second wife is still accepted.

- A Western businesswoman can invite a Thai businessman to dinner. Do not invite his spouse.

- Traditional evenings out are for men only, with fancy dinners, nightclubs, music and dancing with charming hostesses. Spouses are not included.

- If you are a woman traveling alone, try to pair up with others when traveling at night or in remote areas. Urban areas seem relatively safe except for Chiang Mai, where there have been reports of harassment.

HEALTH AND SAFETY

- Medical treatment, especially in Bangkok, is good. Call your embassy or consulate for advice on a good doctor, clinic or hospital. Many newly built hospitals provide 24-hour emergency services. Medical costs are relatively low. However, doctors and hospitals often expect immediate cash payment. Supplemental medical insurance with specific overseas coverage is recommended.

- There are plenty of pharmacies in Bangkok. Prescriptions must be written in Thai.

Over-the-counter drugs are not necessarily of the same composition as those in the United States.

Over-the-counter drugs are not necessarily of the same composition as those in the United States.

- Drink only bottled water or water boiled for at least 10 minutes. Avoid ice, milk and ice cream. Except in top-class hotels and restaurants, eat only cooked or peeled fruits and vegetables. Make sure food is well-cooked.

- Wear shoes at all times, and avoid swimming in fresh water.

- Thailand is a relatively safe country. However, petty crimes are common in areas where tourists gather, particularly on buses and near hotels. Solo women travelers should be careful on arrival at Bangkok Airport, particularly at night.

- Do not fall victim to gem scams, in which a friendly stranger offers to guide you to a vendor selling overpriced gems.

- Don't let vendors take your credit card out of sight; some have been known to run off multiple charge forms and then forge your signature.

- **Emergency numbers: Police 195, Fire 199, Ambulance 246-0199.**

January	New Year's Day (1).
January/ February	Chinese New Year.
March	Makha Bucha Day, Buddhist New Year.
April	Chakri Day (6), Songkran Festival.
May	Labor Day (1), Coronation Day (5), Harvest Festival Day (11), Buddhist Lent (27), Visakha Bucha.
July	Asalaha Bupha Day (28).
August	Queen's Birthday (12).
October	Chulalongkorn Day (23), honoring the beloved monarch (1868-1919) who abolished slavery and introduced many reforms.
December	King's Birthday (5), Constitution Day (10), Christmas (25), New Year's Eve (31).

• Some of the more important Buddhism-related holidays, including Makha Bucha Day, Songkhran (Thai New Year) and Visakha Bucha Day, are set by the lunar calendar and vary from year to year.

29.

VIETNAM
SOCIALIST REPUBLIC OF VIETNAM

VITAL STATISTICS

POPULATION: 77.1 million.

CAPITAL: Hanoi, with a population of 3.1 million.

OTHER MAJOR CITY: Ho Chi Minh City (Saigon), with a population of 3.5 million.

LAND SIZE: 127,246 square miles, slightly larger than New Mexico.

GOVERNMENT: Communist republic since 1976. The Communist Party of Vietnam is the only political party. A 496-member National Assembly is elected every five years; it in turn elects an executive council of ministers and a council of state. The Communist Party, which holds all real power, is led by a 13-member politburo.

LIVING STANDARD: GDP = US$360 per capita.

NATURAL
RESOURCES: Phosphates, rubber, coal, manganese, bauxite, chromate, offshore oil deposits, forests, fisheries.

AGRICULTURE: Accounts for half of GNP; paddy rice, corn and potatoes make up 50 percent of farm output; commercial crops, including natural rubber, soybeans, coffee, tea, bananas and animal products, make up the other 50 percent.

INDUSTRIES: Food processing, textiles, machinery, mining, cement, chemical fertilizer, glass, tires, oil, fishing.

CLIMATE: Climate is diverse due to the wide range of latitudes and altitudes. It can be hot, chilly, dry and wet at the same time, depending on the location. Hanoi has cool winters and summer temperatures approaching 100°F (38°C). Ho Chi Minh City has an average daily high of 88°F (31°C), with temperatures exceeding 95°F (35°C) in March and April and a rainy season that lasts from May to early December.

CURRENCY: *Dong* (d). Notes are in denominations of 2000, 1000, 500, 200, 100, 50 and 20d. There are no coins currently in use in Vietnam.

THE PEOPLE

Correct Name: Vietnamese.

Ethnic Makeup: 84 percent Vietnamese, 2 percent Chinese, remainder comprises more than 50 different ethnic/linguistic minorities.

Value System: A 2,000-year struggle for independence has given the Vietnamese a deep sense of national pride. Although they value their history and culture, Vietnamese are focused on the future. They are pragmatic, industrious and, especially in the south, entrepreneurial. Although Vietnam still officially embraces Marxism, the government is committed to developing a market economy. Most Vietnamese are eager for reconciliation with the United States. Individual Americans and American companies are welcome in Vietnam.

Family: Families are the foundation of Vietnamese society, and family ties can transcend economic and political differences. Ancestors are worshipped and elders are revered.

Religion: 55 percent Buddhist, 8 percent Christian (mostly Roman Catholic). Many Vietnamese practice a combination of Buddhism, Confucianism and Taoism, with elements of animism and ancestor worship.

Sports: Soccer, volleyball, badminton, swimming, tennis; first golf courses recently opened.

IMPORTANT DATES

111 B.C.-937 A.D.	Chinese rule Vietnam.
1288 A.D.	Vietnam defeats the invading armies of Kublai Khan.
1428	Chinese again defeated by Emperor Le Loi.
1776	Tay Son peasant rebellion led by Nguyen Hue.
1858	French attack on Vietnam begins.
1861	French seize Saigon.
1883	French gain total control of Vietnam.
1940-45	Japan occupies Vietnam.
1945	Ho Chi Minh proclaims an independent Vietnam. Japanese surrender to China and Britain; control returned to France.
1946	Indochina War begins as Vietminh attack the French at Hanoi.
1954	French defeated by Vietminh at Dien Bien Phu. Vietnam provisionally partitioned by Geneva accords.
1956	With the support of North Vietnam, the communist Vietcong begin insurgency in South Vietnam.

1964	Tonkin Gulf incident; U.S. air strikes against North Vietnam.
1965	U.S. combat troops arrive in Vietnam.
1968	North Vietnam and Vietcong launch Tet Offensive.
1969	U.S. troop strength in Vietnam reaches high of 543,000.
1973	Cease-fire agreement signed by South Vietnam, United States and Vietcong.
1975	Saigon falls to North Vietnamese and Vietcong troops; exodus of Vietnamese "boat people" begins.
1978	Vietnam invades Cambodia.
1986	Economic reforms approved, moving Vietnam toward a market economy.
1989	Vietnam withdraws troops from Cambodia.
1994	United States lifts economic embargo of Vietnam.

MEETING AND GREETING

- The Vietnamese generally shake hands both when greeting and when saying goodbye. Shake with both hands and bow your head slightly to show respect. Bow to the elderly who do not extend their hand. Vietnamese women are more inclined to bow than to shake hands.

- When greeting someone, say *xin chao ong* (seen chow um) + given name to a man, *xin chao ba* (seen chow bah) + given name to a woman and *xin chao co* (seen chow coe) + given name to a young or unmarried woman. Or you can simply say *chao ong* (chow um), *chao ba* (chow bah) or *chao co* (chow coe), with or without a name.

- It's polite to add the inquiry, *Co manh gioi khong?* (gaw mahn zhoi cum in the north, gaw mahn yoy cum in the south), which means "Do you have good health?"

NAMES AND TITLES

- Vietnamese names can be a little tricky. The family name is written as the first of three parts, the given name the third. Because a huge number of Vietnamese share a relative handful of family names, using them would be confusing. Consequently, the given name is used both formally (with a courtesy or professional title) and informally (only by family and close friends).

Examples: Ly Phuoc Thai should be addressed as Ong Thai or Mr. Thai; Nguyen Cong Ut as Ong Ut or Mr. Ut; Dang Van Phuoc as Ong Phuoc or Mr. Phuoc.

- Female names often include Thi as a second name.

Example: Nguyen Thi Kim Phuong should be addressed as Ba Phuong or Co Phuong (Mrs. Phuong or Miss Phuong).

- Women keep their maiden name after marriage.

- Vietnamese commonly address foreigners by courtesy title + first name.

Examples: John Jones might be addressed as Mr. John and Mary Jones as Mrs. Mary.

LANGUAGE

- Vietnamese is the official language, spoken with different accents in the northern, central and southern regions of the country. Many ethnic minorities speak their own languages.

- English, Russian and French are taught in the schools. Many Vietnamese, mainly older people, speak and understand French. Few people speak English well, although many are learning quickly.

- Vietnamese was written in ideograms until a 16th-century Portuguese missionary devised a system for writing it in Roman characters with diacritical marks that dictate the intonation of the word and the pronunciation of the vowel.

> *Although Vietnamese is a tonal language, most people understand simple phrases spoken without tones by foreigners.*

- Although Vietnamese is a tonal language, most people understand simple phrases spoken without tones by foreigners. They appreciate an effort to speak even a few polite phrases in their language. Listen to these phrases as they're spoken by Vietnamese and try to emulate the pronunciation.

BODY LANGUAGE

- Men and women do not show affection in public.

- Vietnamese of the same gender may hold hands or link "pinkies" while walking.

- Always use both hands when passing an object to another person.

- To beckon someone, extend your arm and hand, palm down, and move your fingers in a scratching motion. Only beckon someone of lower status.

- Never summon someone with your index finger. This is only done by the boss.

PHRASES

English	Vietnamese*	Pronunciation
Hello (greeting for any time of day) goodbye	*Chao ong (Mr.)* *Chao ba (Mrs.)* *Chao co (Miss)*	Chow um Chow bah Chow coe
Please	*Xin or Xin moi*	Seen or Seen moy
I want	*Toi muon*	Toy moo-un
Give me	*Cho toi*	Chaw toy
Thank you	*Cam on*	Kahm un
You're welcome	*Khong co chi*	Cum gaw chee
Yes/Have	*Ya/Co*	Yah/Gaw
No	*Khong*	Cum
Excuse me	*Xin loi*	Seen loy
Pleased to meet you	*Han-hanh gap*	Hahn-hanh gahp
Sir/Madam/Miss	*ong/ba/co*	um/bah/coe
How are you?	*Co manh gioi khong?*	Gaw mahn zhoi cum (north) Gaw mahn yoi cum (south)

* Diacritical marks have been omitted for simplicity; follow the pronounciation guide and emulate the intonation used by the Vietnamese around you.

DINING

- Vietnamese food is eaten with chopsticks, flat spoons and bowls. See "Chopstick Etiquette" in Chapter 10.

- Hold your rice bowl in your hand; it is considered lazy to eat from a rice bowl that is on the table.

- Spoons are provided when soup is served. Hold your spoon in your left hand.

- The host may serve guests, but usually will just invite everyone to begin. Serving dishes are placed in the center of the table and people help themselves.

- Because it has been boiled, soup is a safe food for Westerners, but avoid any garnishes such as fresh greens. A kind of soup called *pho* (feu) with beef, chicken or pork is virtually the national dish. Beef is *bo* (baw), chicken is *ga* (gah) and pork is *heo* (hey-oh). Eat the broth with your spoon and the noodles, meat and vegetables with your chopsticks. Pho is commonly eaten for breakfast.

- Vietnamese cuisine is among the tastiest in the world—combining, say its enthusiasts, the influences of French and Chinese cooking.

A soup called pho is virtually the national dish.

- Rice is the staple dish. You're likely to see it at every meal but breakfast.

- *Nuoc mam* (nook mom), a fermented fish sauce, is the all-purpose seasoning of Vietnam.

- Fresh milk and dairy products are virtually unavailable in Vietnam.

- Cover your mouth when you use a toothpick.

- The person who invites always pays the bill.

Nuoc mam, a fermented fish sauce, is the all-purpose seasoning of Vietnam.

DRINKING AND TOASTING

- Strong tea in tiny cups is a ritual of hospitality at receptions and meetings. Do not refuse.

- Tea, coffee, mineral water, soft drinks and beer are the drinks most commonly served with a meal; "333" (bah-bah-bah) is Vietnam's most famous beer. Tiger Beer and Heineken are the most widely drunk imports.

- Brandy and whiskey are the most commonly consumed spirits.

- Suitable toasts include *Xin can ly* (seen kahn lee), which means "Bottoms up", and *A votre santé* or "To your health."

HOME

- Never visit a Vietnamese home without a specific invitation to do so. If Vietnamese are not prepared for your visit, they will feel unable to offer suitable hospitality.

TIPPING

- Hotels: A service charge is included in the bill at most hotels. An additional tip is not necessary.

- Restaurants: A service charge is generally included in the bill. Most servers are very happy with US$1; the tip in a restaurant should not exceed US$3-4.

- Taxis: No tip is necessary, except late at night.

- Toilet attendants: No tip or small change.

- Bell boys: US$1.

- Maids: US$1.

- For special occasions, Vietnamese women wear the traditional *ao dai*, a long dress with front and back panels worn over satin trousers.

DRESS

BUSINESS

- Men: Conservative, lightweight suits and ties for initial meetings and appointments with senior government officials. Otherwise, the jackets may be dispensed with.

- Women: Conservative dresses or businesslike blouses and pants.

RESTAURANT

- Men: Most restaurants have no dress codes, and you'll see quite a mixture of dress. If your male hosts wear jackets and ties, you should do likewise. If you're on your own, casual attire is suitable almost everywhere.

- Women: Dresses or cotton shirts and pants. Ask about recommended attire.

CASUAL

- Men: Cotton shirts and pants.

For special occasions, Vietnamese women wear the traditional ao dai, a long dress with front and back panels worn over satin trousers.

CASUAL

- Men: Cotton shirts and pants.

- Women: Slacks, casual cotton or knit blouses.

- Never wear shorts in public except at the beach.

GIFTS

- Flowers are normally given only by men to women.

WRAPPING

- Always wrap a gift in colorful paper.

When visiting a Vietnamese home, bring a gift for the hostess. Gifts for children or elderly parents also are appreciated.

HOSTESS

- When visiting a Vietnamese home, bring a gift for the hostess. Gifts for children or elderly parents also are appreciated.

- Give: Items useful for daily activity, like designer soap, cosmetics, lamps, framed pictures for the home.

- Don't give: Handkerchiefs (symbols of a sad farewell). Besides, most Asians consider the Western habit of using a cloth handkerchief and then returning it to your pocket to be barbaric.

BUSINESS

- Give: Whiskey or cognac.

- Don't give a gift in an office setting; it may be misinterpreted as a bribe. Try to save your business gift-giving until you are invited to dinner or to your colleague's home.

DO

- Refer to Ho Chi Minh City as Saigon when you're there, except when talking with government or party officials. Local people prefer Saigon to Ho Chi Minh City, a name imposed by the Hanoi government in 1976. In Hanoi, however, speak of Ho Chi Minh City.

- Allow for a lot of time in customs processing—on the way out of the country as well as on the way in. Customs clearance is a longer and more unfriendly process in Vietnam than elsewhere in Asia. If possible, try to deal with male customs inspectors, who are generally thought to be less hostile than their female colleagues.

- Always take extra passport/visa photos, as well as copies of your visa applications. Applications for visas occasionally are mislaid.

- In Saigon, walk purposefully and avoid eye contact with hawkers, beggars and street people.

DO NOT

- Do not patronize Saigon street hawkers selling gum, candy, newspapers, postcards, etc. If you buy from one, you'll draw a crowd and others may become angry if you refuse to buy from them.

- Never touch anyone on the head— especially children.

- Do not bargain at a shop or street stand unless you intend to buy the item.

PUNCTUALITY

- Vietnamese generally are quite punctual and expect foreigners to be the same.

- That said, Vietnamese can be very flexible and accommodating when situations occur that are beyond the control of one of the parties (a washed-out street or traffic jam, for example). Traffic is much heavier in Saigon than in Hanoi.

BUSINESS CARDS

- Business cards are usually exchanged when meeting for the first time. Give and receive a business card with both hands. Cards in English on one side and Vietnamese on the other can be printed overnight in Saigon and Hanoi.

CORPORATE CULTURE

Structure: The Vietnamese government claims it has ended central planning of the economy, but is still very much involved in all aspects of business. A foreigner doing business in Vietnam will have to deal with government officials. Many newly "privatized" companies are in fact owned by the army or other government ministries.

Find out exactly what agencies and ministries must approve your company's application to do business in Vietnam, and who the responsible individuals are. Continual, direct contact with the ministry officials responsible for granting or approving your permits and licenses is essential. Even if you want to do business in Saigon, the officials ultimately responsible may be in Hanoi. Any one of the approving agencies may have veto power, and difficulties can arise when one official refuses to honor an agreement concluded by another.

Many newly "privatized" companies are in fact owned by the army or other government ministries.

Rule of Thumb

Continual, direct contact with the ministry officials responsible for granting or approving your permits and licenses is essential.

Legal structures are still evolving as Vietnam makes the transition to a market economy. While this is awkward for foreign companies trying to invest in Vietnam, local entrepreneurs are finding the maneuvering room to their advantage.

Meetings: Vietnamese are more likely to get down to business quickly than other Asians. They're somewhat more pragmatic and explicit than some of their Asian counterparts. But they're also wary of being exploited by foreigners, so it's absolutely essential that your proposals and presentations emphasize the benefits that will accrue to Vietnam. Because most decisions are made by committee and no individual holds absolute power, connections are less important than in other Asian countries.

Communication: Because relatively few Vietnamese businesspeople speak English well, an interpreter is usually necessary. Check to see if your host organization is providing one. They usually will, but the interpreter's fee may be billed back to you.

The Vietnamese desire to avoid unpleasantness can sometimes lead to misunderstanding. Vietnamese, like other Asians, will sometimes tell you what they think you want to hear. "Yes" may not mean "yes." When the Vietnamese say "No problem," you should take

it to mean "Yes, there is a problem." Double-
and even triple-check all commitments, and
then monitor them closely.

Telephone installation may take months, and
international communications are expensive. A
one-page fax to Singapore costs $13 from Ho Chi
Minh City and $16 from Hanoi. A one-minute
phone call to the United States costs $18.

BE AWARE

- Your local partner in Vietnam is very
  important and should be chosen very
  carefully.

- Corruption is widespread. The Vietnamese
  government itself has declared that
  corruption has reached "epic proportions."
  That being said, many old Vietnam
  hands say there's less corruption
  than in the South Vietnam of
  the late '60s and early '70s.

- Vietnam has a woefully inadequate
  infrastructure. Less than 30
  percent of Vietnam's surfaced
  roads are usable, and a 1,070-
  mile train trip from Ho Chi
  Minh City to Hanoi takes 48
  hours.

- The Vietnamese have strong sense of cultural identity, but are willing to adopt foreign ideas and practices when their value is apparent.

- The Vietnamese are very enthusiastic about the rapid development of their new "socialist market economy." When treated fairly, Vietnamese are hard workers, quick learners, and adapt easily to changing situations.

ENTERTAINMENT

- There isn't much nightlife in Vietnam, so most entertainment will consist of a meal in a hotel or restaurant.

APPOINTMENTS

- The average workweek is Monday through Saturday.

- Normal business hours are 8 a.m. to 4:30 p.m.; most businesses close at noon for one hour. Shops close for two hours at lunchtime, and are open until 7 or 8 p.m.

Thirty-five years of war and nearly two decades of a U.S.-led economic boycott have helped make the Vietnamese people especially resourceful.

A friend with long experience in Vietnam remembers that his office car in early '70s Saigon was a "Plodge"—front half Plymouth, back half Dodge, welded together between the doors.

On a recent trip, he discovered that this kind of ingenuity is alive and well in Vietnam:

"My Canon EOS camera took a nasty fall, damaging the film-loading circuitry, and I desperately needed photos to accompany a magazine story.

"No camera store in America would attempt to repair a camera like that; they'd send it off to a regional service center, you'd get it back in a couple of weeks if you were lucky, and the bill would be a couple of hundred bucks.

"But I remembered how clever the Vietnamese are at fixing things, and I went looking for a camera repair shop. Less than 200 meters from the Rex Hotel in downtown Ho Chi Minh City, I found a shop that said it could do the job.

"I had the camera back the next morning. It worked fine, and the repairs cost $20."

- In the major cities, little sexual discrimination exists, and Vietnamese women receive equal pay for equal work. In the country, men are still boss.

- Vietnam is generally hassle-free for women travelers. However, women may run into some problems in or around cheap hotels where prostitution is a major part of the business.

- Western women should dress conservatively in Vietnam. Women who wear heavy makeup and revealing clothing are viewed as prostitutes.

In the major cities, little sexual discrimination exists, and Vietnamese women receive equal pay for equal work.

- When dining with a Vietnamese man, a Western businesswoman should arrange to eat in a public place, and should insist upon hosting. If the Vietnamese man hosts, the Western woman is obliged to reciprocate with a meal of equal value.

- Due to the shortage of men, many women are forced to stay single in a society that places enormous pressure on females to marry, and some rural women are choosing to have children out of wedlock. The government grants unmarried mothers six months paid maternity leave—equal to that of married women.

- Vietnam is a highly Confucian society— especially in the north—and no woman can

imagine going through life without a family.
Sons are still preferred to daughters,
especially in the countryside. Sons carry on
family traditions and take care of the
ancestral altars, which are prominent in
many Vietnamese homes.

- In rural areas, women are financially
  dependent on their husbands. Husbands
  are free to have mistresses and wives don't
  dare speak out for fear of divorce.

HEALTH AND SAFETY

- Vietnam is not recommended for people
  who tire easily or are susceptible to
  infectious diseases. Get a gamma globulin
  shot to protect against hepatitis, make sure
  vaccinations are up to date and get tetanus
  and polio boosters if necessary. Malaria
  prophylaxis may be unnecessary for short
  visits to major cities, but many physicians
  advise it.

- Follow precautions to avoid insect bites,
  wear shoes at all times and avoid swimming
  in fresh water.

- Do not drink tap water in Vietnam, and
  avoid ice in your drinks. Drink only bottled
  water, which is readily available and
  inexpensive.

- Make sure food is thoroughly cooked, and
  eat only fruits and vegetables that are
  peeled or cooked.

If you become seriously ill while in Vietnam, get on the first plane to Hong Kong, Singapore or even Bangkok.

- Medical facilities in Vietnam are inadequate, to say the least. If you become seriously ill while in Vietnam, get on the first plane to Hong Kong, Singapore or even Bangkok.

- Petty crime has recently increased dramatically, especially in Ho Chi Minh City. Pocket-picking and purse-snatching attempts are common. Avoid dark streets at night and back away from confrontations.

HOLIDAYS AND FESTIVALS

January	International New Year's Day (1).
January/ February	Tet, the Lunar New Year, is celebrated for three days in late January or early February.
April	Commemoration of the fall of Saigon in 1975, known as Liberation Day or Reunification Day (30).
May	Labor Day (1).
September	National Day (2), Anniversary of Ho Chi Minh's Death (3).
September/ October	Mid-Autumn Festival, a festival for children.

30.

AUSTRALIA
COMMONWEALTH OF AUSTRALIA

VITAL STATISTICS

POPULATION: 18,174,000, approximately the population of the state of Texas. Australia is one of the world's most urban countries–85 percent live in urban areas.

CAPITAL: Canberra, with a population of 331,800.

MAJOR CITIES: Sydney (3,772,700), Melbourne (3,218,100), Brisbane (1,489,100), Perth (1,262,000).

LAND SIZE: 2,966,200 square miles (7,682,300 square kilometers), sixth largest country in the world, about the size of the contiguous U.S. Australia is the world's largest island and smallest continent and the only country to inhabit an entire continent.

GOVERNMENT:	Sovereign democratic nation that is a member of the British Commonwealth. Officially recognizes Queen Elizabeth II as the Queen of Australia. The Head of State is the British monarch, represented by the Governor-General nationally and governors in each state. The Head of Government is the Prime Minister. The Senate has twelve members from each state and two from each territory who are elected for six-year terms. The House of Representatives has 148 members who are elected for three-year terms.
ECONOMY:	Prosperous, western-style economy rich in natural resources. Low growth, low inflation and high unemployment, up to 10 percent since the mid-1980s. Australia is undergoing major economic restructuring and deregulation.
LIVING STANDARD:	GDP = US$23,601 per capita.
AGRICULTURE:	Cereals, dairy, produce, meat, sugar, wine, fruit. World's largest producer of wool.
NATURAL RESOURCES:	Coal, copper, iron, lead, tin, uranium, zinc, light crude oil, LNG (liquified natural gas), gold, bauxite, mineral sands, diamonds, nickel, manganese.
INDUSTRY:	Iron, steel, electrical equipment, chemicals, autos and auto components, ships, machinery, plastics, electronics, aerospace, information technology, paper.

CLIMATE:	The seasons are reversed from the Northern Hemisphere. The climate is tropical in the north and temperate in the south. Australia is the driest inhabited continent.
CURRENCY:	Australian dollar (A$). One dollar = 100 cents. Bills are in A$100, 50, 20, 10 and 5 denominations; each denomination is a different color for easier identification. Coins are in A$2 and 1, and 50, 20, 10 and 5 cent denominations.

THE PEOPLE

CORRECT NAME:	Australians. Adjective: Australian.
ETHNIC MAKE-UP:	78 percent Australian, 6 percent British/Irish, 4 percent Asian, 2 percent Italian, 2 percent New Zealander, 1.5 percent Aboriginal, 1 percent Greek, 1 percent Yugoslavian.
VALUE SYSTEM:	Australians are some of the friendliest people in the world and have an adventurous spirit and independent attitude. They enjoy an easygoing lifestyle and are outgoing and relaxed.
FAMILY:	Australians are family-oriented, with an average family having two or three children. There are increasing numbers of single parent homes and dual-income families. Many couples live together before or instead of marriage.

RELIGION:	26 percent Anglican Church of Australia, 26 percent Roman Catholic, 24 percent other Christian, 10 percent other. 13 percent claim no religious affiliation.
SPORTS:	Australians value physical fitness, exercise and sportsmanship. Popular Australian sports include cricket, surfing, body surfing, yachting, boating, fishing, field hockey, football (called "footy" and played with Australian rules), and rugby (also called "footy" and played in either the Rugby League or the Rugby Union). Soccer is becoming more popular with young people. Women's netball (a combination of basketball and English netball) has the most registered players of any sport in Australia, but this is not commonly known because these teams receive little media coverage.

IMPORTANT DATES

50,000 years ago	Nomadic hunters begin migrating to Australia.
1770	Captain James Cook claims Australia for Britain and names it New South Wales.
1787	Britain begins transporting convicts from overflowing British prisons to Botany Bay (following U.S. independence and refusal to take convicts).
1788	First Fleet raises flag at Port Jackson to establish a settlement.
1813	Exploration of the area inland from Sydney begins.
1852	Gold is discovered.
1880s	Economy booms based on resources and agriculture.
1890s	Depression.
1901	Australia becomes a nation.
1942	Australia is given complete autonomy by the Statute of Westminster Adoption Act.

Australia's history is similar to the United States' history in several ways. The British founded both countries. They were both great unknown, resource-rich lands that were explored and settled upon. Both countries clashed with the native population, discovered gold, built railroads, and used paddleboats to break open a new land with a rich immigrant culture.

MEETING AND GREETING

- "Hello" and "Hello, how are you?" are the best greetings to use. "G'day" (Good day) is a casual Australian greeting. Enjoy this greeting but don't imitate it.

- It is proper to shake hands upon meeting and before leaving with a firm, warm, friendly handshake. Allow a woman to offer her hand first to a man.

- Women generally do not shake hands with other women. Women friends may kiss in greeting.

- Wave to greet someone at a distance but don't shout a greeting.

NAMES AND TITLES

- Australians generally prefer to use first names upon first meeting, but wait until invited to do so or until you are addressed by your first name. Use Mr. and Ms. when first introduced.

Example:

Mr. Moore or Ms. Moore.

- Do not use Miss or Mrs. unless specified.

- Academic or job-related titles are downplayed, although Doctor and Professor should be used.

- A title does not necessarily command respect. That is up to the individual.

- In correspondence use "Dear + title + surname."

Example:

"Dear Mr. Moore."

LANGUAGE

- English is the national language and is spoken by 95 percent of the population. Grammar and spelling include British and American words with British spelling.

- Most Australian schools teach English as the primary language. There are very few Aboriginal schools that teach Aboriginal languages first and English second.

- Australians call themselves "Aussies" (pronounced Ozzies, not Ossies) and they speak "Strine" (Australian).

- Australians may shorten words and add a long "e" sound to the end. For example: "barbecue" is "barbie," "mosquito" is "mozzie," and "Australian" is "Aussie."

- Use standard English, not Aussie terms.

- The words "rooting" and "stuffed" are vulgar–avoid using them.

| HUH? | *A young North American college graduate told me he declined a job offer with an Australian company because he didn't want to learn to speak Australian!* |

PHRASES

Faux Pas

Do not use Australian phrases.

English	Australian
Good day	*G'day*
Afternoon	*Arvo* (very informal)
Thank you	*Ta* (informal)
Australians	*Aussies* (ozzies)
An English person	*Brit* or (derogatory) *pom*, *pommie*
Americans	*Yanks*
Good friend	*Mate*
Bad, defective or ill	*Crook*
Trunk of car	*Boot*
Cookie	*Biscuit*
Druggist or pharmacy	*Chemist*
Flashlight	*Torch*
French fries	*Chips*
Truck	*Lorry*
True, genuine	*Fair dinkum, Dinky-di*
Trash	*Rubbish, garbage*
Across the street	*Over the road*
Eraser	*Rubber*
Hood of car	*Bonnet*
University	*Uni*
Kindergarten	*Kindy*
Television	*Telly*

- Australian men may pat each other on the back, but any further body contact is generally considered unmanly.

- Cover your mouth when yawning and excuse yourself.

- Do not sniff. Blow your nose in private, if possible.

- To beckon a waiter use a quiet hand motion. Never shout or wave your hand.

- Never wink at a woman.

- The "thumbs up" gesture can be vulgar. It can also mean "right on."

The "V sign" gesture (index and middle finger with palm facing in) is obscene.

DINING

- Continental style is used—fork held in the left hand.

- Australians enjoy entertaining in their homes.

- The barbecue is a very informal "cook out" that is a popular get together in Australia. Sometimes guests bring their own meat and other food or drink.

- Breakfast is between 7:30 a.m. and 8:30 a.m. A "cooked breakfast," consisting of sausage, bacon or ham, eggs, toast and jam, and coffee or tea, is very rare. Most Australians eat a "continental breakfast" of cereal, toast, fruit, and coffee or tea.

A barbecue is a popular get together in Australia.

- "Morning tea" is between 10:30 a.m. and 11:00 a.m. and is often tea or coffee with cookies or cake.

- Lunch is usually eaten between noon and 2:00 p.m.

- "Afternoon tea" is between 4:00 p.m. and 5:00 p.m. and consists of tea or coffee with cookies or cake.

- Dinner is the main meal of the day, served between 6:00 p.m. and 8:00 p.m. The meal usually consists of meat (lamb, chicken, beef or pork), vegetables, salad and dessert. Be on time when invited for dinner.

- Dinner and tea are often considered the same thing. If it is by invitation (business contact) it will be for dinner. Tea is more common for the family meal.

- Much ethnic cuisine is available, particularly Asian and Mediterranean.

- Seafood specialties include local fish (John Dory, Bream and Flathead), Sydney rock oysters and Victorian yabbies (like lobster).

- Other popular Australian foods include "carpetbagger steak," beef stuffed with oysters and grilled, lamb, and "Vegemite," an Australian creation of a strong-smelling spread that is eaten the way that peanut butter is eaten in the U.S.

- Beer is the most popular drink and is more potent than in most countries.

- Scotch whisky is popular.

- "White coffee" is coffee with milk.

- Wine is popular and Aussie wine is very good. There are more than 600 wineries in Australia. Every Australian state produces wine, but a third of the production comes from the Barossa Valley in South Australia.

- There is no prescribed ritual for making a toast in Australia, although you may say "Cheers" or "Bottoms up."

- Australians tolerate people with strong opinions, even if they don't agree. Most Australians avoid expressing their own opinions and will fish around for yours. They may "egg you on" to a more and more extreme position and you then discover you have no idea how they feel.

Try "Vegemite" but not with jelly.

Rule of Thumb

Be sure to buy a round of drinks. Never miss your turn to "shout for a round."

CONVERSATION

| DON'T HAVE A COW, MAN | *The great Australian joke: Two swaggies had been on the road together for two weeks. One afternoon as they were walking along the long, dusty road, Bill said, "Hey Jack, did yer see that dead cow lyin' in that ditch?" "T'weren't no cow, were an' orse," said Jack. A while later they set up camp around a fire and settled down for the night. In the morning, Jack woke to find Bill gone. A note in a cleft stick said only, "I'm settin' out on me own. Too many bloody arguments round 'ere for me!" (And that's how Australians feel about arguments!)* |

- Be aware of discussing the "chew the roo" debate: The kangaroo is the national symbol of Australia and is now being served for lunch. There are presently two kangaroos for every person and the latest attempt to cure the problem is to eat the excess. Some are enjoying dining on "the roo" while others are protesting. If offered, try it. It tastes very good and is lean and healthy.

TIPPING

- Tipping is not as widespread in Australia as in the U.S. People in service industries are reasonably paid.

- Restaurants: Tipping is not necessary, but common at better restaurants. Leave 10 percent if service is good.

- Taxi drivers: Round up the fare.

- Porters: $1.00 per bag carried to or from your room.

Tipping is always discretionary.

- Hotels: Hotels do not usually add service charges to bills. A 10 percent tip is appropriate to those providing special services. It is not uncommon to tip for room service or food delivery. It is less important for hairdressers, hotel housekeeping, etc.

DRESSING

- Australians are generally informal and casual.

- European and North American style dressing is popular.

- Never wear dirty or sloppy clothing.

- Many people wear hats in the summer for protection from the intense sun.

- Many homes have no central heating, except in family and entertainment areas. Wear warm clothing in the winter. Offices are heated.

- Check on temperatures before traveling. Remember that seasons are reversed from North America.

- Beaches may be designated as "family" or "topless." Few, however, will be concerned if a woman takes off her top. Any attire or lack of attire is acceptable at most beaches, especially if you are young and gorgeous. Be considerate of those around you, especially families with children. Topless or nude bathing is not recommended on a business trip.

Wear a hat and lots of sunscreen. The sun is very intense.

BUSINESS

- For business dress conservatively–no loud colors or extreme styles.

- Men: Business suit, or jacket and tie. In the summer jackets are often removed. Khaki shorts, long socks, a tie and short sleeved shirt are considered dressy in tropical areas. Sydney, Melbourne and Brisbane are suit territory.

- Women: Suit or dress.

"Smart casual" and "elegant casual" are usual terms for suggested attire.

RESTAURANT

- Men: Jacket and tie (required by better restaurants).

- Women: Dress, skirt and blouse, or dress pants.

CASUAL

- Men: Jeans, shorts or casual pants.

- Women: Jeans, shorts, sundresses, skirts.

Australians are very laid back. If you give an inappropriate gift, they will laugh and tell you why.

HOSTESS

- Flowers, chocolates, books from America or your home region, crafts.

- Australia produces excellent wine. If you give wine, give either a wine from your own region or a good quality Australian one.

- Aussies dislike class structure and distinctions and have a history of "cutting down the tall poppy." Respect is based on your achievements, not your breeding or education.

- Don't be surprised if Aussies disagree with you openly.

- If you are teased, you are expected to reply in kind, with good humor. Such self-confidence will increase an Australian's respect for you. They do not admire a subservient attitude.

Aussies dislike class structure and distinctions.

- Australia is a very clean country. There are stiff fines for littering.

- Australians drive on the left side of the road. Seat belts must be worn at all times. Drunk-driving laws are strict.

- Australians are very open and friendly. They will not like Americans that act as if they are "God's gift to the world."

- Australia has three time zones: Eastern, Central, and Western. Daylight Savings time is observed by everyone except Western Australia, Queensland and Northern Territory.

- Australia has no sales tax added at the point of sale. The price you see is what you pay.

- What to see: Great Barrier Reef, Aboriginal Culture and Art, Ayers Rock (Uluru), kangaroos, Tasmania, koalas, the Queensland rain forest, casinos, Sydney, beaches, opera, the outback, a working sheep station.

- Go to a pub for drinks and conversation.

Rule of Thumb

Be a good sport—win or lose. Good sportsmanship is highly regarded.

DO

- Be prompt.

- Learn as much as possible about Australia. Australians are shocked that "Yanks" know so little about them. Australians are pleased when foreign visitors know something about their country, or about Australian football or other sports.

- Expect a good sense of humor from Aussies.

- Sit in the front seat of a taxi or limousine. A single passenger sitting in the back seat is viewed as "putting on airs."

DO NOT

- Do not say, "I'm stuffed," after a meal. This means you are pregnant.

- Don't try to impress Australians. Be yourself, or you will appear to be stiff, pompous and self-important.

- Never barge into line. Wait your turn.

- Do not be excessively gushy or pretentious.

- Never compare Aussies to Brits or Americans. Respect their uniqueness.

- Never comment on anyone's accent. Accents can distinguish social class, but Australians don't consider themselves to have accents.

- Punctuality is taken seriously in Australia.

- In business, punctuality is a must. It is better to be fifteen minutes early and wait than to be late.

Say "koalas" not "koala bears." Koalas are not bears.

Faux Pas

Do not brag. Aussies dislike people boasting.

PUNCTUALITY AND PACE

STRICTLY
BISINESS

CORPORATE CULTURE

- Aussie business people are pragmatic, efficient, goal-oriented, and interested in productivity and profits. Australians will quickly get down to business.

- Nearly all workers receive four weeks of paid vacation each year.

COMMUNICATION AND PRESENTATIONS

- Communications will be direct, good-humored and to the point. Australians will make fun of anyone who quotes his or her qualifications, title or experience. Australia is an egalitarian society. Treat everyone as equals. Australians will tell you politely if they are dissatisfied.

Treat everyone as equals.

- Straightforward, open presentations will be appreciated. When speaking to a group stand erect but use modest gestures. Eye contact is important.

- Take time to get established and connected. Developing friendships can be important to business success. Connections help get business done successfully. The "Old Boy" network exists between senior executives. An introduction by an established representative will help, but won't guarantee success.

NEGOTIATIONS

- Negotiations proceed quickly. Directness is valued. Knowing where you stand is respected.

- Australians negotiate major issues without over-emphasis on details, but contracts will be detailed and firm. Generally there is little room for haggling and bargaining is not the custom. Leave some allowance for give and take, but make the proposal you expect to accept. Proposals should be presented with acceptable terms.

MEETINGS

- Shake hands with everyone before and after a meeting.

- Take time for brief personal conversation before discussing business.

ENTERTAINMENT

- Take time to dine and party with Australian businesspeople. You will usually be invited for dinner or drinks before you do business. Don't discuss business over drinks unless your host initiates the conversation. Be sure to buy your round of drinks ("shout").

- Spouses are usually invited to business dinners, especially introductory and concluding meetings.

APPOINTMENTS

- Appointments will be easy to schedule regardless of corporate level.

- Make appointments well in advance (four weeks) of a business trip. Business hours are Monday through Friday, from 8:30 a.m. to 5:30 p.m. (later for executives) and Saturdays from 9:00 a.m. - noon (not executives).

- March through November are the best months for business trips. December/ January is a vacation period for Australians. Avoid Christmas and Easter.

ESPECIALLY FOR WOMEN

- Women are generally accepted in business and may hold influential positions in government and business. Women are becoming more aggressive and are making gains. Equal opportunity, non-discriminatory and affirmative action laws are in force.

- Patronizing or sexist attitudes should be rebuffed politely, but firmly, in a businesslike manner.

- It is acceptable for women to eat alone in restaurants, but be cautious of bars or walking alone at night.

January	New Year's Day (1)
	Australia Day (26)
March/April	Good Friday (varies)
	Easter (varies)
	Easter Monday (varies)
April	Anzac Day (25)
	(similar to Veteran's Day)
May	Mother's Day (second Sunday)
June	Queen's Birthday
	(second Monday)
September	Father's Day (first Sunday)
December	Christmas (25)
	Boxing Day (26)

- Labour Day, bank holidays, and holidays for local horse races or cultural festivals vary from state to state. Each state has "Show Day." Bank holidays and show days are generally not public holidays.

- The first Tuesday in November is Melbourne Cup Day, a very popular horseracing event run since 1861.

Thank you to:
Embassy of Australia
Janet Smith

REFERENCES

Aburdene, Patricia, and John Naisbitt. *Megatrends for Women*. New York: Villard Books, 1992.

Acuff, Frank L. *How to negotiate anything with anyone anywhere around the world*. New York: AMACOM, 1993.

Asia & Pacific Review 1993-94. Thirteenth edition. London: Kogan Page and Walden Publishing, 1994.

Axtell, Roger E. *Do's and Taboos of Hosting International Visitors*. New York: John Wiley & Sons, 1990.

Axtell, Roger E., ed. *Do's and Taboos Around the World*. 2nd edition. New York: John Wiley & Sons, 1991.

Axtell, Roger E. *Gestures*. New York: John Wiley & Sons, 1991.

Besher, Alexander. *The Pacific Rim Almanac*. New York: HarperCollins, 1991.

Chambers, Kevin. *The Travelers' Guide to Asian Customs and Manners*. New York: Meadowbrook, 1988.

Chu, Chin-ning. *The Asian Mind Game*. New York: Rawson Associates, 1991.

The Economist World Atlas and Almanac. London: The Economist Books, 1997.

Engholm, Christopher. *When Business East Meets Business West*. New York: John Wiley & Sons, 1991.

Foster, Dean Allen. *Bargaining Across Borders*. New York: McGraw-Hill, 1992.

de Keijzer, Arne J. *China: Business Strategies for the '90s*. Berkeley: Pacific View Press, 1992.

Rearwin, David. *The Asia Business Book*. Yarmouth, ME: Intercultural Press, Inc., 1991.

Rossman, Marlene L. *The International Businesswoman of the 1990s*. New York: Praeger, 1986.

Snowdon, Sondra. *The Global Edge*. New York: Simon and Schuster, 1986.

INDEX